The Archetypes and the Drama of Change

david j. hulings

A guidebook for those in the midst of change, to help them discover and fully incorporate their archetypal characters in their organizational change story.

Copyright © 2017 David J. Hulings

All rights reserved. No part of this book may be used or reproduced by any means, graphic, electronic, or mechanical, including photocopying, recording, taping or by any information storage retrieval system without the written permission of the author except in the case of brief quotations embodied in critical articles and reviews.

This is a work of fiction. All of the characters, names, incidents, organizations, and dialogue in this novel are either the products of the author's imagination or are used fictitiously.

WestBow Press books may be ordered through booksellers or by contacting:

WestBow Press
A Division of Thomas Nelson & Zondervan
1663 Liberty Drive
Bloomington, IN 47403
www.westbowpress.com
1 (866) 928-1240

Because of the dynamic nature of the Internet, any web addresses or links contained in this book may have changed since publication and may no longer be valid. The views expressed in this work are solely those of the author and do not necessarily reflect the views of the publisher, and the publisher hereby disclaims any responsibility for them.

Any people depicted in stock imagery provided by Thinkstock are models, and such images are being used for illustrative purposes only.
Certain stock imagery © Thinkstock.

ISBN: 978-1-9736-1342-8 (sc)
ISBN: 978-1-9736-1343-5 (e)

Library of Congress Control Number: 2018900912

Print information available on the last page.

WestBow Press rev. date: 02/27/2018

TABLE OF CONTENTS

SECTION	PAGE
Preface	3
Where are we going?	4
Introduction to the Archetypes	6
Warrior	10
Caregiver	11
Innocent (Idealist)	13
Orphan (Realist)	14
Seeker	16
Lover	17
Destroyer (Revolutionary)	19
Creator	20
Ruler	22
Magician	23
Sage	25
Jester	26
The Drama of Change - Act I - The Developmental Archetypes	32
Seeker	33
Lover	44
Destroyer	56
Creator	66
The Drama of Change - Act II - The Structural Archetypes	78
Warrior	79
Ruler	89
Orphan	98
Sage	109
The Drama of Change - Act III - The Attitudinal Archetypes	121
Caregiver	123
Magician	132
Innocent	141
Jester	150
Conclusion	162
Addendum	169

CHANGE IS A STORY - WHAT PART DO YOU PLAY?

Any change in a person's life or an organization is a story. It is a story that has acts, stage props, lights and curtains. And, of course, like a story, there must be characters ... actors. Some actors in the story of change are heroes. Some are villains. Some are key actors and have powerful and influential roles in the change narrative. Others have bit roles; they seem insignificant and less important. Each person in the change dialogue, however, will tell the story over and over. Generations later will give an account of, "remember when we had to change that ...". Sometimes the story is a good story. Often it is a bad story. This book is a guidebook, a script, to help assure we have more purposeful actors creating more positive stories of change. Those successful stories would replace what we often hear: Negative narratives of failed and incomplete ventures.

Simply stated, these negative narratives are seldom pretty. Those telling the story will tell THEIR version of the events. They will speak of everyone's part and how so and so tried to roadblock the change. They will speak of the fellow who tried to change everyone's attitude. They will tell the story of the character who tried to legislate the change and almost created an insurrection. They will speak of all the roles. They will seldom speak of their own role, however. Depending on how the change unfolded, they may pretend to be in the audience of change, simply watching and evaluating each act in the drama of change. But everyone knows they had a role as well. This book is a guidebook to identify the roles ... everyone's role.

The roles played by each actor and actress vary in many ways. But, be assured, in each change paradigm each role WILL BE played. Sometimes the role is played by a strong actor/actress. We love those who show up to the change process and make a positive contribution. However, some of the roles are played in a shadowy manner; the actor or actress has slipped into a funk and is not only failing to contribute in the role they were intending to play, they are undermining the entire change process. This book is a guidebook to identify the strengths and the shadows of each role and to make sure each actor or actress knows when they are crossing from strength to shadow as the change drama unfolds.

When change happens, every role must be played. If there is no "intent" to assign these roles to a viable character within the organization (who can successfully play a specific role), the jobs, duties and responsibilities of that role will not be carried out during the change process. This book is a guidebook to make sure all roles are being assigned with intent and played out with intent.

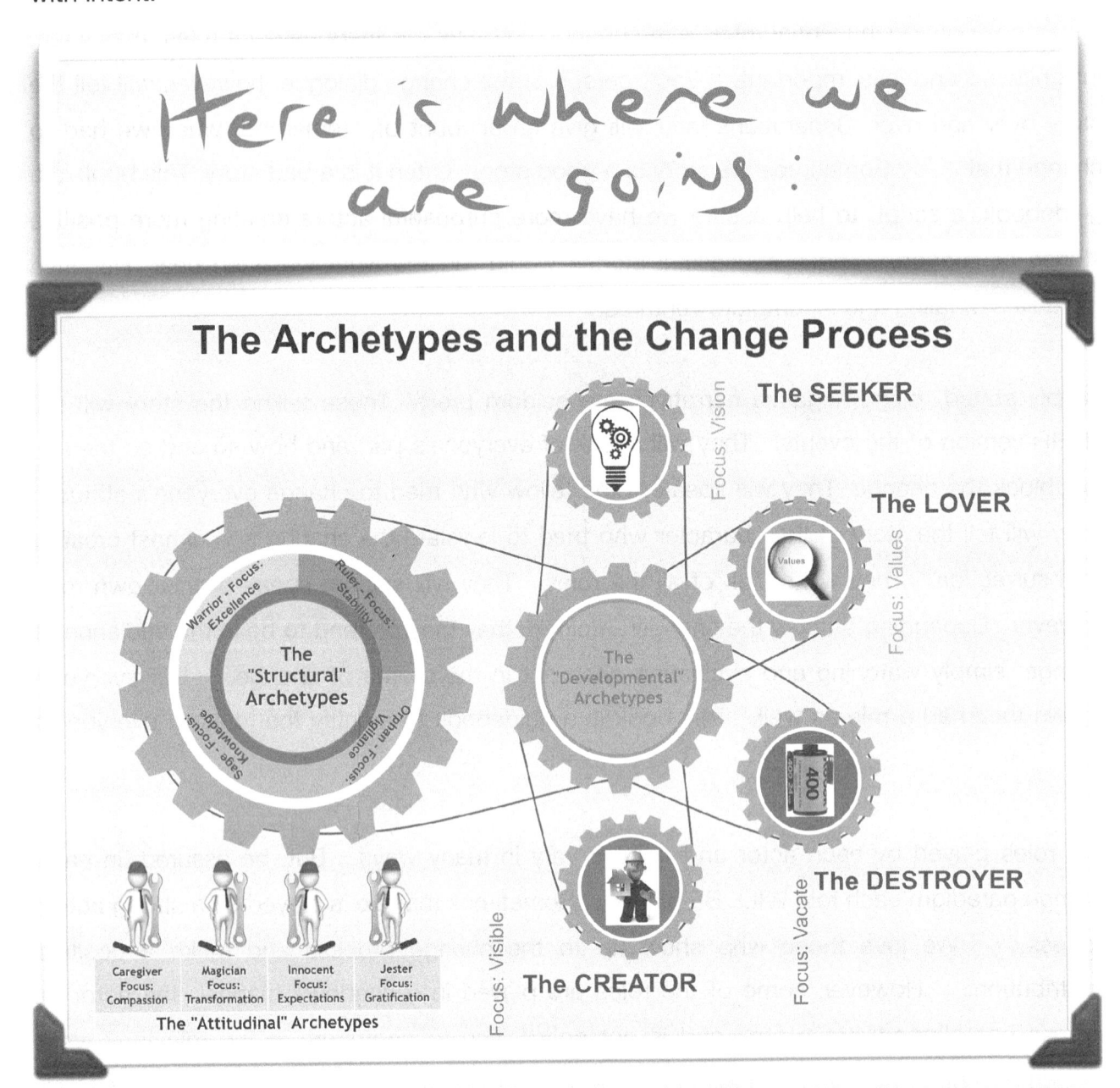

Here is where we are going:

The Archetypes and the Change Process

The SEEKER — Focus: Vision

The LOVER — Focus: Values

The DESTROYER — Focus: Vacate

The CREATOR — Focus: Visible

The "Structural" Archetypes:
- Warrior - Focus: Excellence
- Ruler - Focus: Stability
- Orphan - Focus: Vigilance
- Sage - Focus: Knowledge

The "Developmental" Archetypes

The "Attitudinal" Archetypes:
- Caregiver — Focus: Compassion
- Magician — Focus: Transformation
- Innocent — Focus: Expectations
- Jester — Focus: Gratification

How do we get there?

What Role Do You Play In Change? The Archetypes and the Change Process

THE ROLE YOU PLAY OUT TO FLOW FROM YOUR ENERGY SOURCE

Where does your energy come from?		Check a Box		
When change happens (and you are in the midst of it), where do you get the most energy?	Couch Potato	Candle Flame	Hot Stove	Fully Inflamed
You get energy when you are the one who comes up with the idea?				
You get energy as the one who passionately remembers the past and wants to make sure it is not lost?				
You get energy when you see the waste in the status quo and seek to get others to let non-profitable areas go in order to make room for the new?				
You get energy by coming up with processes and tangible tools to make the change happen successfully?				
You get energy by making sure the change accomplishes the goals and desired end(s) it was intended to reach?				
You get energy by making sure that the necessary rules, policies and procedures are established and followed?				
You get energy by making sure any obstacles that others missed or dangers in the way are pointed out and someone is making sure they don't stop the change?				
You get energy by making sure we are learning something during each phase of the change?				
You get energy by making sure everyone is being cared for during the change?				
You get energy by making sure that the change is also changing the hearts and souls of those engaged in the change?				
You get energy by making sure no one loses hope in the change?				
You get energy by making sure we enjoy life during the change?				

What Role Do You Play In Change? The Archetypes and the Change Process

INTRODUCTION TO THE ARCHETYPES

Change happens whether we want something to change or not. Since change will happen, the only real question is our response(s) to change. When change takes place, we all have a variety of responses toward the change and are motivated differently by it. *The Archetypes and the Drama of Change* is a guidebook to discover and direct those internal, subconscious imprints. These imprints are often described as *archetypes*. These *archetypes* are subconscious patterns of behavior that have been pressed into the deeper portions of our lives. We can find archetypal language in literature, marketing, dramas, movies, television commercials, political campaigns and many other avenues. Archetypes can often be connected or described in the context of personality. It should be noted that archetypes are only one small aspect of our personality, however.

The good way to describe archetypes in the context of personality is to think of an archetype as something like the apps on our phone. The archetypes are NOT our phone, but they are the software on our phone. We can use the apps on our phone as we desire. Some apps we use often, and some apps we use less. The apps we use the most are the apps we enjoy and find some profit while using them. The apps on our phone we use less are the apps we find less beneficial. Archetypes are like those apps. Some we are very familiar with, and we find them very useful. Some are not. When we *call* upon an archetype, we subconsciously *open* that subconscious imprint, and the *app* impacts our behavior. We ought not think of the archetype as defining our personality. We are not defined by archetypes ... at least we should not find our definition in an archetype. We should think of them as tools in our lives we use to express our behavior. If we saw three carpenters holding a hammer, a saw and/or a drill, we would not say, "He is a hammer; he is a saw; or he is a drill." We would say, "He is using a hammer; he is using a saw; he is using a drill." That is how we ought to think of archetypes, especially while navigating the change process.

Archetypes are great tools we can use to manage and work our way through change, whether we initiated it or it was an initiative of someone above us or around us.

The change process is like the famous Psalm: In the valley of change, we can have *cups that are overflowing* and valleys of the *shadow of death*. The archetypes give us tools to enjoy the former and avoid the latter. It is our desire in this guidebook to provide tools and scripts that can be used to activate and flourish with every archetype needed in the change process. Failure to use one of the archetypes during the drama of change (or to use one improperly) will result in a negative change story. Using them correctly will tell a great story about the change.

There are many descriptors for an archetype. There are hundreds of different ways to describe an archetypal imprint. One powerful method to identify them was created by Dr. Carol Pearson and Dr. Hugh Marr. The Pearson-Marr Archetype Indicator (PMAI) instrument identifies twelve archetypes. Pearson and Marr have provided a very powerful tool to assist us in identifying our more favorable archetypes and those that are less favorable. See below to find a link to take the instrument. It would be advised for each reader to take the PMAI. Until then, let's look at the titles for each of the twelve descriptors Pearson and Marr have chosen to describe these archetypes. They are listed below as six pairs (more on this later).

Pearson-Marr Archetype Descriptors
(Colors are not significant, except in highlighting the archetype pairs.)

Past or Current Names	Warrior	Caregiver	Innocent	Orphan	Seeker	Lover	Destroyer	Creator	Ruler	Magician	Sage	Jester
New Names Changed 2017			Idealist	Realist			Revolutionary					

For further understanding of archetypes:

Dr. Carol Pearson explains her understanding of archetypes in her book, *Awakening the Heroes Within: Twelve Archetypes to Help Us Find Ourselves and Transform Our World* (October, 2015; HarperSanFrancisco, a division of HarperCollins Publishers).

This author's book, *Just Middle Manager - Next Great Leader; Expanding the Range of Your Leadership Style* (May, 2017; WestBow Press, a division of Thomas Nelson & Zondervan)

To take the PMAI assessment: www.capt.org (Select Assessments > PMAI > Purchase). After you take the assessment, you will receive both the assessment and a document to assist you in the understanding of your results.

Or, you can read further here …

Before we venture into the relationship between the archetypes and the change process, let's take just a moment to briefly understand each of the twelve archetypes. In the following pages, each archetype is described using:

My Headgear Options	Strength Words	Shadowy Words	Leadership Value	Situation Room	Great Day	Illustrative Examples
If I had to pick headgear(s) to wear to describe me, what would it (they) be?	Words that describe the archetype favorably	Words that describe the archetype less favorably	What they value in followers	How would they respond if they came in on Monday at 8:00 and saw that the work was piled up and HAD to be done by Friday at 4:00?	How would they describe a perfect day?	Various industries, brands, leaders, and/or stories

The material presented in the next twelve pages attempts to give a summary of the twelve archetypes. It is not meant to be an exhaustive handling of the archetypes, but rather a quick reference as we work through the archetypes and the change process. It is highly recommended that the three references listed above be used to better understand each archetype, prior to reading further. As the archetypes are applied to the change process, they will be further explained and developed as this guidebook unfolds. However, the best approach would be to read fully the material listed above to know the archetypes in the most in-depth possible manner.

To understand archetypes, there are a few things we should be aware of before we simply dive into their descriptions.

Areas we need to be aware of to understand archetypes:

1. Every archetype has a strength and a shadow. There are aspects of the archetype that are strong and pleasing to us, and there are aspects of the archetype that are shadowy in nature and less appealing to us.
2. We tend to view the archetypes we enjoy and that give us energy in their strength words. Those we think of as less favorable we tend to view in their shadowy words. If we see someone acting out during the change process and they are demonstrating the archetype we favor, we tend to see them in a positive light. If they are acting out during the change process and they are demonstrating an archetype we do not favor, we tend to see them negatively.
3. The archetypes should be viewed in their pairs (Warrior-Caregiver; Seeker-Lover; etc., see above). We should seek to balance each pair in our behaviors. Using the archetypes in their strength form in equality will result in a more balanced approach to life's situations.
4. The archetypes are ways we can describe the actions and behaviors of leaders, followers and colleagues during the change process.

The Archetype Descriptions - Warrior

WARRIOR

Strength Words	Shadowy Words	Leadership Value	Situation Room	Great Day	Illustrative Examples
Words that describe the archetype favorably	Words that describe the archetype less favorably	What they value in followers	How would they respond if they came in on Monday and the work was all piled up and HAD to be done by Friday at 4:00?	How would they describe a perfect day …	Various industries, brands, leaders, and/or stories
Disciplined Courageous Determined Skilled Powerful Bold	Arrogance Ruthlessness Fear of losing power Win at all cost Combative	Leader Warrior will inspire and desire those they lead to be competitive and battle sound.	Warrior wants everyone to roll up their sleeves and get to work; they would lead by example. They might falsely see those who don't roll up their sleeves as *lazy* or *not part of the team*.	At the end of the day, the Warrior would say it was a great day because he or she won; he or she was victorious in battle and secured the reward.	Sports Teams: Nike, Adidas Military Movies: *Rocky*, *Saving Private Ryan* Leaders: Powell, Eisenhower, Joan of Arc
Possible Headgear Options (Stereo-Typical)					What hat would you pick as a Warrior?

Strength Vanity Plate: IWIN

Shadow Vanity Plate: ULOSE

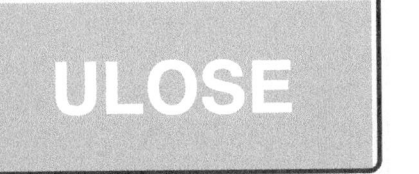

PLAYLIST

We Are The Champions By Queen

What Role Do You Play In Change? The Archetypes and the Change Process

The Archetype Descriptions - Caregiver

CAREGIVER

Strength Words	Shadowy Words	Leadership Value	Situation Room	Great Day	Illustrative Examples
Words that describe the archetype favorably	Words that describe the archetype less favorably	What they value in followers	How would they respond if they came in on Monday and the work was all piled up and HAD to be done by Friday at 4:00?	How would they describe a perfect day ...	Various industries, brands, leaders, and/or stories
Community focus Nurturing nature Compassion driven Generosity Giving Helpful	Enabling others Martyrdom nature Motivated by guilt Sacrifice too much Accommodating	Leader Caregiver will inspire and desire those they lead to be caring and concerned about others.	Caregiver will seek to help everyone and try to help them get their work done. They might not focus on their own work and enable others. They will order pizza for late night work to show they care for others.	At the end of the day, the Caregiver might say it was a great day because he or she helped someone; they served others sacrificially in a great way and enabled others to accomplish their journey.	Johnson & Johnson Health Care Service Hospice All State Insurance Leaders: Saint Theresa, Princess Diana, Jimmy Carter
Possible Headgear Options (Stereo-Typical)					What hat would you pick as a Caregiver?

Strength Vanity Plate

IHELPU

Shadow Vanity Plate

HELP!

▶ PLAYLIST

Lean On Me
By Bill Withers

The Warrior-Caregiver Archetype *Alone* vs. in *Balance*

(The archetypes should always be viewed in their pairs. When the archetype pairs are in balance, some great results can transpire from our lives and our behaviors during the change process.)

<u>Warrior</u>
when acting alone
(win-w-win)
Ruthless

<u>Caregiver</u>
when acting alone
(give-give-give)
Enabling

In Harmony with Each Other

Discovering Responsibility

True Responsibility is when you know when to help and when to teach others to help.

The Archetype Descriptions - Innocent (*Idealist*)

(NOTE: See addendum #1 in regard to the change of the descriptor *Innocent* to *Idealist*)

Innocent (*Idealist*)

Strength Words	Shadowy Words	Leadership Value	Situation Room	Great Day	Illustrative Examples
Words that describe the archetype favorably	Words that describe the archetype less favorably	What they value in followers	How would they respond if they came in on Monday and the work was all piled up and HAD to be done by Friday at 4:00?	How would they describe a perfect day …	Various industries, brands, leaders, and/or stories
Optimistic Trusting Hopeful in all things Faith in all things Simple virtue Untarnished	Naïveté Denial Oblivious Childish Can be blindsided	Leader Innocent will inspire and desire those they lead to be positive and always looking on the bright side of the day through a world of possibility.	They might say, "Hey, where did all this work come from?" Innocent might offer hope that the work CAN get done. However, they might overlook the seriousness and create a false sense of hope.	At the end of the day, the Innocent might say it was a great day because everything worked out just as he or she thought it would, inspiring others to have an equally great outlook.	Ivory Soap Switzerland Churches TV/Movies: *Mr. Rogers*, *Mary Poppins* Leaders: Walt Disney, President Obama
Possible Headgear Options (Stereo-Typical)					What hat would you pick as an Innocent?

Strength Vanity Plate: RAINBOW

Shadow Vanity Plate: STILHOPE

▶ PLAYLIST

The Sun Will Come Out Tomorrow
Orphan Annie

The Archetype Descriptions - Orphan (*Realist*)
(NOTE: See addendum #2 in regard to the change of the descriptor *Orphan* to *Realist*)

Orphan (*Realist*)

Strength Words	Shadowy Words	Leadership Value	Situation Room	Great Day	Illustrative Examples
Words that describe the archetype favorably	Words that describe the archetype less favorably	What they value in followers	How would they respond if they came in on Monday and the work was all piled up and HAD to be done by Friday at 4:00?	How would they describe a perfect day ...	Various industries, brands, leaders, and/or stories
Realist Alert Independent Vigilant Seldom blindsided	Cynicism Victimized Complaining Overly Critical Untrusting	Leader Orphan will inspire and desire those they lead to be vigilant and watchful.	They might say, "I told you so!" Orphan was probably warning everyone all along that the work was piling up. They might be negative and point out future problems.	At the end of the day, the Orphan might say it was a great day because he or she survived it, recusing self and others from the edge of destruction or certain peril.	Unions Journalist Newspapers Insurance companies Leaders: John McCain, Jack Welch
Possible Headgear Options (Stereo-Typical)					What hat would you pick as an Orphan?

Strength Vanity Plate

HEADSUP

Shadow Vanity Plate

TOLDUSO

PLAYLIST

Danger Zone
Top Gun

What Role Do You Play In Change?   The Archetypes and the Change Process

The Innocent-Orphan Archetype *Alone* vs. in *Balance*

(The archetypes should always be viewed in their pairs. When the archetype pairs are in balance, some great results can transpire from our lives and our behaviors during the change process.)

<u>Innocent</u>
when acting alone
("It's all okay")
Naïveté

<u>Orphan</u>
when acting alone
("It's all bad")
Negativity

<u>In Harmony with Each Other</u>

Discovering Discernment

True Discernment is when you can see the bad (danger) and the good (hope) at the same time.

The Archetype Descriptions - Seeker

Seeker					
Strength Words	**Shadowy Words**	**Leadership Value**	**Situation Room**	**Great Day**	**Illustrative Examples**
Words that describe the archetype favorably	Words that describe the archetype less favorably	What they value in followers	How would they respond if they came in on Monday and the work was all piled up and HAD to be done by Friday at 4:00?	How would they describe a perfect day …	Various industries, brands, leaders, and/or stories
Autonomy Dreamer Possibility Adventurous Imaginative	Lack Commitment Alienation Loneliness Disappointment Head in the clouds Wanderer	Leader Seeker will inspire and desire those they lead to be inquisitive and adventurous about everything.	Seeker will want to discover new ways to solve the problem, looking for new methods. They might get so lost in the new ways that they forget THIS work has to get done.	At the end of the day, the Seeker might say it was a great day because he or she left society's norms and found a new idea, new place, or a new path others missed.	Starbucks Levi Startup tech companies Travel Agencies Movies: *Huck Finn*, *Apollo 13* Leaders: John F. Kennedy, Bill Gates
Possible Headgear Options (Stereo-Typical)					What hat would you pick as a Seeker?

Strength Vanity Plate

IDEAGUY

Shadow Vanity Plate

ROAMIN

PLAYLIST

Still Haven't Found What I'm Looking For
U2

What Role Do You Play In Change?   The Archetypes and the Change Process

The Archetype Descriptions - Lover

Lover					
Strength Words	**Shadowy Words**	**Leadership Value**	**Situation Room**	**Great Day**	**Illustrative Examples**
Words that describe the archetype favorably	Words that describe the archetype less favorably	What they value in followers	How would they respond if they came in on Monday and the work was all piled up and HAD to be done by Friday at 4:00?	How would they describe a perfect day …	Various industries, brands, leaders, and/or stories
Passionate Committed Enthusiasm Love cures all Perseveres Vintage	Objectifies Things Entanglement Values the past Kumbaya	Leader Lover will inspire and desire those they lead to be unified and passionate in their concerns and causes.	Lover will see this as an opportunity to create a team and call a team meeting. They might make team shirts or take photos to post on Facebook.	At the end of the day, the Lover might say it was a great day because he or she established a new relationship, saved a damaged one or was able to hold onto something.	Hallmark Cards Victoria's Secret National Historical Society France & Italy Movie: *Titanic* Leaders: Reagan, Mandela
Possible Headgear Options (Stereo-Typical)		Kentucky Derby			What hat would you pick as a Lover?

Strength Vanity Plate

GRPHUG

Shadow Vanity Plate

HOLDON

▶ PLAYLIST

Stand By Your Man
Tammy Wynette

What Role Do You Play In Change?   The Archetypes and the Change Process

The Seeker-Lover Archetype *Alone* vs. in *Balance*

(The archetypes should always be viewed in their pairs. When the archetype pairs are in balance, some great results can transpire from our lives and our behaviors during the change process.)

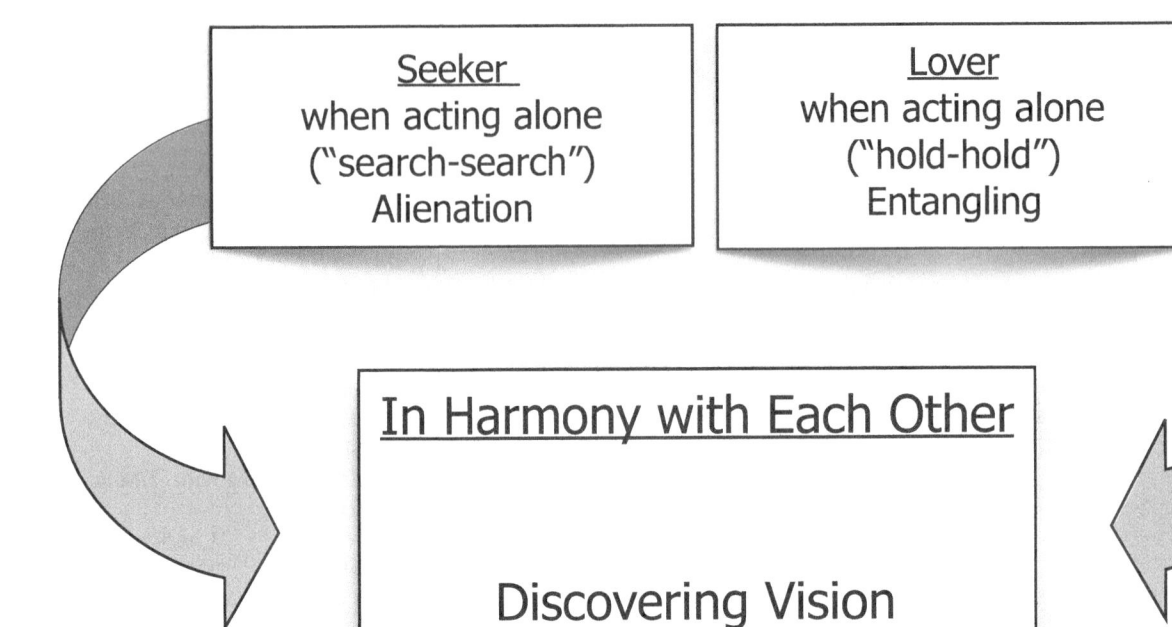

<u>Seeker</u>
when acting alone
("search-search")
Alienation

<u>Lover</u>
when acting alone
("hold-hold")
Entangling

<u>In Harmony with Each Other</u>

Discovering Vision

True Vision is when you can see the values of the past and the possibilities of the future.

The Archetype Descriptions - Destroyer (*Revolutionary*)
(NOTE: See addendum #3 in regard to the change of the descriptor *Destroyer* to *Revolutionary*)

Destroyer (*Revolutionary*)

Strength Words	Shadowy Words	Leadership Value	Situation Room	Great Day	Illustrative Examples
Words that describe the archetype favorably	Words that describe the archetype less favorably	What they value in followers	How would they respond if they came in on Monday and the work was all piled up and HAD to be done by Friday at 4:00?	How would they describe a perfect day ...	Various industries, brands, leaders, and/or stories
Metamorphosis Ability to let go Moving on Break status quo Ability to dismantle	Tearing apart Harming others Tossing out values Quitting Simple in approach to problems	Leader Destroyer will inspire and desire those they lead to be useful and calculating in all tasks.	Destroyer might ask, "What can we stop doing?" Destroyer will look the work over and select what is useful to do. They will discard anything that is no longer profitable or worthy. They might toss out tasks indiscriminately.	At the end of the day, the Destroyer might say it was a great day because it was the beginning of a revolution; they were able to let go of something "they" deem unprofitable.	Boston Tea Party Harley Davidson (let go of past life) Movie: *Robin Hood* Leaders: Gandhi, Thoreau
Possible Headgear Options (Stereo-Typical)					What hat would you pick as a Destroyer?

Strength Vanity Plate: LETITGO

Shadow Vanity Plate: LEFTHER

▶ PLAYLIST

Let It Go
Frozen

What Role Do You Play In Change? The Archetypes and the Change Process

The Archetype Descriptions - Creator

Creator					
Strength Words	**Shadowy Words**	**Leadership Value**	**Situation Room**	**Great Day**	**Illustrative Examples**
Words that describe the archetype favorably	Words that describe the archetype less favorably	What they value in followers	How would they respond if they came in on Monday and the work was all piled up and HAD to be done by Friday at 4:00?	How would they describe a perfect day …	Various industries, brands, leaders, and/or stories
Inventive Resourceful Practical Solutions Tangible Tools Phoenix	Self-Indulgent Overwhelmed Prima-Dona Self-Governed Wasteful of resources	Leader Creator will challenge and inspire with creativity those they lead to be as equally creative in their work.	Creator will introduce a new method or procedure they are working on to accomplish all the work faster. However, it may take more time to learn the new method and fail to finish THIS work on time.	At the end of the day, the Creator might say it was a great day because it was practical; he or she was able to create something concrete or, better, take an idea to something tangible.	Linux Free Software Hobby Lobby Apple, Google Leaders: Steve Jobs, Mark Zuckerberg
Possible Headgear Options (Stereo-Typical)					What hat would you pick as a Creator?

Strength Vanity Plate

I N VNT

Shadow Vanity Plate

I MADE I OWN IT

PLAYLIST

I Did It My Way
Frank Sinatra

What Role Do You Play In Change?   The Archetypes and the Change Process

The Destroyer-Creator Archetype *Alone* vs. in *Balance*

(The archetypes should always be viewed in their pairs. When the archetype pairs are in balance, some great results can transpire from our lives and our behaviors during the change process.)

Destroyer
when acting alone
("toss-out & toss-out")
Emptiness

Creator
when acting alone
("create more & more")
Indulgence

In Harmony with Each Other

Discovering Revolution

True Revolution can only happen when you toss out what is no longer working and create something to take its place.

The Archetype Descriptions - Ruler

**Ruler**					
Strength Words	**Shadowy Words**	**Leadership Value**	**Situation Room**	**Great Day**	**Illustrative Examples**
Words that describe the archetype favorably	Words that describe the archetype less favorably	What they value in followers	How would they respond if they came in on Monday and the work was all piled up and HAD to be done by Friday at 4:00?	How would they describe a perfect day …	Various industries, brands, leaders, and/or stories
Responsible In Control Sovereign System Person Order Driven	Rigidity Over Controlling Limited Vision Entitlement My way or the highway	Leader Ruler will direct and guide with policies and procedures those they lead.	Ruler will begin to organize and structure the work making sure everyone has a part and that this won't happen again. NOTE: Actually, IF Ruler were in charge, the work would not be piled up anyway.	At the end of the day, the Ruler might say it was a great day because things were put in order and the kingdom is at peace for all the subjects (even though the peasants didn't know it needed order).	IRS United Nations Office Managers Vatican Military Police Officers Lawyers Leaders: Steve Jobs, Iacocca, Castro
Possible Headgear Options (Stereo-Typical)					What hat would you pick as a Ruler?

Strength Vanity Plate

ORDR

Shadow Vanity Plate

LRGNCHG

PLAYLIST

Working 9 to 5
Dolly Parton

The Archetype Descriptions - Magician

Magician					
Strength Words	**Shadowy Words**	**Leadership Value**	**Situation Room**	**Great Day**	**Illustrative Examples**
Words that describe the archetype favorably	Words that describe the archetype less favorably	What they value in followers	How would they respond if they came in on Monday and the work was all piled up and HAD to be done by Friday at 4:00?	How would they describe a perfect day …	Various industries, brands, leaders, and/or stories
Transformer Catalyst for change Influential Sees ways to change others and organizations	Manipulator Cultist Guru Lack Reality Kool-Aid approach	Leader Magician will inspire those they lead to see what can become of people, projects or circumstances; they will look to transform someone or something.	Magician will use this as a time for personal transformation and metamorphosis. They might say, "This week will transform everyone into something better and make us all stronger."	At the end of the day, the Magician might say it was a great day because they were able to change someone or something, whether it wanted to be changed or not.	MasterCard (Priceless Ads) Consultants Pastors, Social Workers Movies: *Harry Potter* Leaders: MLK, Obama, Jim Jones
Possible Headgear Options (Stereo-Typical)					What hat would you pick as a Magician?

Strength Vanity Plate

CHANGE

Shadow Vanity Plate

ICHNGU

PLAYLIST

Man in the Mirror
Michael Jackson

The Ruler-Magician Archetype *Alone* vs. in *Balance*

(The archetypes should always be viewed in their pairs. When the archetype pairs are in balance, some great results can transpire from our lives and our behaviors during the change process.)

> **Ruler**
> when acting alone
> ("rules-rules-rules")
> Controlling

> **Magician**
> when acting alone
> ("poof-poof-poof")
> Manipulate

> **In Harmony with Each Other**
>
> Discovering Transformation

> *True Transformation can only happen when you have guidelines, principles and rules to follow as you help people change from the inside out.*

The Archetype Descriptions - Sage

Sage					
Strength Words	**Shadowy Words**	**Leadership Value**	**Situation Room**	**Great Day**	**Illustrative Examples**
Words that describe the archetype favorably	Words that describe the archetype less favorably	What they value in followers	How would they respond if they came in on Monday and the work was all piled up and HAD to be done by Friday at 4:00?	How would they describe a perfect day …	Various industries, brands, leaders, and/or stories
Wisdom Knowledge Truth seekers Healthy skeptic Insightful	Overly Critical Pomposity Impractical Fake empathy Overly skeptical Know-it-all	Leader Sage will inspire those they lead to seek truth and the power found in it.	Sage may either use their tribal knowledge (*we have been here before*) or learned knowledge and attempt to tell everyone the lessons learned before or that can be learned through this week.	At the end of the day, the Sage might say it was a great day because they were able to pass their knowledge on to the lesser souls, enlightening them to the greater truth(s) to be learned.	Ivy League Schools Alan Greenspan E.F. Hutton Research Labs Know-it-all at work Leaders: Kerry, Gore, Ben Franklin
Possible Headgear Options (Stereo-Typical)					What hat would you pick as a Sage?

Strength Vanity Plate

ASKME

Shadow Vanity Plate

INOMORE

The PLAYLIST

Smarter Than You
The Undertones

What Role Do You Play In Change?   The Archetypes and the Change Process

Archetype Descriptions - Jester

Jester

Strength Words	Shadowy Words	Leadership Value	Situation Room	Great Day	Illustrative Examples
Words that describe the archetype favorably	Words that describe the archetype less favorably	What they value in followers	How would they respond if they came in on Monday and the work was all piled up and HAD to be done by Friday at 4:00?	How would they describe a perfect day …	Various industries, brands, leaders, and/or stories
Humor Living in the moment Joyous Light hearted Zest for life	Irresponsible Insensitive humor Slothful Con artist Practical joker	Leader Jester will inspire those they lead to seek fun and fulfillment of life through enjoyment.	Jester will tell someone to crank up the music, get us some costumes and turn it into a fun game or party. They will assure the week isn't taken too seriously.	At the end of the day, the Jester might say it was a great day because they enjoyed their life and made others laugh and/or enjoy their lives.	Beer ads Ben & Jerry's Ice Cream Movies: *Indiana Jones*, *Dumb and Dumber* Leaders: George Bush, Abe Lincoln
Possible Headgear Options (Stereo-Typical)					What hat would you pick as a Jester?

Strength Vanity Plate

ENJOY

Shadow Vanity Plate

JOKSONU

PLAYLIST **The**

Eat It
Weird Al Yankovic

Sage-Jester Archetype *Alone* vs. in *Balance*

(The archetypes should always be viewed in their pairs. When the archetype pairs are in balance, some great results can transpire from our lives and our behaviors during the change process.)

Sage
when acting alone
("think-think-think")
Superiority

Jester
when acting alone
("laugh-laugh-laugh")
Juvenile

In Harmony with Each Other

Discovering Transparency

True Transparency can only be discovered when you can laugh at yourself and allow others to see that, even though you might know things, you don't take yourself too seriously.

The Archetype Description Summary

We have briefly described the twelve archetypes we are going to use to navigate the rough waters of change. It would be suggested that the reader take the Pearson-Marr Archetype Inventory (PMAI ... see above for website link). The PMAI will identify, of those twelve archetypes, which are more familiar and currently active in your life, as well as those less familiar and/or less active.

When you take the PMAI, you will receive a report and a document with further explanation of the archetypes. The more familiar you are with the twelve, the easier it will be to make the applications to the change process and to understand this guidebook. The reader can also read the books mentioned above. Familiarity of the archetypes is paramount to the application to change or any dynamic of human development and interaction.

In summary, however, there are some key thoughts to review before moving forward:

1. Each archetype has a strength and a shadow. If you score high in a particular archetype, that doesn't mean you only use it in the strength form of the archetype and never use it in a shadowy manner. For example, even though someone might score high in the Magician, they can slip into the shadowy side of the Magician as well.

2. We should not refer to ourselves as being "A" Warrior or "A" Caregiver. These are simply tools we use to express ourselves in certain situations. Knowing how we are expressing ourselves or how others are expressing themselves, in known terms, gives us a language to work together. The archetypes should not become identifiers of our "personality" but rather "descriptions" of our behavior at that time.

3. We should not be fearful of using a lessor known archetype. If we score low on a particular archetype, there are some reasons for us to consider as to why we may have scored lower than the other archetypes. Here are some reasons we *might* score low on a particular archetype:

    A. The archetype is **Unfamiliar** to us: For example, we may have grown up in a home where the Warrior archetype was seldom used. When family game night came around, each game was ended before there was a winner or loser. Pushing yourself was foreign in the family dynamic, and there was a *laissez-faire* approach to life. Each family member was simply accepted the way they were. The family mantra was, "Everyone is a winner." With these family imprints, it would not be surprising for a person in an organization to score low on Warrior. Is this a reason you might score low; it is *unfamiliar* to you?

B. The archetype is **Uncomfortable** to us: We may be familiar with the archetype, but we have tried to use the archetype in our lives and had a bad experience. Perhaps when we used the Caregiver archetype we were treated like a rug in someone's life, and they just used us and wiped their feet on us. We gave and gave and gave and someone took advantage of us. It would be natural for someone who was asked questions about the Caregiver archetype to score low as they had this *uncomfortable* experience. Is this why you might have scored low on an archetype; it is *uncomfortable* to you?

C. The archetype is **Unfriendly** to us: We may have had someone use the Magician archetype in our lives, and they attempted to manipulate us for the purpose of changing us into their version for us. Perhaps they didn't like the way we lived our lives, and they simply wanted a different person, so they attempted to "poof" us into the "perfect" image. Someone experiencing the Magician in such a way would not score high on this archetype. Is this why you might have scored low on an archetype; it is *unfriendly* to you?

D. The archetype is **Unneeded** in our lives: We might have gone through a real life experience of purging and cleaning things out of our lives and, therefore, at this time, have little or no need for the Destroyer archetype. We can, at times, go through a real season using a particular archetype and then, in another season, not currently need that archetype. Is this the reason you might have scored low on an archetype; it is *unneeded* to you?

E. The archetype is **Uncomplimentary** to something in our lives: Perhaps we work in a culture that does not support the Orphan archetype; this would cause us to score low on this archetype. If we have a spouse or significant other who scores high in a particular archetype, we might not score high in the archetype of balance, as that might cause stress in the relationship. You might be perfectly comfortable with the Orphan voice, but someone important in your life is not. You might score low because this archetype is *uncomplimentary*. For instance, if the societal normative supports women being smart and intelligent over funny, they might score high in Sage and low in Jester. If, in the same society, a man believes he will be more popular being funny and not being serious, he might score high in Jester and less in Sage. Is this the reason you might have scored low on an archetype; it is *uncomplimentary* to your surroundings?

F. The archetype is **Unbalanced** in our lives: We might score high in one pair of the archetype (Sage) and, therefore, not score high in the complimentary pair (Jester). This might be the most dangerous of the reasons to score low. We might find that an archetype conflicts with the pair and that using it will somehow cause conflict with the complimentary archetype. Is this the reason you might have scored low on an archetype; it is *unbalanced* in your life?

G. NOTE: The above six reasons are for you to identify. Perhaps talking it over with a leadership coach, spouse, colleague, or friend would provide some feedback as to which of the above reasons might best fit your situation in relationship to how you scored on a particular archetype. The key is to identify a reason(s) and begin to work through the imprint with a better understanding of how to use that particular archetype. This guidebook is not designed for this purpose. It is, however, imperative to know why you scored low in a particular archetype, so that during the change drama, when asked to live out a particular archetype necessary for the change, you know how to use it in the archetype's strength form.

4. You are not limited in your use of the archetypes. Each of the archetypes has an important role to play in the change story. You should not lock in on one or two and maintain those as your "go to" roles. Although it is true you will be more proficient and practical with some of the archetypes over some of the others (see later chapter of this book), you can and should incorporate them all into your life. When change takes place, no one is exempt from having to play one of the roles we will identify. If asked to play a particular archetypal role, no one person should be limited in that role. We certainly want to live in the areas where we have more strength and comfort, but this isn't always possible in the midst of the reality of a fluid change process.

THE DRAMA OF CHANGE

- Three Acts -

Act I - The Developmental Archetypes

Scene 1 - The Seeker

Scene 2 - The Lover

Scene 3 - The Destroyer

Scene 4 - The Creator

Act II - The Structural Archetypes

Scene 1 - The Warrior

Scene 2 - The Ruler

Scene 3 - The Orphan

Scene 4 - The Sage

Act III - The Attitudinal Archetypes

Scene 1 - The Caregiver

Scene 2 - The Magician

Scene 3 - The Innocent

Scene 4 - The Jester

ACT I - THE DEVELOPMENTAL ARCHETYPES

When we discuss the change process, we can get deep into many moving and *changing* parts. This book is provided to assist us in navigating roles in the drama of the change process. Change theory is broad in variety and open to many interpretations. It is the hope of this writer (the "Innocent" archetype coming through) that this work can be applied to many different forms of change theory and is beneficial to all. Let's look again at where we are going:

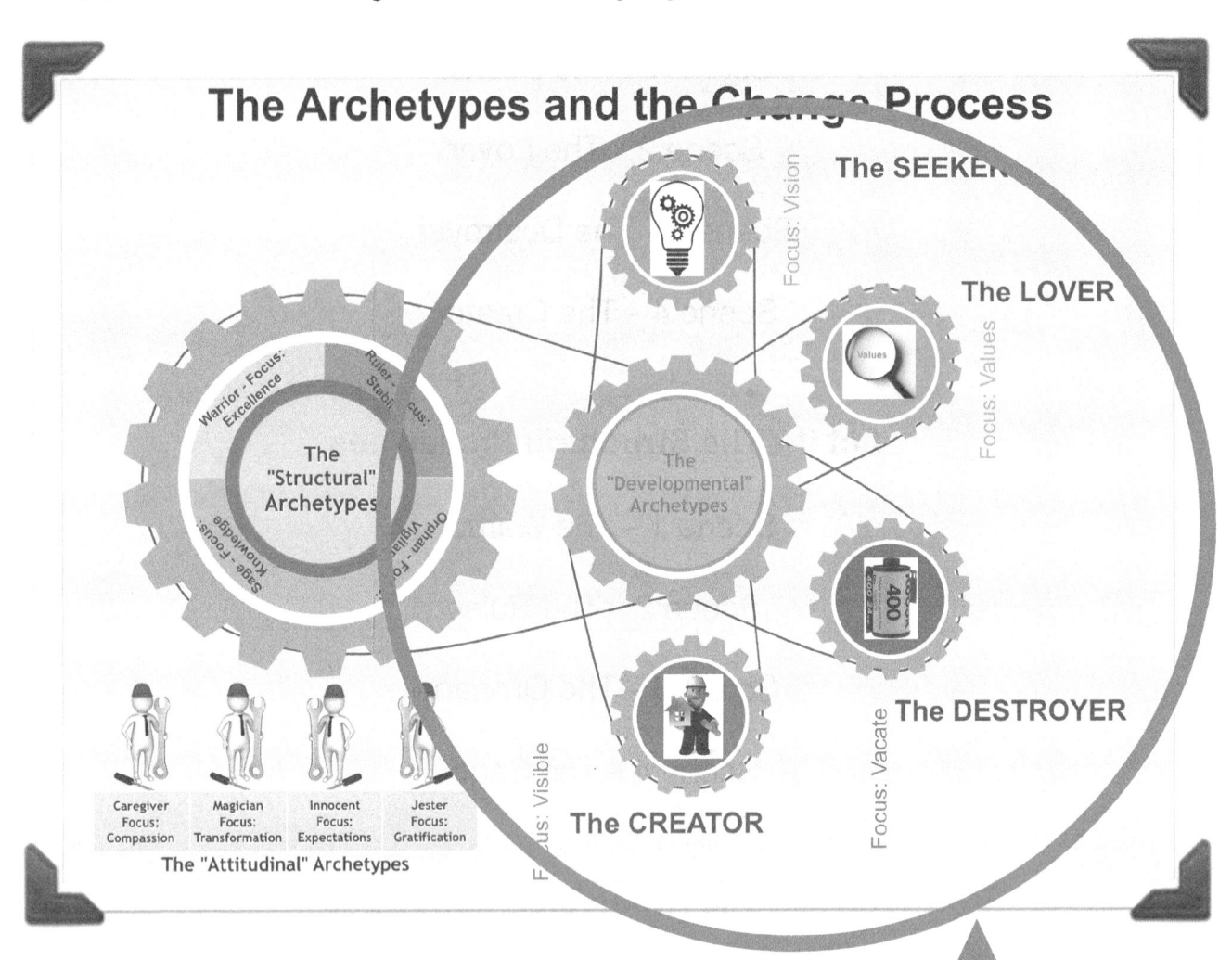

The Archetypes and the Change Process

The SEEKER — Focus: Vision
The LOVER — Focus: Values
The DESTROYER — Focus: Vacate
The CREATOR — Focus: Visible

The "Structural" Archetypes: Warrior - Focus: Excellence; Ruler - Focus: Stability; Sage - Focus: Knowledge; Orphan - Focus: Vigilance

The "Developmental" Archetypes

The "Attitudinal" Archetypes:
- Caregiver — Focus: Compassion
- Magician — Focus: Transformation
- Innocent — Focus: Expectations
- Jester — Focus: Gratification

> In Act I we are going to focus on The Developmental Archetypes. These are the archetypes that are the most important during the incubation of any idea for the change drama. These four are often overlooked in regard to their "unity." What typically happens during the change process is that the Seeker and the Creator archetypes work well together, while the Lover and Destroyer archetypes are overlooked. Act I is about using all four of these archetypes during the early stages of the change process, in unison and harmony. Failure to do so can subvert the change before it ever starts.

ACT I - THE DEVELOPMENTAL ARCHETYPES
SCENE ONE - *SEEKER* CENTER STAGE

During the beginning days of change, each of these four archetypes begin to increase their role(s) and their voice(s). The Seeker is often the initiator of any proposed change. The Seeker is the one who one day woke up and said, "I am tired of pushing dirt. From now on I am going to suck dirt." That was the day the vacuum cleaner was created. The Seeker is the one who thought it was odd that we had a phone attached to a wall that was connected to a line held in the air by a pole cemented in the ground. How odd is that? The Seeker is the one who thought Polio could be cured, automobiles were better than horses for travel and man, without wings, could fly. A Seeker thought we should go to the moon. A Seeker thinks food can be purchased online and delivered to your home by drones. There is a current Seeker who probably thinks drones are so yesterday. Seekers change the world. The iPhone alone has impacted dozens of other industries. Apple wants to disrupt the world in a positive manner with their products. That is the world of the Seeker in the change process. The Seeker thinks cancer can be cured. The Seeker doesn't have limits on their propositions. They dream. They dream big. They dream big and don't allow others to quench their thirst for their ideas.

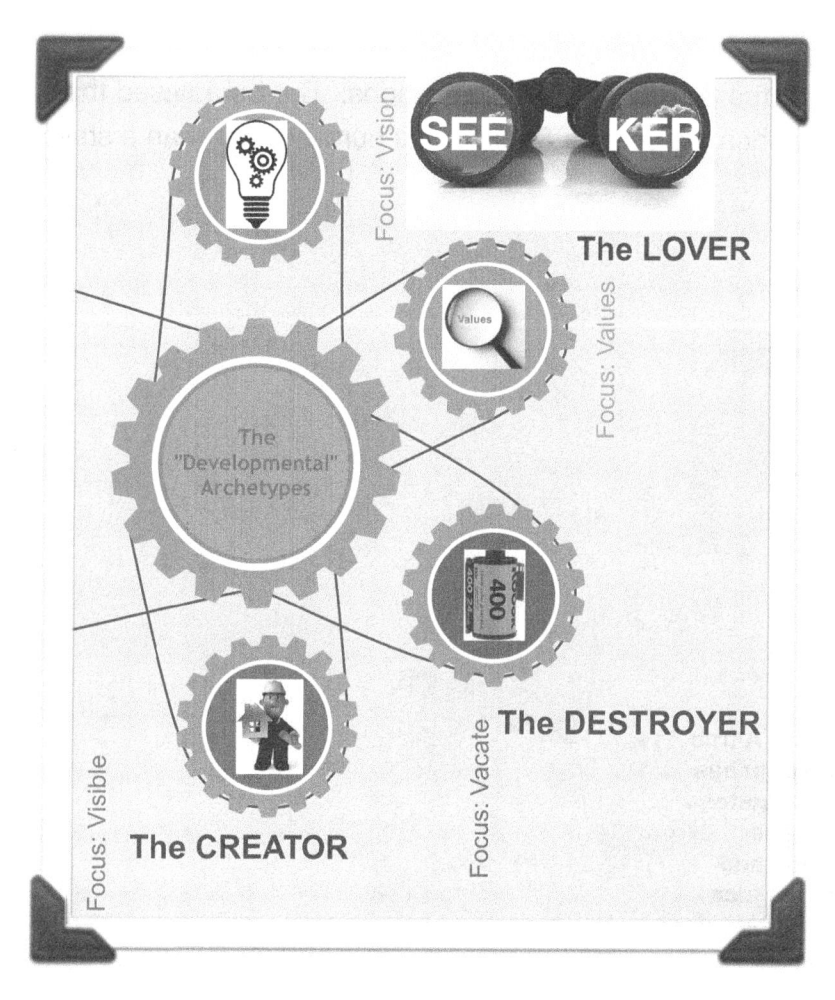

The Seeker can be very disruptive to the status quo. The Seeker sees the status quo as something to be conquered. They see status quo as an anchor that prevents the full sail of their ideas to flourish. The worst thing you can say to a Seeker is, "But we don't do it that way." It is not the worst comment to make because it holds them back. It is the worst words you would want to say if you want them to stop dreaming. The words, "But we don't do it that way," are fuel for the Seeker. They look for places where people are holding dearly to the status quo. A place with the *status quo* mantra is like the Wild West to the Seeker … it is a place yet to conquer. Seekers are the world's natural challengers. They challenge everything. They seek to explore and to leave society's norms, looking for new ventures to capitalize upon.

The Seeker is the **Vision** of the change process. The Seeker is always looking above and beyond the norms. This is what makes them so vital to organizations and so disruptive to organizations at the same time. There might be a reason why, in generations past, the R&D department was in another building.

Here are some reasons we struggle with the Seeker in our organizations. But be advised that we have static and dying organizations when we see the Seeker as a hurdle rather than a stair step to something great.

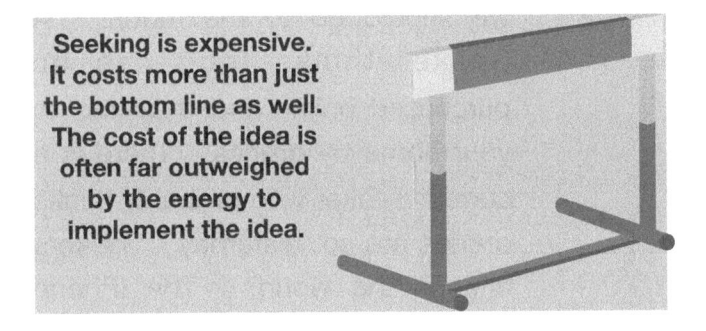

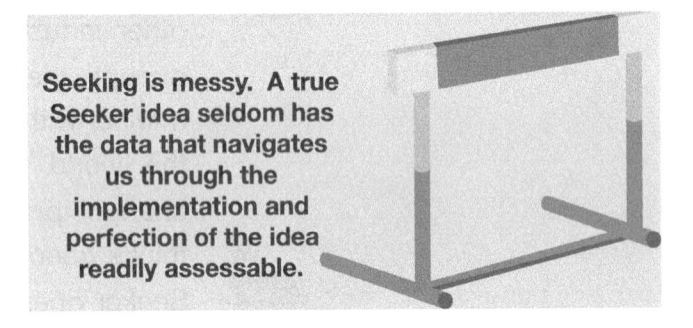

Seeking is expensive. It costs more than just the bottom line as well. The cost of the idea is often far outweighed by the energy to implement the idea.

Seeking is messy. A true Seeker idea seldom has the data that navigates us through the implementation and perfection of the idea readily assessable.

Seeking is risky. We never really know if the idea will actually work. (Thomas Edison comes to mind.) We hear about the ideas that do work but seldom about the ideas that fail.

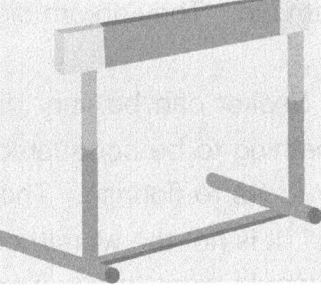

If we want to promote the Seeker, we have to be willing to take an expensive, messy risk. That is not on the top of ANY of the other archetypes (maybe the Creator ... IF they can catch the Seeker's **Vision**).

During the change process there are two problems that arise with the Seeker, however. The Seeker must be fully engaged and operating on the strength side of the archetype with the entire organization. But, often, when change is introduced to the broader organizational body, the Seeker work is considered already done. This is a problem with the Seeker world. The Seeker has the idea and delivers it to others, assuming they will carry out their idea. Often others "hear" about the idea as it is ready to be implemented. Early in the change drama, to those further down the organizational food chain, the idea is already "fully baked" and, therefore, they have little or no voice in the development of the idea. This already causes a hinderance to the change, as those asked to implement the idea feel they have no real voice. The majority of the organizational body are often simply the "doers" and are left out of the "developmental" stages of the idea. This creates a problem that cannot be ignored.

The second challenge with the Seeker is that once the idea is "accepted" the Seeker may "check out" of the process. The Seeker gets energy from thinking of the idea and not necessarily during the implementation period. They love to incubate an idea but get far less energy from the implementation of the same idea. Resentment of the organizational body can be created at this point in the change process. To the working body, the "idea guy" simply throws out ideas and then leaves them for others to solve. This is also a problem in the Seeker world. Once the Seeker believes their "work is done" and they are no longer engaged in the change process, the organization can lose the **Vision** behind the idea. The Seeker, the idea, and the organization all suffer when this problem exists.

The key to solving these two problems is the same for both: The Seeker has to know their role in the story of change as it applies to the rest of the cast. To assure that the change process is successful, the Seeker must begin with the body of the organization and must end with the body of the organization. Seekers don't like this because, again, they get energy from creating ideas. However, their ability to dream up many ideas for the organization (and therefore get much energy from each idea) is completely dependent upon the body of the workers in the organization to be engaged with them.

Getting the Seeker to engage with the body of the organization can be difficult, however. Seekers tend to want to be distant from anyone who might criticize their dreams. Remember, others do not share the Seeker's desire to disrupt the status quo. Criticism can come fast and furious for the Seeker's work. This is why the culture of the organization has to promote the Seeker mindset in addition to providing a platform for individual Seekers. The role of the

Seeker in the change process cannot be a "bit" role. Seeker is a major player in the change process. When the culture promotes a Seeker culture, everyone in the body of the organization comes to understand that no single idea or change is the product of an individual, but it is the product of the entire organization. In organizations where the Seeker is limited to a single individual, there is a chance for greater resistance to ideas. *Politics* over *ideas* is easier when the idea is connected to a single individual Seeker. But in a culture of Seeking, each Seeker is valued by other Seekers, because all are playing a part in the Seeker idea. In this type of approach, the organization becomes a place where all ideas are valued, and that makes change an expectation, not a hurdle. There might still be hurdles surrounding implementation, but there is a new level of desire to see ideas fostered and developed. Status quo is no longer King of the Castle in such an organization. The hurdles presented earlier are still real. The Seeker's world is still expensive, messy and risky. But the value of organizational success is changed when the Seeker archetype runs deep into the organizational body. The idea is developed and is further promoted as the Seeker sticks with the idea to the very end of the implementation. Giving a voice to the body emboldens the other archetypes and improves the change process.

Fostering a culture for Seekers to thrive, of course, creates another problem, the possibility of Failure! What organization wants to foster failure?

Outside the YMCA where I grew up there is a skateboard park. After finishing exercising, I would sit and watch these young people attempt some incredible tricks on their boards. Often they would not complete the trick they wanted and end up on their backsides. When

this happened, I was amazed at the response of the skateboarder who was on his/her back … they simply got up, laughed with their friends and tried the same trick again. In this culture it was perfectly permissible to fail. Imagine the same young person in their school's algebra class making a mistake while solving a problem on the white board in front of the class. What if everyone laughed? Would they be inspired to "try again?" Failure has not always been an option in that environment.

These skateboards are not, of course, spending public dollars or investor's retirement money or costing the organization resources. This is probably a stretch of a comparison for the Seeker, but maybe not. Skateboarding used to be a back-street-side-street, kid activity. The skateboard park I was observing was created with public dollars. The skateboard industry today is in the millions of dollars' type industry. All this around a bunch of kids who said to each other, "you can fail here." The Seeker said this can be a recognized sport. ESPN picked up the "sport" in their Extreme Games. Don't underestimate a place where you are allowed to fail. To the Seeker, failing only happens when you are not allowed to Seek.

On the next page is a "script" for the role of the Seeker during the change process. Each Seeker needs to find a way to play their role from the beginning of the change process to the end. That means the culture has to support the role and assure their character in the change process is valued.

The Seeker's Script in the Change Drama

The Seeker's script in the drama of change includes three scripts:

Seeker Script #1 - Center Stage

01 ADAPTABILITY

Don't get so locked in on your idea that all aspects of it are "holy" to you. Be willing to compromise in the beginning, and make sure you alert others that you are flexible and fluid in your thoughts. Just because it is an idea doesn't make it good.

02 CRITICAL THINKING

Yes, you will be criticized for your idea (early and often). Don't think of the criticism as a hurdle. Think of it as a "purification gate." The criticism will shape your idea and make it worthy to become the next status quo. Listen to the criticism, and learn from it. Allow it to shape your idea.

03 STRATEGIC PACE

Don't start to bake your idea until you have all the ingredients. Asking questions deep down into the body of the organization can solve problems well before they get a chance to disrupt the change. Your idea can and should include the other voices in the organization. This will enable you to be supported by others in the organization because you are supporting others in return.

04 CONVERSATIONS

Make sure you start conversations early with the rest of the organization about your idea. Engage with them individually, and let them speak early into your thoughts.

Seeker Script #2 - Moving Off Stage

Remember, you are not the center of the idea. The organizational mission and the people who make the mission happen must take the center stage. The other archetypes need to be heard and get a chance to speak into the change process. Your idea may have started it, but you are moving from the center spotlight because it is not about you. It is about the change that this idea can accomplish in regard to the mission of the organization.

Walk the idea through the other archetypes. Pay particular attention to the voice of the Lover archetype. This is status quo speaking (as we will see in the next scene). Remember, the other archetypes might object to your idea, all for different reasons. Note the following chart. Remember, each archetype has a role they are trying to play as well. If you remain at center stage, they can't play their part. You have to respond to their objections, and then, also bring them into your world by winning them over to your idea, early and often. Here is your script.

Seeker's script to interact with the other archetypes

Archetype	Possible objections they may have with the change	Goal Association Work (See Addendum #4)
Lover	They may want to hang on to the status quo. They may value the wrong thing, but, nevertheless, they see your idea is dangerous to their status quo.	You have to show them how this idea will still allow them to reach what they really value. If you fail here, your idea will fail, and the change initiative will fail.
Destroyer	They need to see what the idea is replacing and will need to agree that "something" needs replacing.	You have to show them early that your idea can help the organization replace something that is simply no longer profitable.
Creator	They can't always see the real practical application or design of the idea. They need to know the vision has something tangible behind it.	You have the role to help them see the tangible parts of your vision. It can't simply be a vision to the Creator, however. You have to help them touch it, not just see it.
Warrior	They might reject the idea if they think it will fail. They will want someone to show them that the change is successful or has the ability to be successful.	You have to show them that this will allow them to be the best. They are less interested in being the first if it doesn't translate to increased performance to be the best.
Caregiver	They might reject the change because of all the work that will be put on the plates of the workers to accomplish the idea.	You will have to show them that once the idea is fully implemented this will relieve the worker. You can't tell them; you have to show them.
Innocent	They might reject the change because they either don't see the need (naïveté) behind it or because they think it will be a hopeless pursuit.	You will need to convince them the idea can inspire the organizational body to reach greater possibilities. Get them to look at the positive aspects of the idea.
Orphan	They might reject the change because of failure to solve some of the problems the change will create when implemented.	You will need to hear the problems they present (they will be your biggest critic). Don't shut them down. They can improve your idea if you listen to them.
Ruler	They might reject the change because they don't see structurally how the change will work. They will want to policy and procedure any change.	The Ruler might want to put your idea into a box that fits nicely with the status quo of their processes. You will need to make sure you show them how the idea can fit into policies.
Magician	They might reject the idea if they think the idea lacks any ability to see transformation. They will be the least resistor since they see "change" as good for anyone or any organization.	Simply show them how "transformative" the idea is to the organization, individuals or mankind in general. Get them on board early in that thought, and you will have a great advocate to sell your idea to others.
Sage	They might reject change because they see the change as foolish and lacking substance or because it has little research (and it probably does because it is a new idea).	You should listen and learn from the Sage. You will have to decide if you want credit for the idea or if you want it to work. The Sage likes to lead in the ideas ... even if it is not their idea. Make it their idea for success.
Jester	They might reject the change because they think it will be boring, too much work (that will steal the joy of the current work), or because they see the change as too complicated (the Sage will make it so).	You will have to make sure they have a vision for enjoyment in the idea. This might be tough, depending on the idea. The enjoyment might not be in the idea, but in the way the idea interacts with the organization or how it is implemented.

Seeker Script #3 - Backstage

The Seeker must make sure that during the implementation process the **Vision** for the idea is not lost. That means making sure that the **Vision** is well defined and can be seen by everyone in the organization. When the **Vision** is lost, people parish with their support for the idea. Their objection is not, necessarily, rejection of the idea. They simply may not be able to see the idea in fruition. How do you keep the **Vision** in front of the other archetypes during the drama of change?

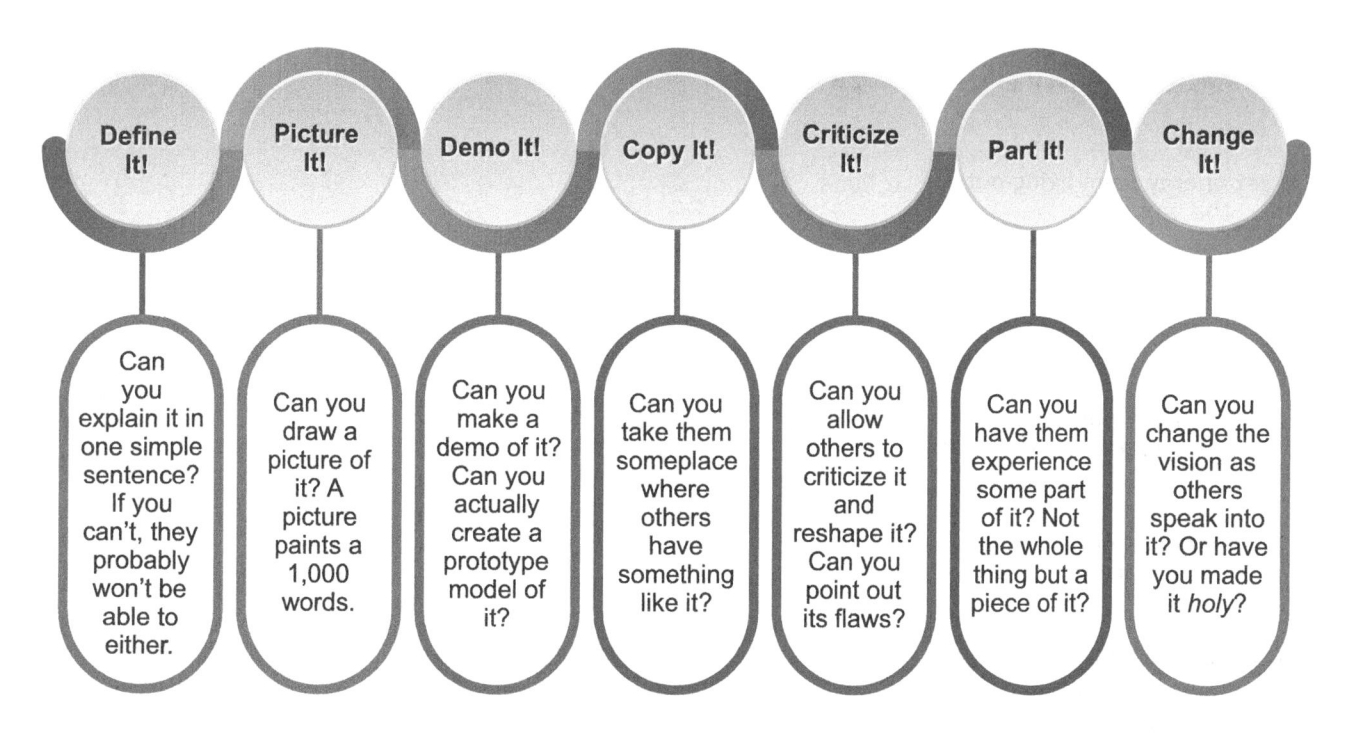

Define It!	Picture It!	Demo It!	Copy It!	Criticize It!	Part It!	Change It!
Can you explain it in one simple sentence? If you can't, they probably won't be able to either.	Can you draw a picture of it? A picture paints a 1,000 words.	Can you make a demo of it? Can you actually create a prototype model of it?	Can you take them someplace where others have something like it?	Can you allow others to criticize it and reshape it? Can you point out its flaws?	Can you have them experience some part of it? Not the whole thing but a piece of it?	Can you change the vision as others speak into it? Or have you made it *holy*?

Conclusion - an Email to the Seeker

Dear Seeker,

Let's face it; change doesn't happen without you. If it wasn't for you, we would still be living in caves and have no reclining chairs. As a foolish society, we have to admit you rule!! We can't live without you and your often flaky ideas. We owe you for plungers (thanks so much), Chia Pets, Polaroid film and pagers. Seriously, thanks for all you bring to us. The smart phone is great. We can't wait until it is obsolete. Texting is so cool.

Just one thing, however, could you slow down a bit, and let us process? The rotary phone was around for almost 70 years. The push button phone is still here … someplace. Can you just slow down?

Thanks again … the other 11 archetypes.

Seeker Audition Checklist
(You think you are equipped for the Seeker part in the Drama of Change?)

The following activities give the Seeker energy:	Never	Seldom	Sometimes	Often	Always
I get energy from dreaming of new ways to do things:	☐	☐	☐	☐	☐
I get energy from living outside the box:	☐	☐	☐	☐	☐
I get energy from challenging the status quo:	☐	☐	☐	☐	☐
I get energy from taking new ways to get to old places:	☐	☐	☐	☐	☐
I get energy from solving complicated problems:	☐	☐	☐	☐	☐
I get energy when others say there is no solution:	☐	☐	☐	☐	☐

- ☐ I like adventure stories
- ☑
- ☐ My vacations vary in type
- ☐ I am comfortable with risks
- ☐ I am not always organized
- ☐ I like to color outside the lines

Secrets for a Success Callback for a *Seeker* Role

❖ You have spent time or are willing to spend time researching and understanding innovation theory.

❖ You are interested in growing the organization through new things.

❖ You don't scare easily when confronted by those who are protecting the status quo.

❖ You are willing to study entrepreneurs and what makes them tick.

❖ You can recall a time in your life where you have failed and overcome the failure to accomplish something bigger.

❖ You are willing to take criticism of your ideas.

ACT I - THE DEVELOPMENTAL ARCHETYPES
SCENE TWO - *LOVER* CENTER STAGE

No drama can be written without some conflict. If you are going to have a Seeker in your organization (and you must ... unless you want to be Kodak, Atari, Blockbuster, etc.), you will have conflict. Seekers introduce a challenge to the status quo. Status quo is what makes a culture a culture. The status quo of a culture never changes. To have a culture, you have to have consistency. That is what makes it a culture. It is the culture's greatest strength and its Achilles heel. As change begins to take shape in the mind of the Seeker, at the same time a cold feeling of resistance might be forming in the Guardian of Status Quo: The Lover.

The Lover is the archetype that wants to hold on to the very thing that makes the culture what it is. Lovers love to hold. When the wind of change begins to blow, the Lover wants a warm blanket, a hot cup of coffee and a good friend to talk with about past accomplishments and glory. In the context of change, the Lover protects the way things are, and that is what gives them their greatest strength and deepest shadow.

The Lover wants to make sure that the change does not move us from our moorings. In the long run this is vital to any organization. As stated above, the greatest strength of an organization's culture is that it is identified, known and stable from day-to-day. The Lover, therefore, protects the organizational culture from chasing every wind of change. If the Seeker is the wind in the sail of the organization, the Lover is the compass to assure that the organization stays on course with the desired mission - based upon the steady adherence to the **Values** of the organization.

The Lover is often misunderstood (especially by the Seeker). The Lover, in the strength side, is not about "resistance." They are about "protection." They so much want to make sure that the *Values* of the organization are not lost, that they can take a stand against change, thinking they are doing something good. There are some reasons they may be doing good:

1. The *Values* of the organization can and should change to adapt to the constant demands of the world around us. However, when the *Values* change, the entire organization MUST BE in complete knowledge of such a change. The Lover makes sure everyone knows that any proposed change may be impacting a **Value**.

2. When *Values* change, the Lover is who we call on to make sure we know how to change them. Any change that impacts a core *Value* is a change that will take the greatest toll on the organization. An organization that doesn't know how to adjust their **Values** and shape and re-shape them (see the next page) will begin to either never change or experience unhealthy change.

3. The Lover enables us to see any change through the eyes of what we *Value*. In fact, a change suggested by the Seeker will actually put an organization in the best place to evaluate their *Values*.

The Lover is essential in the midst of change.

Before the real script of the Lover can be outlined, there needs to be understanding of *Values* and how they work within an organization. Again, this guidebook is not designed to be a full explanation of all things *Value*, but there needs to be a brief understanding about *Value* work within an organization or industry. For the sake of developing the Lover archetype in relationship to the drama of change, it should be noted that there is a difference in an organizational core value and a non-core value. To illustrate this, let's look at a current change happening in the educational industry.

In education, teachers are valued for many reasons. In the past, however, if you had to layoff any teachers, the mantra, *last-in-first-out,* would apply. The most recent teachers hired would be let go before a teacher with years of service. Seniority ruled. The term used to express this *Value* for teachers was *tenure*. A *tenured* teacher was *Valued* over a non-tenured teacher.

This mantra is, today, changing, however. Today, teachers are being evaluated using an evaluation tool. Ineffective teachers are being identified. Highly effective teachers are being identified. At least this is the current change drama taking place in the educational industry. This is not to say that, in the past, teachers were not evaluated and identified based upon their abilities. The change, however, is that when it comes to layoffs, tenure has been replaced with effectiveness. Education always *Valued* effectiveness. But they would still layoff a more effective teacher for a tenured teacher. That was the *Value* system. The industry *Value* was years of service. The current change is changing a core *Value* of education. They are now introducing the *Value* of effectiveness to replace tenure. This is a change in a core *Value*. It could be argued by some that the *tool* used to evaluate teachers is unfair or not representative of the teachers' skills or even highly flawed. The point here is that what the industry *Values* is being changed. The *tool* used to evaluate teachers is changing from year-to-year and, in some cases, month-to-month. The change in a *tool* is not a core *Value* change. A *tool* or a *method* or a *process* or a *procedure* are non-core *Value* changes. Changing what the *tool*, *method*, *process* or *procedure* is meant to *accomplish* is a core **Value** change.

This is where the Lover can become confused in their protection of the status quo. Lovers CAN and often DO hang onto the method or the tool or the procedure and/or process, instead of the core **Value** the tool, method, procedure or process they intended to accomplish. In our example of education, the question would be, "Did the change process introduce to the body of the industry that this was going to be a change in a core **Value**?" If not, the drama in the change process would be significant. The Lovers in the industry would have significant concern in the change to an evaluation tool that identified "effectiveness" as the new *Value*, if they highly *Valued* tenure.

To illustrate further the struggle with this Lover **Value** driven world, let's play a game. I have an empty house, and you are allowed to bring in one of three items. You can only bring in one thing into the house. Which of the three would you bring into the house? Again, you can only bring one!

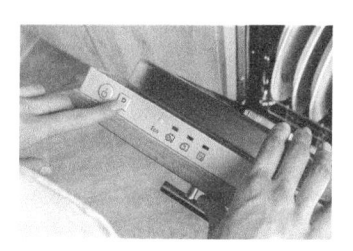

Dishwasher?

Washing Machine?

Which would you pick?
(You can ONLY pick ONE.)

Television?

What Role Do You Play In Change?   The Archetypes and the Change Process

Let me add to the game from the previous page. I will give you the empty house but let you bring one of *four* items into the house, only one. You can bring a dishwasher, a washing machine, a television or a ...

Refrigerator?

Can you see the struggle a Lover might have? In this illustration you are calling upon your Lover archetype to make a choice about your **Value**. In some countries the **Value** choice is, "Do I eat or do my children eat?"

The **Value** choice is tough to make. If you have children, you might choose the washing machine. If you like food, you might take the refrigerator. Whatever you choose, it is a **Value** decision; which one of the four do you **Value** more? (The only real choice here is a TV by the way! The house is empty, so you have no dishes, clothes or food. There is no need for a dishwasher, washing machine or refrigerator. The choice was to bring ONE thing in. The only logical choice would be a television. But who says we do **Value** choices on *logic*?)

This is a silly game, but the Lover makes choices like this every day in regard to **Values**. This is why the Lover is so important to us during the change process. Let's go back to our illustration of education and the change in **Value** from tenure to effectiveness based upon an evaluation process. The industry still **Values** tenure, just not as much as it did in the past. If in the game you switched from dishwasher to refrigerator, you can see the Lover's challenge as applied to the teacher. They certainly all **Value** effectiveness. But they also **Value** tenure (for more reasons than just job security). This is the **Value** struggle of the Lover. Always having to choose between the **Values** of the past and the Seeker's **Vision** for the future.

Too many industries and organizations hold on to non-core **Values**, thinking they are the most important **Value** when, in reality, they have simply objectified the tool, item, or thing they say they **Value**. The thing they **Value** is not the tool, but they think it is. Here are some examples of this approach:

Example #1 - Somewhere in a large office building in a small town in western, upstate New York, someone may have said, "They (customers) will always want 35mm film!" The town was Rochester, New York. The company was Kodak. However, across the country around the same time, someone else said, "They may not always want 35mm film. We better develop (no pun intended) other products." That company was Fuji film. Fuji **Valued** capturing images, the core **Value**. Kodak **Valued** 35mm film, the tool that allowed them to capture images. The Lover archetype can objectify something, mistaking it for the main thing.

Example #2 - Somewhere in any town in America someone said, or is saying, "They will always want a newspaper." You might remember the time you stayed in a hotel and when you woke up each morning and looked down the hallway of any floor there was a copy of the USA Today at every door. Today, you might find newspapers at the front desk. There are many who made their living off the newspaper news business that were in love with newspaper print. There were others who were in love with conveying news. One **Valued** the tool (the actual newspaper), and there were others who **Valued** the core **Value**, conveying news.

Example #3 - In the educational industry there is a movement to change the way we teach today's students. The old method was a teacher standing in front of the class as the person with the content, who conveyed that content to the students. They called that teaching. Today we see that engaging students in a variety of methods in the learning process is far better. Some teachers are in love with teaching. They **Value** teaching. There is a movement changing that paradigm, however. Some teachers today are now in love and **Value** learning. They see teaching as only one method for learning to take place. Students can actually learn without a teacher (this is why we don't let them spend hours in front of a computer on their own … we are afraid of what they might learn). If a teacher **Values** learning, they will have a completely different classroom look and feel than a teacher who **Values** only teaching.

These are but three examples of the Lover archetype and the difference in what they may **Value** and how that, in turn, impacts how they may play their role in the drama of change.

The Lover's Script in the Change Drama

The Lover's script in the drama of change includes three scripts:

Lover Script #1 - Center Stage

Make sure as you identify the **Value** you hold on to, that you also identify if it is a core **Value** or a non-core **Value**. Are you holding onto a mission-sensitive **Value**, or are you holding on to a **Value** that is a tool, method, process or procedure.

Make sure when you hear about the change, you don't react in regard to simply being the Guardian of Status Quo! You have a responsibility to hold on to the organization's **Values**, but remember, every status quo was, at one time, a new idea.

When you see the change idea, spend some time trying to help the Seeker connect it to a current **Value** the organization holds. The job of aligning new ideas to current **Values** is important. You are the best fit for that job.

Take a key role in introducing and selling the idea to others. Show them how this new idea can be used to help the organization better reach their established **Values**. Who better to show this connection. Make the connection for them.

Lover Script #2 - Moving Off Stage

Remember, you too are not the center of the idea. The mission of the organization is at the center. Your role in the change process is, yes, guard the **Values**. But you are also responsible to make sure others can see the connection of the idea to the core **Values** of the organization. If this is a core **Value** change, you have much work today. Resisting is not work. Obstruction is not work.

Walk the idea through the other archetypes. Pay particular attention to the voice of the Destroyer archetype. That voice will frighten you (as we will see in the next scene). Remember, the other archetypes might object to the idea based upon how you react. They will all have different reasons. Note the following chart. As stated previously, each archetype has a role they are trying to play as well. If you remain at center stage, they can't play their part. The Lover has to respond to their objections, and then, also bring them into your world by winning them over to the idea and how it impacts the organizational **Values**, early and often. Here is your off stage script.

Lover's script to interact with the other archetypes

Archetype	Possible objections they may have with the change	Goal Association Work (See Addendum #4)
Seeker	They may want to take the organization into a new direction. This isn't always bad and, in fact, necessary at times.	You have to help the Seeker remember the values of the organization. Don't make them prove to you how their idea reflects the values.
Destroyer	They need to see what the change is replacing and will need to agree that "something" needs replacing.	Remember, this is your toughest archetype. You will be challenged that your values are still relevant. If they are, fight. If not, change!!
Creator	They can't always see the real practical application or design of the change. They need to know the vision has something tangible behind it.	Your real work with the Creator is to make sure that with the tangible portion of the work, we keep on track to identify the values we are trying to reach with the creation.
Warrior	They might reject the change if they think it will fail. They will want someone to show them that the change is successful or has the ability to be successful.	You have to help the Warrior see the fight is worth fighting. They have to connect their desire for the best performance to the value the idea is trying to reach. Show them!
Caregiver	They might reject the change because of all the work that will be put on the plates of the workers to accomplish the change.	You can help them know the difference from helping just to help and helping for a real reason, the extension of the identified value(s).
Innocent	They might reject the change because they either don't see the need (naïveté) behind it or because they think it will be a hopeless pursuit.	The Innocent wants to inspire others to keep going. What is more inspirational than the value the idea in the change process is attempting to reach and complete?
Orphan	They might reject the change because you failed to solve some of the problems the change will create when implemented.	The Orphan can be a great ally for you. They see danger. Make sure they don't misread the values. They can often see the wrong values.
Ruler	They might reject the idea because they don't see structurally how the change will work. They will want to policy and procedure any change.	The Ruler might get lost in the value discussion. You might have to help them see that policies and procedures are there to further the values. Policies and procedure are not the values.
Magician	They might reject the change if they think it lacks any ability to see transformation. They will be your least resistor since they see "change" as good for anyone or any organization.	The Magician is often value driven. The problem might be that they are not driven by the organization's value but their own values. Help them see that true transformation can only happen when guided by "shared" values.
Sage	They might reject change because they see the change as foolish and lacking substance or because it has little research (and it probably does because it is a new idea).	The Sage needs to see that their knowledge base has to be connected to the values of the organization and the idea driving the change. Help them connect all three. New knowledge can tie true values to valid ideas of change.
Jester	They might reject the change because they think it will be boring, too much work (that will steal the joy of the current work), or because they see the change as too complicated (the Sage will make it so).	Jesters are not always driven by the values of the organization. They value enjoyment no matter the mission. You will have to work to show them that the shared organizational values are worthy to be enjoyed.

Lover Script #3 - Backstage

The Lover must make sure that during the implementation process the **Value** for the idea is not lost. That means making sure that the **Value** is well defined and can be seen by everyone in the organization. When **Value** is lost, people drift with any idea that is mentioned. They may not know the **Value**(s). They simply may not be able to remember them as the idea blows them in a different direction. How do you keep the **Value** in front of the other archetypes during the drama of change?

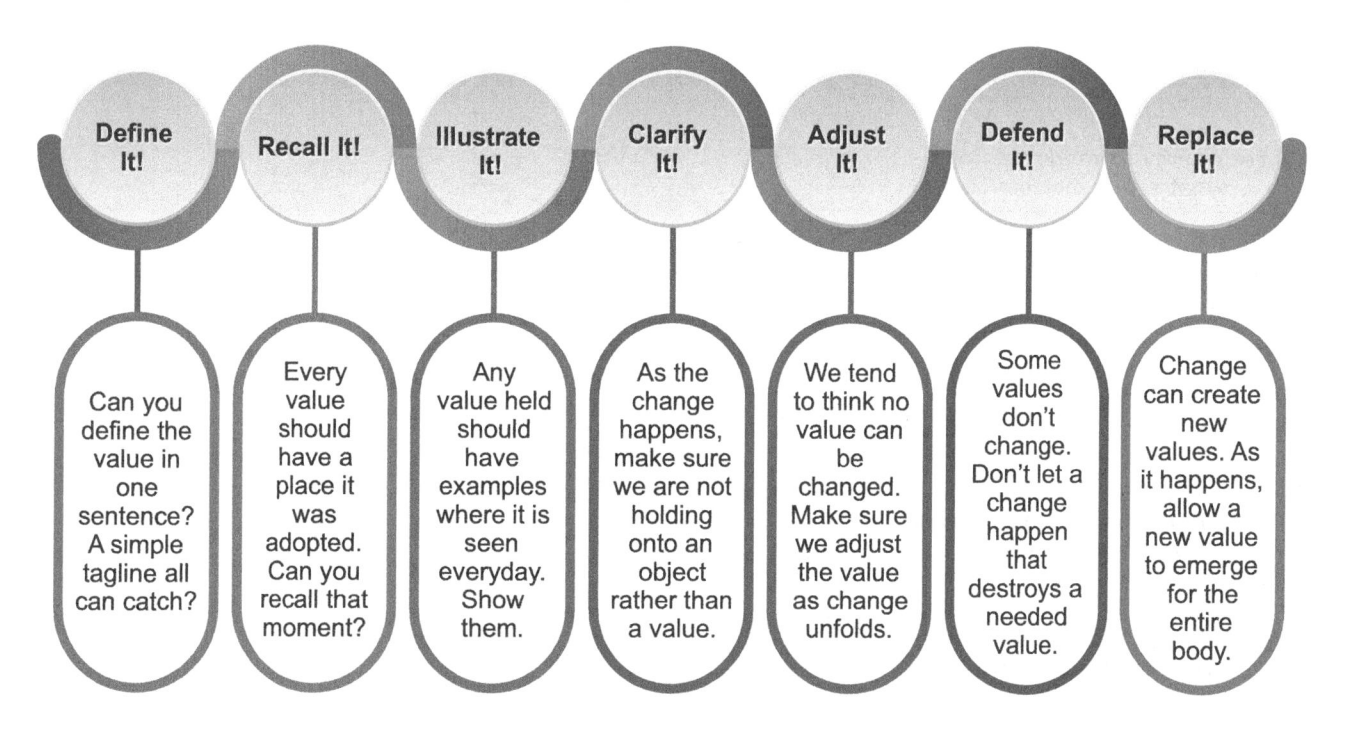

Define It!	Recall It!	Illustrate It!	Clarify It!	Adjust It!	Defend It!	Replace It!
Can you define the value in one sentence? A simple tagline all can catch?	Every value should have a place it was adopted. Can you recall that moment?	Any value held should have examples where it is seen everyday. Show them.	As the change happens, make sure we are not holding onto an object rather than a value.	We tend to think no value can be changed. Make sure we adjust the value as change unfolds.	Some values don't change. Don't let a change happen that destroys a needed value.	Change can create new values. As it happens, allow a new value to emerge for the entire body.

Conclusion - an Email to the Lover

Dear Lover,

Thank you. Without you, our organization would be adrift. You play such an important role in our holding on to what matters. So many organizations change, just to change. We appreciate your remembering the past and keeping us tied to it.

But can you see the beauty and the beast in that statement? You so often remind us of a great moment from the past, but also keep us so tied to that moment we can't create new moments. We see that the past was great, but it had many challenges that you sometimes forget. Progress can be difficult for you, we know. But we also know the past was not always the best. If we were still in the past, we would still be roasting some animal on a stick over an open flame. Sometimes change can create new moments. We want our memories of the past to support the future, not prevent it. Thanks again ... the other 11 archetypes.

Lover Audition Checklist
(You think you are equipped for the Lover part in the Drama of Change?)

The following activities give the Lover energy:	Never	Seldom	Sometimes	Often	Always
I get energy from making sure things stay the same:	☐	☐	☐	☐	☐
I get energy from identifying what really matters to us:	☐	☐	☐	☐	☐
I get energy recalling highlights from the past:	☐	☐	☐	☐	☐
I get energy from creating a team approach to things:	☐	☐	☐	☐	☐
I get energy from remembering those from the past:	☐	☐	☐	☐	☐
I get energy when others say we stand for something:	☐	☐	☐	☐	☐

- ☐ I like team building stories
- ☑ My vacations don't vary much
- ☐ I am comfortable with what I know
- ☐ I love harmony
- ☐ I like traditions

What Role Do You Play In Change?   The Archetypes and the Change Process

Secrets for a Successful Callback for a *Lover* Role

❖ You have spent some time or will spend time studying team development.

❖ You get annoyed by conflict but want to work through it to protect the harmony of the team.

❖ You enjoy learning about what makes team members tick and how they interrelate.

❖ You have or are willing to study failed teams and what made them fail.

❖ You have or are willing to study your culture to discern what makes it tick and strong.

ACT I - THE DEVELOPMENTAL ARCHETYPES
SCENE THREE - *DESTROYER* CENTER STAGE

(NOTE: The descriptor *Destroyer* has been changed to *Revolutionary*. Please see Addendum #3 as to why this author is using the *Destroyer* descriptor.)

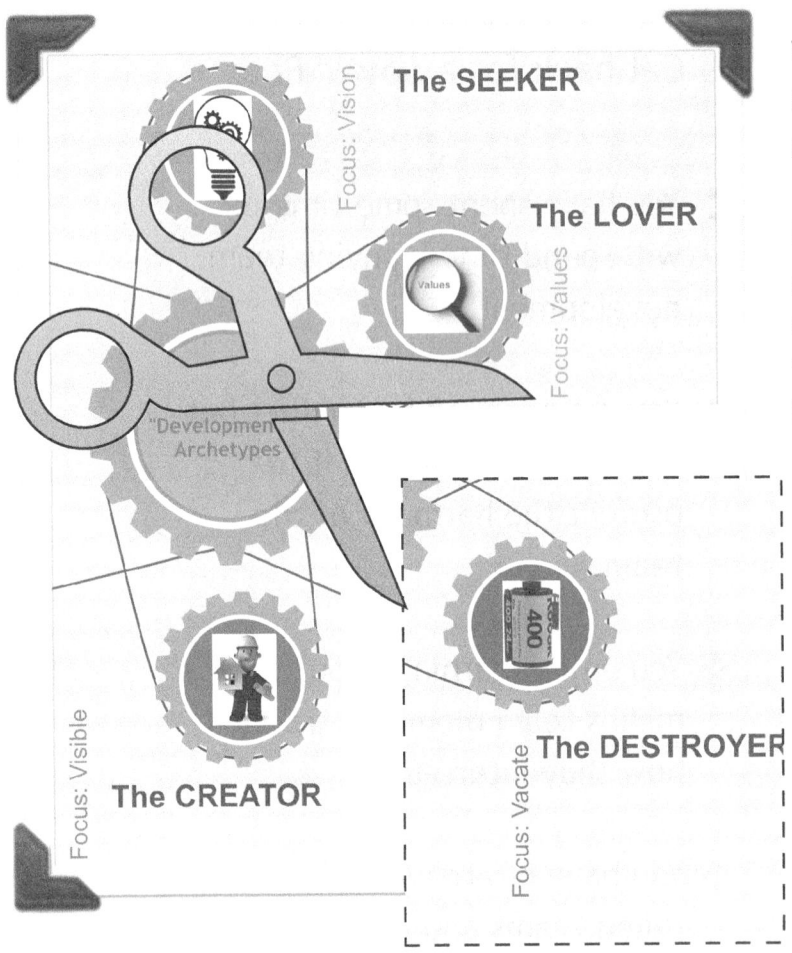

What is the favorite phrase of the Destroyer? Cut it out!! (A little archetype humor ... very little.)

During the change process, the greatest area for pressure and conflict will be where the change is forcing or asking for something to be let go, replaced, cut out, and/or to quit something. The classic book, *Who Moved My Cheese*, is a book about how the Destroyer archetype came to work one day and did what the Destroyer archetype does during the drama of change: Dismantled the system and moved the cheese.

The Destroyer archetype is a difficult archetype for the other archetypes to engage. It is obvious why those who developed the PMAI assessment wanted to change the name to Revolutionary (see Addendum #4). Who wants to be known as a Destroyer? Yet, you can't have change, especially significant change, without someone playing the role that is best defined by the term Destroyer. If you want to have change, you will have to let something go. If you want to see change take place in your life or organization, you will have to do some destroying of something. The concept of "letting go" is a prerequisite for change. Simply changing the name of the archetype does not change the need or importance of letting go of something to allow change to take place.

The truth of the matter is that the name of this role is secondary to the function it plays in the drama of change. The Destroyer reminds us, identifies for us, and teaches us how to **Vacate** something to allow the change to take place. We can't do change from one thing to the other without the Destroyer's work of **Vacating** something.

What Role Do You Play In Change?   The Archetypes and the Change Process

If you have ever visited an art museum and gazed upon a great sculpture, you could come to appreciate the Destroyer archetype even more. As you stand on the clean carpet of the museum, while listening to a Kenny G playlist in the background, you can enjoy the beauty of the sculptured piece. You take in the design, the message being conveyed by the artist, and the meaning of the artist's choice of medium. Yet, what you see before you in the confines of the museum's pleasant nature is nothing like what you would have seen if you would have been in the artist's studio the moment he/she finished the sculpture you now admire. If you could look down at the studio floor, what would you see? What would be at the feet of the artist? You would see everything the artist DID NOT WANT in his/her sculpture. The Destroyer archetype is in the artist's heart, mind and hands. The artist destroys and cuts away what is not wanted, needed or contributing to the change the artist is introducing to the medium they have chosen to convey their vision.

The Destroyer archetype is about how to choose what to **Vacate** and what to validate - what needs to stay in the finished product. This role in the drama of change is crucial. Without the role of the Destroyer, we might "add" to the status quo, but we don't necessarily change the status quo. Change implies letting something go to replace it with something else. That is the Destroyer-Creator archetypes in action (see Creator in the next scene).

The struggle with incorporating the Destroyer archetype into the change process might be one reason why workers have so much "stuff" in their lives and in their work processes. They simply have a struggle "letting go" of something. The Warrior archetype in particular struggles with the concept of "quitting" something. Warriors simply don't quit … quitting is for losers. The only way we can get a Warrior archetype to quit is to reframe the quitting as *strategic abandonment*. *Strategic Abandonment* is the ability to destroy something in your life you no longer see as profitable, needed or important. That is the work of the Destroyer archetype.

What Role Do You Play In Change?   **The Archetypes and the Change Process**

In the change process, in order to play the Destroyer role, you have to understand and appreciate the art of *chiseling*. Woodworkers know how to chisel. They have a specific tool for each away they wish to accomplish. The ability to chisel ideas, individuals and/or the interests of others is an art form. We can be destructive with the chisel, but it is much more beneficial to use the chisel to shape rather than to smash, shatter or sabotage.

There are, however, some reasons why we dislike the chiseling process:

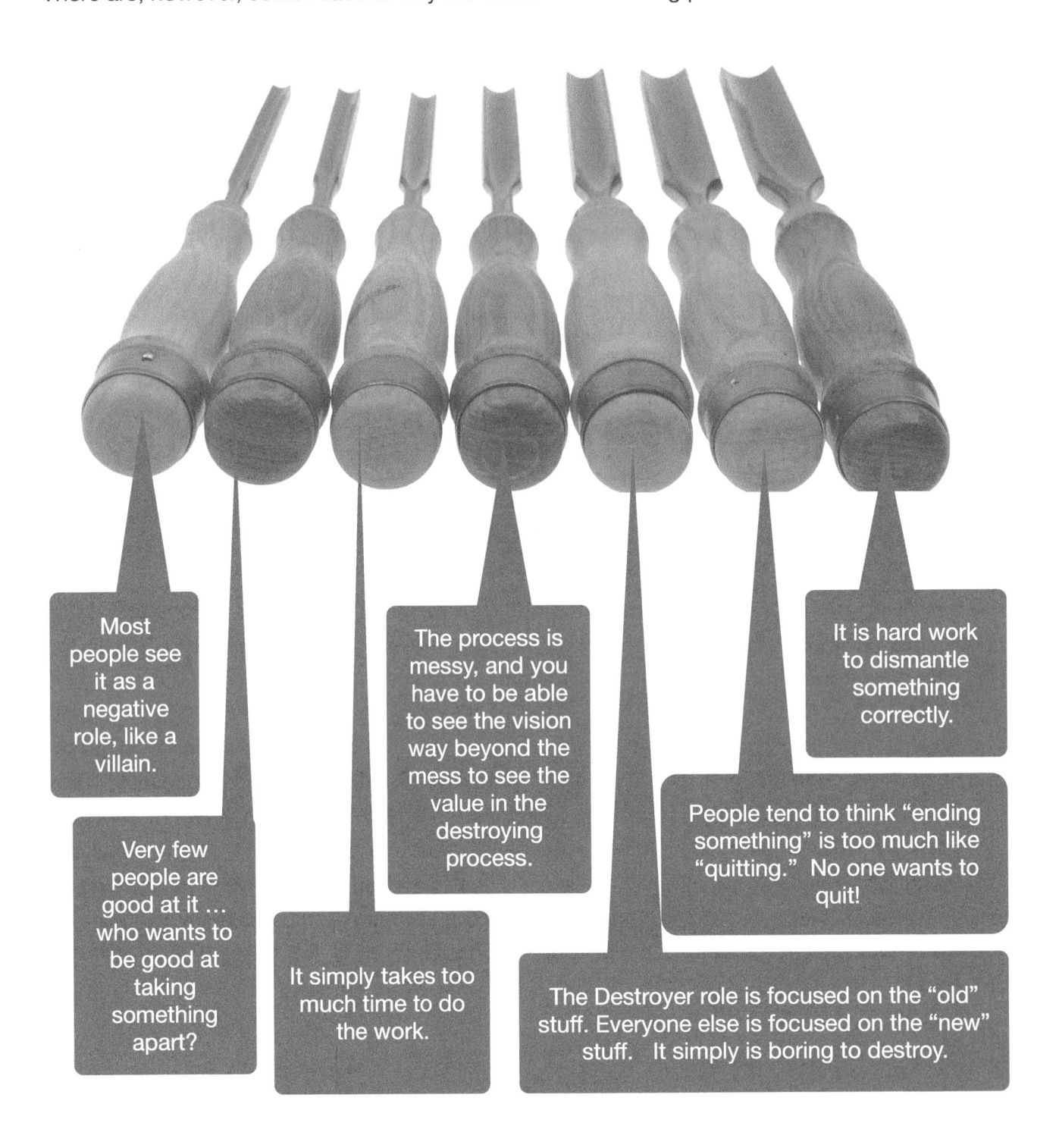

- Most people see it as a negative role, like a villain.
- Very few people are good at it ... who wants to be good at taking something apart?
- It simply takes too much time to do the work.
- The process is messy, and you have to be able to see the vision way beyond the mess to see the value in the destroying process.
- The Destroyer role is focused on the "old" stuff. Everyone else is focused on the "new" stuff. It simply is boring to destroy.
- People tend to think "ending something" is too much like "quitting." No one wants to quit!
- It is hard work to dismantle something correctly.

The Destroyer's Script in the Change Drama

The Destroyer's script in the drama of change includes three scripts:

Destroyer Script #1 - Center Stage

The Destroyer should focus on three ares when assisting those around them to *let go* of something:

INVESTIGATE

The Destroyer must spend time investigating the work, always looking for what is profitable and what is not profitable. They must spend time putting the work under a spotlight to investigate what is serving the mission and what is not. Their role is to look at the change process and the areas of change to assure that if anything is not working it is reported and investigated. This needs to be the first step in their role: Investigate the work.

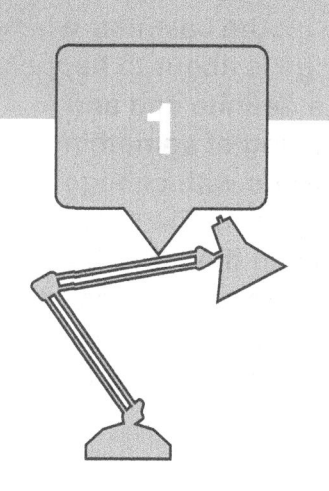

1

IDENTIFY

The tendency of the Destroyer is to toss the *baby out with the bathwater*. The Destroyer can't just point out work that isn't working. They must take time to identify if there is anything within the parts of the work that might have some profit. All parts of a particular task, tool, procedure, process, etc., are not always bad and without merit. The Destroyer must spend time to identify what might have some profit and what no longer benefits the organization.

2

INDULGE

If the Destroyer has done a great job in these previous steps, they have separated the wheat from the chaff. Now the Destroyer's work really begins. At this point, they may think it is time to take a trip to the dumpster. That time will come, but it is important to remember that what they now see that needs to be tossed out, *once* was important to someone; it once served a purpose. Before tossing it, it is time to celebrate that service. It's time to indulge. Turn page ...

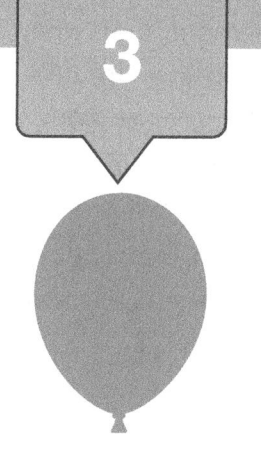

3

What Role Do You Play In Change? The Archetypes and the Change Process

INDULGE - THE DESTROYER'S SECRET WEAPON

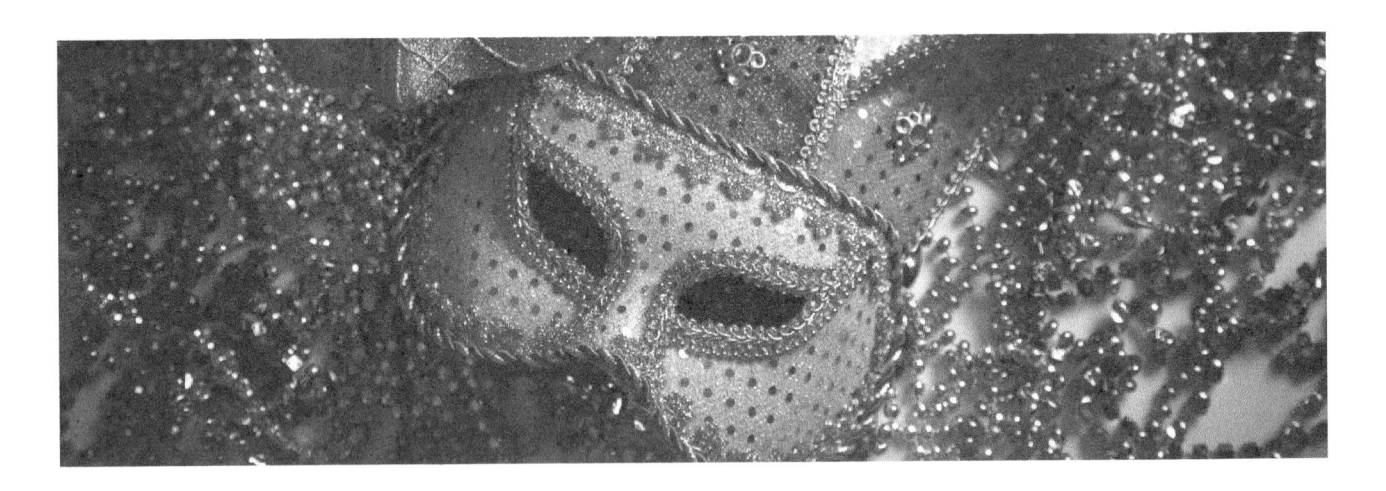

Do you know what a Mardi Gras is all about? A Mardi Gras is a party we have that leads up to Fat Tuesday. On Fat Tuesday we have a great time gorging ourselves. The reason we gorge ourselves on Fat Tuesday is because the next day is Ash Wednesday, and that is the day we have committed ourselves, or others with us, to *let go* of something, or *toss something out of* our lives, or *quit* something. Mardi Gras is a party that a Destroyer invented to indulge over something they were about to quit. (It should be noted that Mardi Gras is much more than this for many, but the basic premise is a celebration over the death of something.)

The key thought in here is that there is a celebration prior to a separation. One of the reasons the Destroyer term is so important is that it allows us to remember that when we ask someone to let go of something in the change process, they feel *destruction* on their side of the story. We think it is a necessary purging. They feel like it is a punishment. The thing we are asking them to *get over* was, at one time, an important part of their status quo. We are asking them to move away from it, but they see it as valuable.

Four reasons you should celebrate destroying:

1. It shows you value the person(s) who originally developed the thing you're letting go.
2. It shows you value past work and product. It is not simply a "throw-away."
3. It shows that the letting go process can have meaning and purpose.
4. It provides an important date on the calendar where change is about to happen. It is a definite end and beginning of something. The issue with change is the ambiguity of the date one ends and the other begins. (Software companies are great at *sunset dates* - a time the software ends.)

If a husband goes away and, while gone, his wife tosses out his old college sweatshirt, upon return he feels destruction. If, on the other hand, his wife goes away and he cleans his closet, tossing out the sweatshirt, he feels cleansed. He had a choice in the purging. This is why it is so important to make sure that before we toss something out we know to be no longer profitable, we take time to celebrate and indulge those who had a part in the birth and sustainability of the thing we are tossing. We need to celebrate how the *thing* served us. We need to have a Fat Tuesday celebration. Why? Because Ash Wednesday is coming for the *thing*. The Destroyer would do well to ask for help from the Caregiver and/or Jester for this moment in their script. But whether with another archetype or alone, the Destroyer must master the art of *indulging* before destroying.

Destroyer Script #2 - Moving Off Stage

Remember, you, like the others, are not the center of the idea. The mission of the organization is at the center. Your role in the change process is, yes, to look for what to **Vacate**. But you are also responsible to make sure others can see the reason something needs to be **Vacated**. They need to see why it is no longer useful. They will each have a different need when it comes to quitting something they have been doing for a long time. They also need to see that you are aware that there might still be parts that are important and needful ... if only small parts. Your work in this area is key to them understanding the Destroyer role in the change process. You will want to give them a voice in that work.

Walk the idea through the other archetypes. Pay particular attention to the voice of the Lover archetype. That voice may not see you kindly (as we saw in the previous scene). Remember, the other archetypes might object to what you see needs to be *Vacated* to make the change successful. You might have to show the Seeker what part of their idea needs to be *Vacated*. Each archetype will have a different reason to see how the **Vacating** work is done. Note the following chart. As stated previously, each archetype has a role they are trying to play as well. If you remain at center stage, they can't play their part. The Destroyer has to respond to their objections, and then also bring them into your world by winning them over to the idea. They need to see both the reason something has to be *Vacated* and how to do the **Vacating**. They need to be taught to let go of something. Here is your moving off stage script.

Destroyer's script to interact with the other archetypes

Archetype	Possible objections they may have with the change	Goal Association Work (See Addendum #4)
Seeker	They may want to take the organization into a new direction. This isn't always bad and, in fact, necessary at times.	You may have to investigate and identify the Seeker's idea. The Seeker often thinks that all parts of their ideas are great. You might not.
Lover	They may want to hang on to the status quo. They may value the wrong thing, but, nevertheless, they see change as dangerous to their status quo.	This may be your most difficult archetype. Your job is to help them see what is still important in the status quo and what is not. They will very much need your indulging work.
Creator	They need to see what the change is replacing and will need to agree that "something" needs replacing.	As the Creator begins to put tangibility to the idea, you will want to make sure that they are not overcommitting the organization and team to unprofitable tasks and roles.
Warrior	They might reject the change if they think it will fail. They will want someone to show them that the change is successful or has the ability to be successful.	Getting a Warrior to quit something is tough. You will have to teach them strategic abandonment. Once they see the thing you want to quit can cause loss, they will let go.
Caregiver	They might reject the change because of all the work that will be put on the plates of the workers to accomplish the idea.	The Caregiver needs to see that *letting go* of something can *help* others. If you can't show them how, they will struggle *letting go*.
Innocent	They might reject the change because they either don't see the need (naïveté) behind it or because they think it will be a hopeless pursuit.	The Innocent may not see the *letting go* as hopeful or inspiring. You will have to show them that letting go will *open the door* to something more inspiring and hopeful.
Orphan	They might reject the change because of failure to solve some of the problems the change will create when implemented.	Orphans can let go as soon as they see the *thing* to let go is dangerous and not beneficial to the entire group. They might be helpful in your *investigation* step.
Ruler	They might reject the change because they don't see structurally how the change will work. They will want to policy and procedure any change.	Along with Lover, it can be hard for Ruler to let go. You have to show them a better rule, policy, etc., they can use to replace what you are asking them to let go. They will want a voice in the process of how to let go.
Magician	They might reject the change if they think it lacks any ability to see transformation. They will be the least resistor since they see "change" as good for anyone or any organization.	You can use the Magician's transforming ability to help others learn how to let go. If you struggle with how to let go, the Magician may be your best resource. They get energy using the *letting go step* to transform others.
Sage	They might reject change because they see the change as foolish and lacking substance or because it has little research (and it probably does because it is a new idea).	The Sage is another valuable resource as to what needs to be let go and what needs to stay. They would be helpful in the *identification* stage, knowing what should stay.
Jester	They might reject the change because they think it will be boring, too much work (that will steal the joy of the current work), or because they see the change as too complicated (the Sage will make it so).	As stated earlier, the Jester can help in the *indulging* step. The Jester can throw a mean party. They don't like the idea of destroying. It does not sound like fun. But they would love to help you make destroying enjoyable.

Destroyer Script #3 - Backstage

The Destroyer must make sure that during the implementation process the **Vacating** of useless steps, processes and/or procedures is ongoing. This means they have to be vigilant in watching for what may be wasteful. But it is not simply a matter of pointing it out. The Destroyer has an obligation to prove the wasteful enterprise and to make sure others know how to move away from the non-profitable to the profitable. How do you keep the **Vacate** idea in front of the other archetypes during the drama of change?

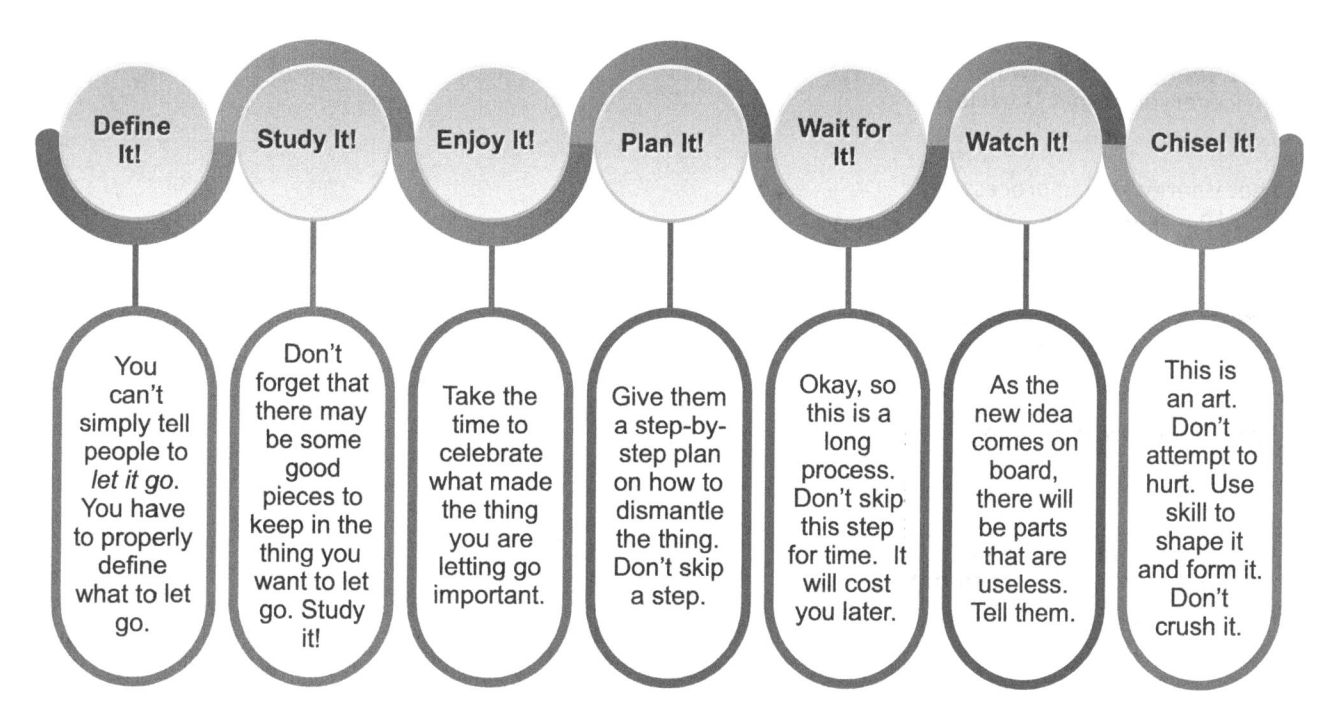

Define It!	Study It!	Enjoy It!	Plan It!	Wait for It!	Watch It!	Chisel It!
You can't simply tell people to *let it go*. You have to properly define what to let go.	Don't forget that there may be some good pieces to keep in the thing you want to let go. Study it!	Take the time to celebrate what made the thing you are letting go important.	Give them a step-by-step plan on how to dismantle the thing. Don't skip a step.	Okay, so this is a long process. Don't skip this step for time. It will cost you later.	As the new idea comes on board, there will be parts that are useless. Tell them.	This is an art. Don't attempt to hurt. Use skill to shape it and form it. Don't crush it.

Conclusion - an Email to the Destroyer

Dear Destroyer,

You are sometimes hard to take. We are just being honest. We know that there are things we all need to let go, but sometimes you can be rather cruel and blunt about it. Please be patient with us. We will get it. We really like the celebration part. Can we do that for like … years? Just kidding(?) We do need help knowing how to quit. It is not like we had any classes on *how to quit*. Our parents taught us never to give up on something. You will really need to take the time to show us how to let go. We just don't know how to do it. If you don't show us how to let go of something, the only thing we will really want to let go of is you! Just kidding(?)

Thanks again … the other 11 archetypes.

Destroyer Audition Checklist
(You think you are equipped for the Destroyer part in the Drama of Change?)

The following activities give the Destroyer energy:	Never	Seldom	Sometimes	Often	Always
I get energy from taking things apart:	☐	☐	☐	☐	☐
I get energy from showing everyone what is useless:	☐	☐	☐	☐	☐
I get energy seeing processes that don't work, ended:	☐	☐	☐	☐	☐
I get energy from watching change take place:	☐	☐	☐	☐	☐
I get energy from cleaning days:	☐	☐	☐	☐	☐
I get energy watching others move away from tradition:	☐	☐	☐	☐	☐

- ☐ I like revolutionary stories
- ☑
- ☐ My vacations need to change
- ☐ I am comfortable with letting go
- ☐ I love breaking habits
- ☐ I dislike clutter

Secrets for a Successful Callback for a *Destroyer* Role

❖ You have spent time or would spend time studying industries that went through change.

❖ You would be willing to study how to dismantle something.

❖ You would be willing to learn how to celebrate something that needs to go but needs to be honored.

❖ You have experience or would be willing to learn how to identify cultures (especially yours) for what is broken.

❖ You have stories of when you saw something that wasn't working, and it helped yourself and others.

ACT I - THE DEVELOPMENTAL ARCHETYPES
SCENE FOUR - *CREATOR* CENTER STAGE

The Creator archetype is a real action figure. The Creator will take us from ideas to instrument, talk to tangible, and fantasy to substance. It is at this point of the change process that something starts to take shape - or should. The Creator's main focus is the **Visible**. Their job is to make sure we have some product or tangible evidence at the end of the change process. This is their function. But that function can come with some incredible challenges. The issue with the Creator,

Focus: Visible

The CREATOR

however, is the focus. What, who or where does the Creator put their primary focus? Of the three archetypes already discussed, which one of the three does the Creator typically spend their time concentrating upon for this productivity? Should the Creator put their focus on the

The SEEKER   The LOVER

The DESTROYER

Seeker? If they don't, how will they know the Vision of the change? This is one of the main challenges in the drama of change: The Creator typically ONLY has an eye for the Seeker's ideas. But if they only focus on the Seeker and they don't focus on the Lover, they might start to create something that takes the organization away from what they collectively Value. But if they focus on the Lover, they might neglect the work of the Destroyer and create, without consideration for the process of letting go. This is the challenge in the drama of change. The Creator is not *simply* the archetype to make sure the Seeker's ideas are translated into some instrument of change. The Creator must create something **Visible** that brings together the Vision of the Seeker, the Value of the Lover and what the Destroyer has identified as needing to be Vacated. If the Creator fails to partner with each one of these three archetypes, they can create a calamity instead of a construction. The Creator has to create harmony between the Seeker, Lover and Destroyer. If they fail to orchestrate harmony between the three, the more drama occurs during the change process. The more they can bring the three together, the less drama the organization experiences.

The difficulty for the Creator is recognizing the above mentioned need. Those who score high in the Creator archetype get so much energy from hearing the Seeker's ideas. They are bogged down by the Lover's focus on what we should not change. They can be equally deflated by the work of the Destroyer. They are creators; destruction, for the sake of destruction, lets the wind out of their sails.

My favorite parking space at my favorite restaurant.

One morning there was a sign on the door that read, "Perkins Restaurants are no longer operating in lower Michigan." I was devastated!!

Perhaps the best example of the Creator pulling together the Seeker-Lover-Destroyer struggle is seen in a recent change near the mall of my home town. This picture is where I would eat breakfast and have my morning coffee. It was a Perkins restaurant. I would be served hot coffee and great oatmeal each morning. That is when the bad things began to happen. Perkins had pulled out of our state.

It was two years later that something began to change. The east side and the south side of the building began to be torn down. Most of the roof and the west and north side of the building were somewhat left in tack. Someone began to change the building ... not all of it ... parts of it. I was told a Five Guys Burgers was going into this old Perkins building. In my mind I had only seen a Five Guys in a strip mall setting. Would this be the first one I would see in a stand-alone building? I made several calls to Five Guys and discovered that they were NOT going to have a Five Guys in a stand-alone building, at least not on this site. Their past practice (what they Valued) was to keep the Five Guys in a strip mall. The Lover voice would prevail. But this was the BEST location in this county for a restaurant. Why not just knock down the whole building? Those were my questions. Instead, this picture shows what happened as they developed their **Vision** for the site. Instead of **Vacating** via

complete destruction (Destroyer in the shadowy role), they found worth in some of the established construction. They were able to hold to their **Value** (Lover archetype in the strength side) and were able to capture the Seeker's **Vision** for having a fine restaurant in one of the most profitable sites in the county. This is a perfect picture of the Seeker-Lover-Destroyer process in the hands of a great Creator. The Creator gave them a **Visible** concept, uniting the other three archetypes. This is the perfect picture of the drama of change via the loss of one eatery and the beginning of another. This is the role of the Creator.

The political year of 2017 will be known in history for many things, perhaps, mostly bad. But one *change drama* that will be written about for years is the attempt to reform the USA healthcare system. This might be a second example of the Seeker-Lover-Destroyer-Creator process. It is happening right in front of us, albeit not so successful. This is the scene as it is playing out in front of the USA public:

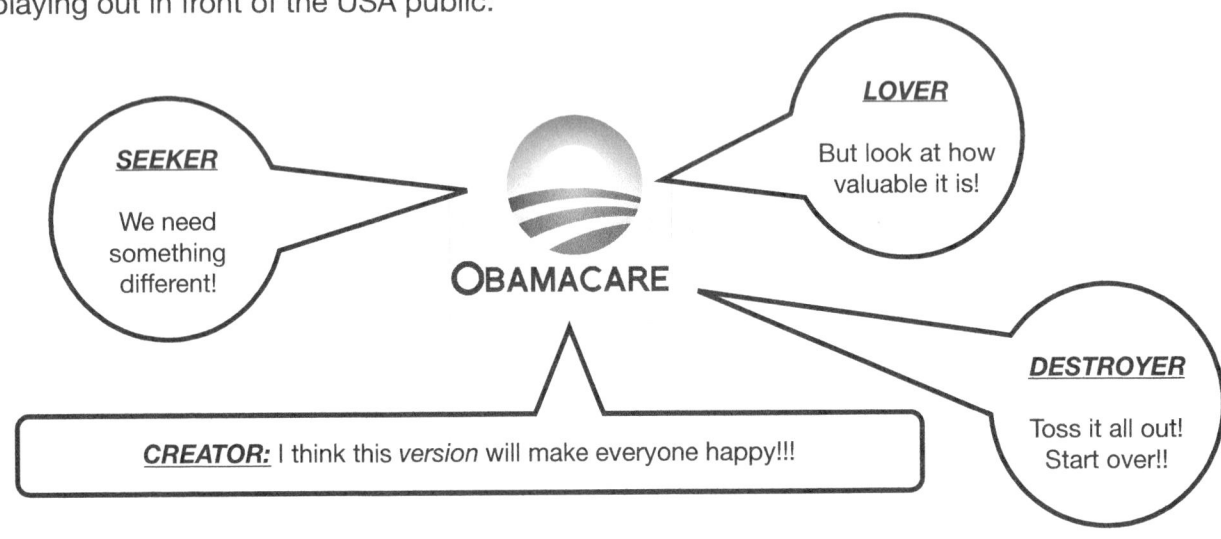

SEEKER
We need something different!

LOVER
But look at how valuable it is!

DESTROYER
Toss it all out! Start over!!

OBAMACARE

CREATOR: I think this *version* will make everyone happy!!!

The Creator's Script in the Change Drama

The Creator's script in the drama of change includes three scripts:

Creator Script #1 - Center Stage

The Creator MUST orchestrate bringing the Seeker-Lover-Destroyer archetypes together. That is the focus of the Creator's first work.

SEEKER

Steps to catch their Vision:

1. Spend time making sure you know what they want to accomplish. This can be difficult. The tendency might be to hear part of the idea and start to move forward without the entire picture. Make sure you both communicate what you hear and what you are saying.

2. Make sure you don't hear part of the idea and take the project in a direction *you alone* see and leave the Seeker not understanding why. Remember, a pure Seeker might only see the Vision and not the Visible. It might be hard for them to see how your *Visible will reach their Vision.* The two of you have great power over change when you are working together. Unite, don't fight!

3. Sometimes the Seeker has an idea, and they lose energy once the idea is delivered to others. Prod them into developing the idea further and deeper. Don't settle!!

LOVER

Steps to catch their Value:

1. The Lover wants to make sure that, as you create, you understand their connection to the past (tool, procedure, etc.). They will adapt to your knew creation when they have a connection to it. Bring them into your creation early so that they have a voice into it and feel connected to it.

2. Make sure you identify what the Lover values in their current approach. As you create something to replace it and they begin to see the tangible side of change, they need to see that this new creation will allow them to reach their past value. You may have to demonstrate that.

3. Your most difficult struggle in the creative process will occur if the new idea introduced by the Seeker is changing a currently held value. The Lover will need to see that the new value you are going to have to reach with your creation is better than the old value reached in the past.

DESTROYER

Steps to catch what they Vacate:

1. The visible change you are introducing is replacing something. You might not have knowledge of what it is as it was created by another. Make sure you KNOW what is being replaced. The Destroyer has this information.

2. As you create, ask the Destroyer if there might be a piece, part or portion of the thing being replaced that can be incorporated into your creation. In doing so, you will also show the Lover that you value past work, tools, and procedures. Don't let the Destroyer toss out the baby with the bath water.

3. The Destroyer has a role: To let the thing go that your creation is replacing. Don't be surprised that they will see parts of your creation that need to be *let go*. Let them have a voice in your creation. The Destroyer might see some unprofitable waste you don't see.

Creator Script #2 - Moving Off Stage

Remember, even though Creators create the tangible aspects of change, they are not the center of the idea. The mission of the organization is at the center. Your role in the change process is, yes, to put the idea into productive form. But be careful you don't slip into the prima-donna mode. If you keep in mind that what you really want is your creation to come to fruition, you won't mind stepping off the center stage and letting the other archetypes play their roles.

The success of your creation will depend upon how you work with and utilize the skills and the roles of each of the archetypes. They have their own ideas and will want to have a voice into the creation. This might be the most difficult step for the Creator. Once the tangible piece of the idea is laid out, everyone will have a voice to share. They all will have an opinion as to what will make the work better. Take writing as an example. This manuscript is the work of the Creator archetype. As the author, I will complete the work and then pass it on to others. They will want to change the creation as they view the manuscript via their archetypal eyes. I will, if I am smart, utilize what they see. My ability to allow them to do their part is vital to the completion and success of the work. Resistance to their voice will damage and undermine the actual work I want to accomplish. I have to interact with the other archetypes and allow them to have center stage for their role. It will make my creation better.

Creators must incorporate the other archetypes. Here is your moving off stage script.

Creator's script to interact with the other archetypes

Archetype	Possible objections they may have with the change	Goal Association Work (See Addendum #4)
Seeker	They may want to take the organization into a new direction. This isn't always bad and, in fact, necessary at times.	As you develop their idea, you will need to draw them into the creation. Don't let them drop it at your feet and move on to more ideas.
Lover	They may want to hang on to the status quo. They may value the wrong thing, but, nevertheless, they see your idea is dangerous to their status quo.	The more physical touching of your creation you can muster the better. Lovers need to be connected. Allowing them to try it out and take it for a spin will enable connection.
Destroyer	They need to see what the change is replacing and will need to agree that "something" needs replacing.	The Destroyer needs to make sure that this idea is a better replacement for what they see is unprofitable. Is it better?
Warrior	They might reject the change if they think it will fail. They will want someone to show them that the change is successful or has the ability to be successful.	New creations are difficult for the Warrior to see as successful. You will have to show them that you are willing to continue to shape it as they try to make it work. Adapt to their needs.
Caregiver	They might reject the change because of all the work that will be put on the plates of the workers to accomplish the idea.	Does your creation help others or make their life more difficult? Make time for them to learn the creation so they see it can be helpful.
Innocent	They might reject the change because they either don't see the need (naïveté) behind it or because they think it will be a hopeless pursuit.	Does your creation inspire? The Innocent will have to see that this creation can produce possibility. Beware: They might adapt early because they don't really see the depth of it.
Orphan	They might reject the change because of failure to solve some of the problems the change will create when implemented.	Be prepared for the Orphan to see difficulty in your creation. They can really help you refine and improve your work. Get their voice early.
Ruler	They might reject the change because they don't see structurally how the change will work. They will want to policy and procedure any change.	New creations don't always have instant structure and order. The Ruler can help with this. They can give your creation order, structure, procedure and stability.
Magician	They might reject the change if they think the change lacks any ability to see transformation. They will be the least resistor if they see "change" as good for anyone or any organization.	The Magician can adapt early to new creations when they see that the creation has a purpose in the change process. They will focus more on the *why you created it* of your creation than the *what it does*.
Sage	They might reject change because they see the change as foolish and lacking substance or because it has little research (and it probably does because it is a new idea).	The Sage can provide you the research and truth you need to hear as the creation is implemented. The Sage can accelerate the growth of your creation. Learn from their feedback.
Jester	They might reject the change because they think it will be boring, too much work (that will steal the joy of the current work), or because they see the change as too complicated (the Sage will make it so).	The Jester can find ways to make the early versions of the creation enjoyable. People are willing to try things if they see that failure is not a scary thing. The Jester can add fun to the early mistakes your creation might produce.

Creator Script #3 - Backstage

The Creator must make sure that during the implementation process the **Visible** creation is improved and completed. As they allow the archetypes to speak into their creation, they can get to the best possible creation. They will get a better creation if they listen to the other archetypes during the drama of change. The biggest question backstage for the Creator is, "Can they let others improve and reshape their creation?"

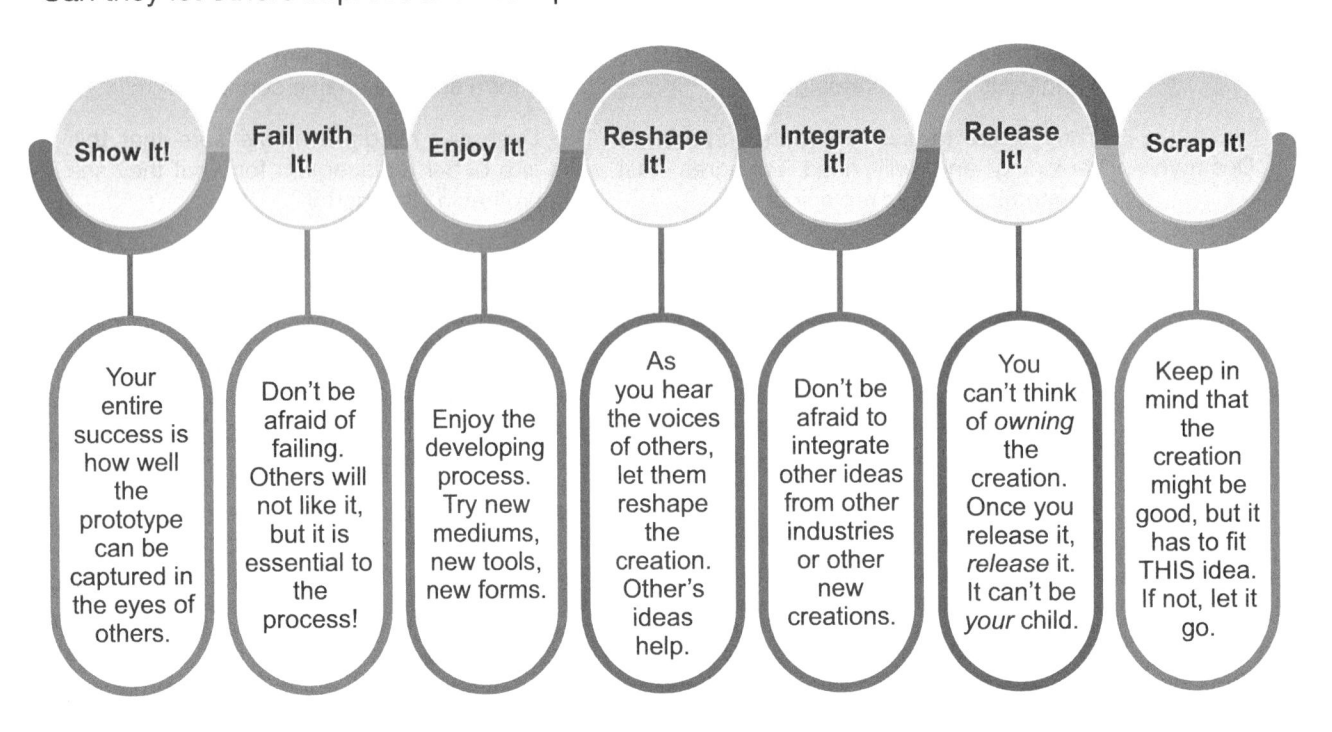

Show It!	Fail with It!	Enjoy It!	Reshape It!	Integrate It!	Release It!	Scrap It!
Your entire success is how well the prototype can be captured in the eyes of others.	Don't be afraid of failing. Others will not like it, but it is essential to the process!	Enjoy the developing process. Try new mediums, new tools, new forms.	As you hear the voices of others, let them reshape the creation. Other's ideas help.	Don't be afraid to integrate other ideas from other industries or other new creations.	You can't think of *owning* the creation. Once you release it, *release* it. It can't be *your* child.	Keep in mind that the creation might be good, but it has to fit THIS idea. If not, let it go.

Conclusion - an Email to the Creator

Dear Creator,

Where would we be without you? Yes, the Seekers give us the ideas, but without you we would only have the ideas. You make things **Visible**!! We can touch your products, experience your services, and live an easier life due to your innovative approaches to life's challenges. Necessity is, indeed, the mother of invention, and you seem to have mastered it.

We just need you to remember that not everything you create is profitable for us. Just because the Seeker thinks it, doesn't mean you have to create it. But if you do create it, please listen to us, and allow the creation to take on new shapes. Yes, Henry Ford thought everyone wanted a black car. But that is no longer true. We MAY NOT know what we want, but, once we do get it, we know how we want to use it. So, listen to us as the creation takes shape. We don't like it when you tell us, "We can't do that." We might not know how, and we probably don't want to pay for it, but we know it can be done. Thanks to you!!

Thanks again … the other 11 archetypes.

Creator's Audition Checklist
(You think you are equipped for the Creator part in the Drama of Change?)

The following activities give the Creator energy:	Never	Seldom	Sometimes	Often	Always
I get energy from building things:	☐	☐	☐	☐	☐
I get energy from putting things back together:	☐	☐	☐	☐	☐
I get energy when someone says, "I have an idea!"	☐	☐	☐	☐	☐
I get energy from watching parts come together:	☐	☐	☐	☐	☐
I get energy from finding new resources piled up:	☐	☐	☐	☐	☐
I get energy watching the parts all come together:	☐	☐	☐	☐	☐

- ☐ I like stories about building things
- ☑
- ☐ I like making vacations happen
- ☐ I am comfortable with construction
- ☐ I love to show progress
- ☐ I dislike unfinished ideas

What Role Do You Play In Change? The Archetypes and the Change Process

Secrets for a Successful Callback for a *Creator* Role

- ❖ You have a history of building things.

- ❖ You spend time on weekends with many hobbies.

- ❖ You would be willing to learn a new skill if it includes using a new tool.

- ❖ You have, or are willing to, study how things are put together.

- ❖ You have many things that are not finished in your life.

- ❖ You read books about how to build things.

The Seeker-Lover-Destroyer-Creator Dynamic

The drama of change has many elements. However, using some of the basic elements, compare the Seeker, Lover, Destroyer and Creator to each other. Note the different ways they approach the change process:

THE DEVELOPMENTAL ARCHETYPES OF CHANGE in relationship to four ELEMENTS OF CHANGE

FOUR ELEMENTS FOR SUCCESSFUL CHANGE	LOVER	SEEKER	DESTROYER	CREATOR
TRUST	They will trust you if they believe the change can still allow them to embrace the values they embrace.	They will trust you if they believe the change will allow them to find a new area that takes them to a new place.	They will trust you if they believe the change will replace something that is no longer useful.	They will trust you if they believe the change allows them to build or develop something.
OWNERSHIP (Will-Power)	They have to have a say in _why_ the change is being considered.	They have to have a say in _where_ the change is taking them.	They have to have a say in _what_ the change is replacing.	They have to have a say in _how_ the change will be developed.
VISION	They have to see _how they fit_ into the change - _connection_.	They have to see _how the change fits_ into their journey - _exploration_.	They have to see _the freedom_ in the change - _liberation_.	They have to see _how to develop_ the change - _expression_.
APPLICATION (Way-Power)	They have to be in control of the _focus_ of the change. They are fearful of losing long held values.	They have to be in control of the _destination_ of the change. They are fearful of losing the joy of movement.	They have to be in control of the _reason_ for the change. They are fearful of adapting another useless ...	They have to be in control of the _steps_ of the change. They are fearful of losing their imagination.
Language Key - Words & Phrases	Embrace; Value; Team; Hold on to; Relate; Connect	Journey; Experience; New; Discovery; Reach; Explore	Let go; Release; Move on; Replace; Improve; Get beyond	Build; Structure; Process; Create; Medium; Form

As an example of the dynamic between these four in regard to the development of a change, note the language and terms between just the Lover and the Destroyer. Imagine the discussion between the two over lunch in the break room of any organization. What would happen if they were discussing the latest change and didn't understand each other's preferred language? They both might have the same values and see the current change as positive. However, at the end of the lunch break, they might think they are on complete opposite sides of the change.

During the change process, these four archetypes play a major role in the success or failure of the proposed change. When working in concert, they can launch a change in a way that propels the change forward. When working in conflict with each other, they can sabotage the change before it gets to the implementation stage of the change drama. It is difficult enough to implement change, much less when the incubation portion of change disregards the Four Developmental Archetypes. There is such power in their cooperation. There is much destruction in their antagonism.

THE CHANGE STORY

- Three Acts -

Act I - The Developmental Archetypes

Scene 1 - The Seeker

Scene 2 - The Lover

Scene 3 - The Destroyer

Scene 4 - The Creator

(crossed out with a large X)

Act II - The Structural Archetypes

Scene 1 - The Warrior

Scene 2 - The Ruler

Scene 3 - The Orphan

Scene 4 - The Sage

Act III - The Attitudinal Archetypes

Scene 1 - The Caregiver

Scene 2 - The Magician

Scene 3 - The Innocent

Scene 4 - The Jester

ACT II - THE STRUCTURAL ARCHETYPES

Act I ended with The Developmental Archetypes (Seeker-Lover-Destroyer-Creator) all working together to incubate a change idea to the fullest. In Act II we are going to see what happens when we start to implement a proposed change. Structurally, change has so many mountains to climb. Change, by nature, is unstable. Like a small child learning to walk, change needs structure. It wants to grab something to stand up. It wants to reach for something to give stability. The archetypes that provide structure are the Ruler, the Warrior, the Orphan, and the Sage. There are four archetypes that play powerful roles in ensuring that structure holds and makes change possible. When these four are disjointed, change can fail simply because structure fails.

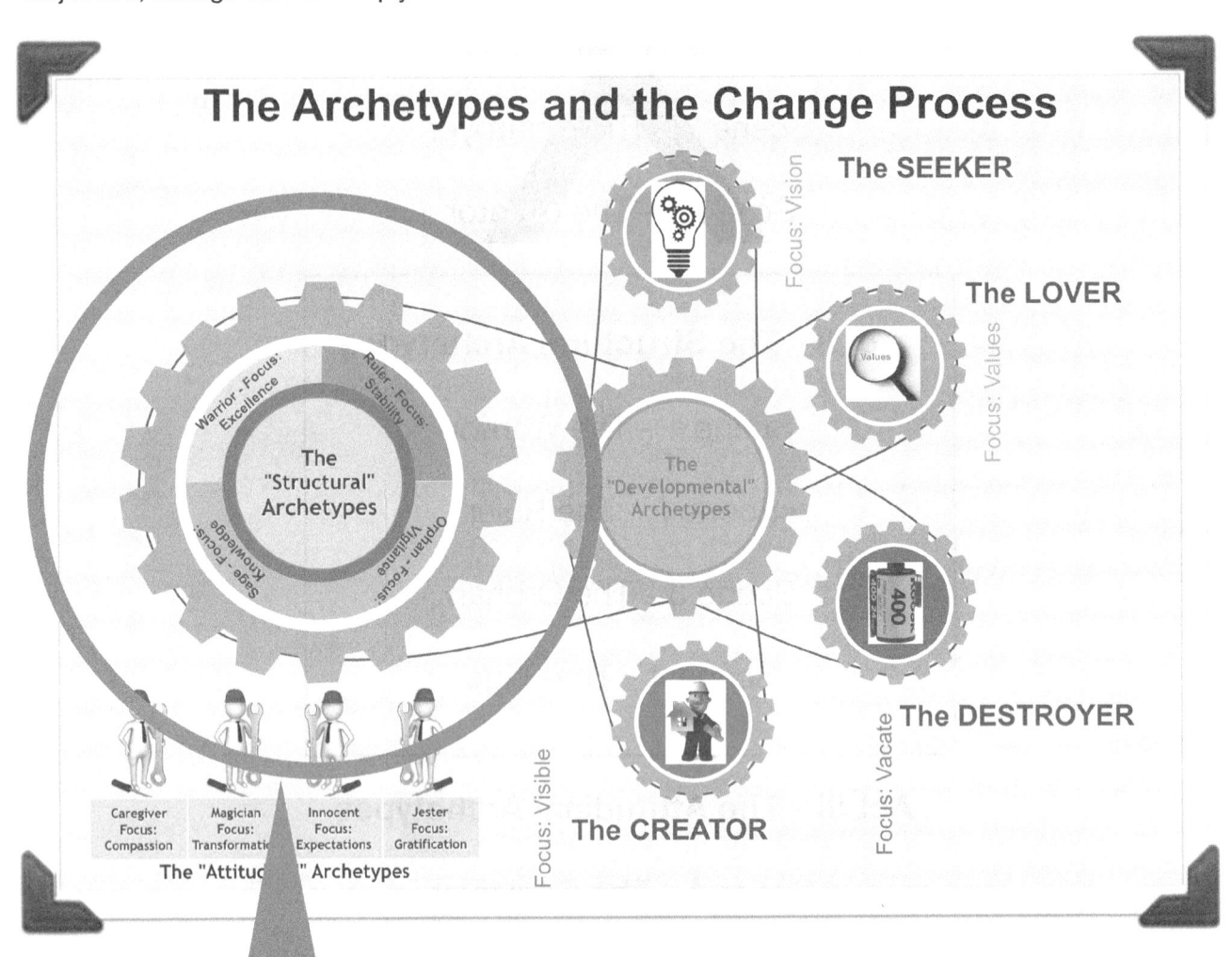

Act II will see The Structural Archetypes take center stage. These four archetypes may have the harshest voices during the change process. The Ruler, the Warrior, the Orphan and the Sage MAY BE the most dominate archetypes in organizational change. They are probably the most honored in our society in regard to leadership. Would you follow someone who saw the dragon before anyone else (Orphan) and knew (Sage) how to and was capable of (Warrior) slaying the dragon based upon established structures (Ruler)? This is what makes these four so powerful in the drama of change.

ACT II - THE STRUCTURAL ARCHETYPES
SCENE ONE - *WARRIOR* CENTER STAGE

CHANGE PUNCH CARD

- EXCELLENCE ✓
- SUCCESS ✓
- BEST EFFORT ✓
- QUALITY ✓
- WINNERS ✓
- TOP SHELF ✓

There is no doubt about the Warrior mindset during the drama of change: They want to make sure they reach the ultimate in performance, **Excellence**. The most dangerous aspect of the Warrior life is that of failing. Therefore, their view of change is through the lens of how they define success. Since everyone defines success differently, no two warriors are the same, except for the fact they have to be successful, however they define it. When change is introduced into the warp and woof of an organization, the Warrior can be both the most resistant to the change and the most adamant that the change should take place. If they see that the change will enable them to reach their version of success, they are on board with that change. If, however, they sense that the change will not allow them to reach their definition of success, they often *fight* against the proposed change.

Change to the Warrior can be dangerous. Their motto is to be the *best at something*, but not necessarily the *first to try something*. As stated in The Developmental Archetypes, the Warrior has to know that there is success in the change. They don't mind fighting for the success, but they have to see that it is possible. When the Warrior takes center stage, they want to know that *Excellence* can be reached. They might define **Excellence** differently than others in the organization, however. This is why their approach to change has to be interpreted through that lens.

To understand the Warrior and their view of excellence for the change process, it would be beneficial to identify some key elements of success for the Warrior as they strive for **Excellence**. Below are offered pieces to the puzzle of **Excellence** for the Warrior. It is the thought that every Warrior, no matter how they define success, strives to put this puzzle together for each change drama they are asked to support. A Warrior, as they enter the change drama, will want to define their success through these five elements:

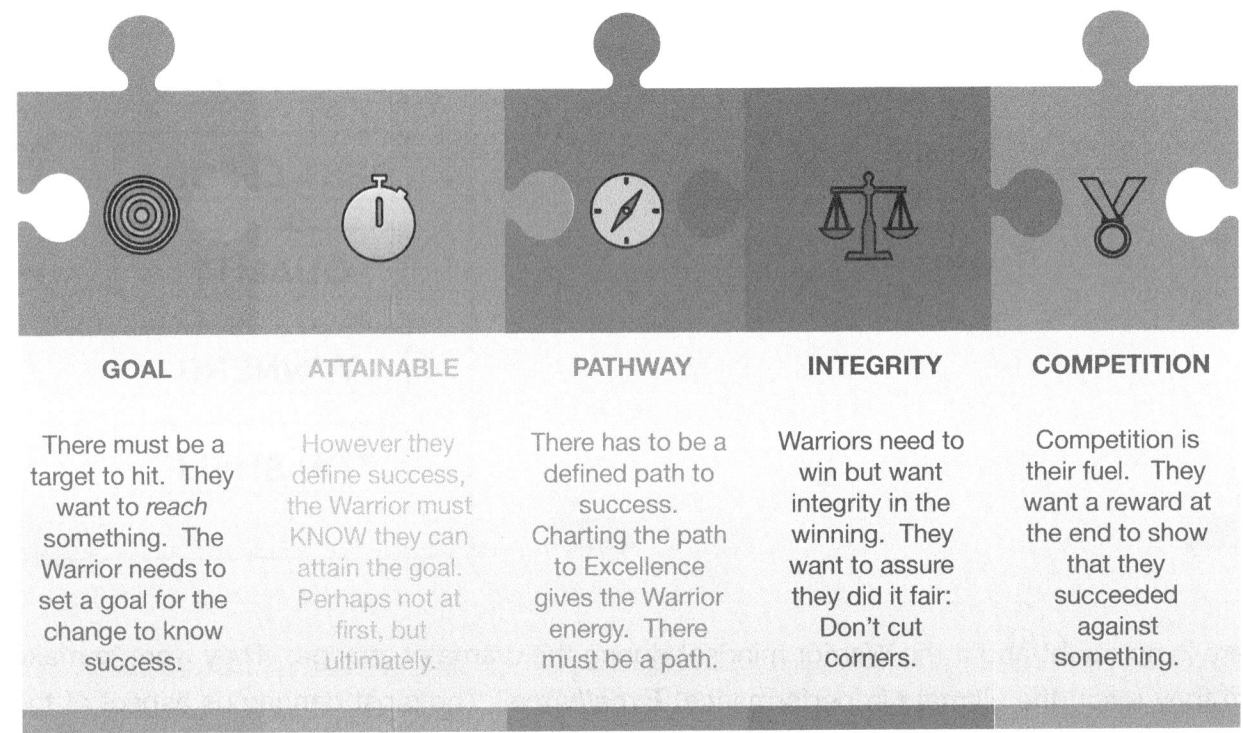

GOAL	ATTAINABLE	PATHWAY	INTEGRITY	COMPETITION
There must be a target to hit. They want to *reach* something. The Warrior needs to set a goal for the change to know success.	However they define success, the Warrior must KNOW they can attain the goal. Perhaps not at first, but ultimately.	There has to be a defined path to success. Charting the path to Excellence gives the Warrior energy. There must be a path.	Warriors need to win but want integrity in the winning. They want to assure they did it fair: Don't cut corners.	Competition is their fuel. They want a reward at the end to show that they succeeded against something.
The stronger the Warrior the tougher the target. The Warrior does not move forward without a target out front. In the shadowy side, the Warrior can have a higher, tougher, more difficult target for others than they do for themselves. They can rely on past victories and not set new heights to reach. Their glory days can be highlighted.	The stronger the Warrior the more difficult the target is to attain. The Warrior will work hard to reach it and won't accept failure. In the shadowy side, the Warrior may redefine what *attaining* the goal looks like. Since they can't fail, they might redefine what it looks like rather than admit they lost. They can often create excuses.	The stronger the Warrior the less defined the path needs to be. The strong Warrior can adapt and create the path as they go forward. In the shadowy side, the Warrior may complain the path is not clear enough to go forward with the change. Again, they can't have failure, and an undefined pathway can be an adopted *reason* they failed.	The stronger the Warrior the more accurate the weights of integrity. They will want equal weights for everyone. No one gets a break. In the shadowy side, the Warrior may put their thumb on the scale of integrity. Their desire to win might trump being fair. A bad call in their favor is just *how the game is played*. The bad call against them will be an excuse.	The stronger the Warrior the tougher the competition. They want to beat the best, even if the best is a thing and not a person(s). In the shadowy side, the Warrior looks for weaker competition to show their superiority. They so much want to win that they are okay with beating a "B" team or *average* goal. They will diminish the goal to win!

The Warrior's Script in the Change Drama

The Warrior's script in the drama of change includes three scripts:

Warrior Script #1 - Center Stage

AREA	STRENGTH SIDE	SHADOW SIDE
Goal Setting	Aim high. Surround yourself with people who want to push you to set high goals. When change comes along, don't think of it in regard to winning or losing, but how can this new change help you reach a current goal or another goal or a better goal.	Avoid setting low goals to just let yourself *feel* successful. Others will see through this. The glory days of the past are past. Keep stretching yourself. Failure is just a step in that process.
Attainability	Attainability is that balance between challenge and capacity. When we don't have the capacity to reach a goal, we think failure. When we have such an easy goal, the Warrior can be bored with the *game*. Attainability is being able to stretch capacity to reach a challenge. Know your capacity and stretch it.	Failure often happens when we don't know our capacity, and we overshoot what we can and can't do. Make sure you don't redefine what the final product looks like in order to say, "I made it."
Pathway	Remember in a new change the path is less known. Often, change is a *build it while the car is moving* process. You might have to use your Warrior skills to set the mark for others. Mark the path if it is unseen. Your ability to forge ahead when others can't see the path is the mark of a great Warrior.	You can find yourself frustrated when there is no clear method to reach your target. Make sure you don't use a lack of a path as an excuse for missing a target in the change process.
Integrity	Integrity is what separates strong Warriors from weak Warriors. Make sure as you strive for your goal and set a pathway, that it assures attainability in the right way. Develop a set of principles you will follow in life as you reach tough goals. Live by principle, not by popularity or product.	Have others watch the ethics of your approach. Allow them to challenge you to stay pure in the work it takes. Cutting corners might be missed by some now, but by all later (when you are weaker at the end).
Competition	There is a reason their is a finish line or a final score; Warriors need to know the order everyone finished. Just because someone is not competitive doesn't mean they are not working, however. Not everyone likes to compete. Some can work without it being a competition.	Make sure you don't make everything a contest, however. Working hard for the sake of working hard is acceptable. Take pride in knowing you can work hard without having to work harder than someone else.

Warrior Script #2 - Moving Off Stage

Remember, even though when it comes to change Warriors can get things done, they are not the center of the idea and change. The mission of the organization is at the center. Your role in the change process is, yes, to ensure the change gets done to the highest quality. But be careful you don't slip into battle mode. If you keep in mind that what you want is to help everyone succeed (and that their definition of success might be different than yours), you can better help everyone reach success. Change is a team sport. You are not running a race by yourself. In an organization, this is a combined effort to strive for the highest level of change.

The success of the change will depend upon how you work with and utilize the skills and the roles of each of the archetypes. They have their own ideas and will want to contribute to the change. This might be the most difficult step for the Warrior. Once the change process actually starts to move forward, your desire might be to just *take over*. Granted, to make sure the effort reaches the performance of **Excellence** you desire, you might think you have to *push* others. Or you might think you have to *pull* them along. It might be better to think of supporting them and utilizing and incorporating the unique skills of the other archetypes, rather than pushing (or pulling them) along to keep up with you … The Famed Warrior.

The Warrior must bring out the **Excellence** of the other archetypes. Here is your moving off stage script.

Warrior's script to interact with the other archetypes

Archetype	Possible objections they may have with the change	Goal Association Work (See Addendum #4)
Seeker	They may want to take the organization into a new direction. This isn't always bad and, in fact, necessary at times.	For the Warrior, a new direction can be dangerous. New doesn't always translate as the best for them. Don't simply reject "new."
Lover	They may want to hang on to the status quo. They may value the wrong thing, but, nevertheless, they see change as dangerous to their status quo.	The proven and tried can be perfected and can hit the mark over and over. Be careful that you don't accept status quo for the sake of *attaining* it over and over.
Destroyer	They need to see what the change is replacing and will need to agree that "something" needs replacing.	If the Warrior and Destroyer team up on the shadowy side, life can be tough. Be sure that you show Destroyer the *best* way to let go.
Creator	They can't always see the real practical application or design of the change. They need to know the vision has something tangible behind it.	As the Creator puts tangibility to the idea make sure you are working side-by-side to show how it might happen. You will want to get their creation off the ground; you have to know it!
Caregiver	They might reject the change because of all the work that will be put on the plates of the workers to accomplish the change.	Caregiver wants to enable others, and you can see that as a weakness. Show them how to help others to learn how to do things themselves. Help them help others better.
Innocent	They might reject the change because they either don't see the need (naïveté) behind it or because they think it will be a hopeless pursuit.	The Innocent can be very inspirational. They like to point out to others what CAN be done. Your job is to make it happen. Help them see the *work* behind their inspirational *talk*.
Orphan	They might reject the change because of failure to solve some of the problems the change will create when implemented.	The Orphan can help you see the dangers in your own work. Pull their voice into your work. But they can be negative. Show them it can happen.
Ruler	They might reject the change because they don't see structurally how the change will work. They will want to policy and procedure any change.	The Ruler will help you find a path to reach your goal. They are great with structure and putting the path together. They might be limited because they don't see your power.
Magician	They might reject the change if they think the change lacks any ability to see transformation. They will be your least resistor if they see "change" as good for anyone or any organization.	The Magician can see the strength in the Warrior. They can help you find a path, as well as see the transformation you are trying to achieve, even when you can't see it. They might, however, cut corners. Watch them.
Sage	They might reject change because they see the change as foolish and lacking substance or because it has little research (and it probably does because it is a new idea).	They will see your hard work and effort as useless if they don't see the attainability of the work. They can give you knowledge necessary to adjust your goal or path. Their intellectual approach can differ from yours.
Jester	They might reject the change because they think the change will be boring, too much work (that will steal the joy of the current work), or because they see the change as too complicated (the Sage will make it so).	The Jester can be seen as foolish to the Warrior. To the Warrior, they seem to lack work effort. They will enjoy competition if they see it as a game. That will enable them to join into the work. Don't be fearful of the joy in their work. Sweat doesn't have to crush humor.

Warrior Script #3 - Backstage

The Warrior must make sure that during the implementation process that change reaches **Excellence**. This means that as they allow the archetypes to speak into the change, they can get to the best possible change. They will get a better change if they listen to the other archetypes during the drama of change. The biggest question back stage for the Warrior is, "Can they get others to work at their best so that the change can be successful?"

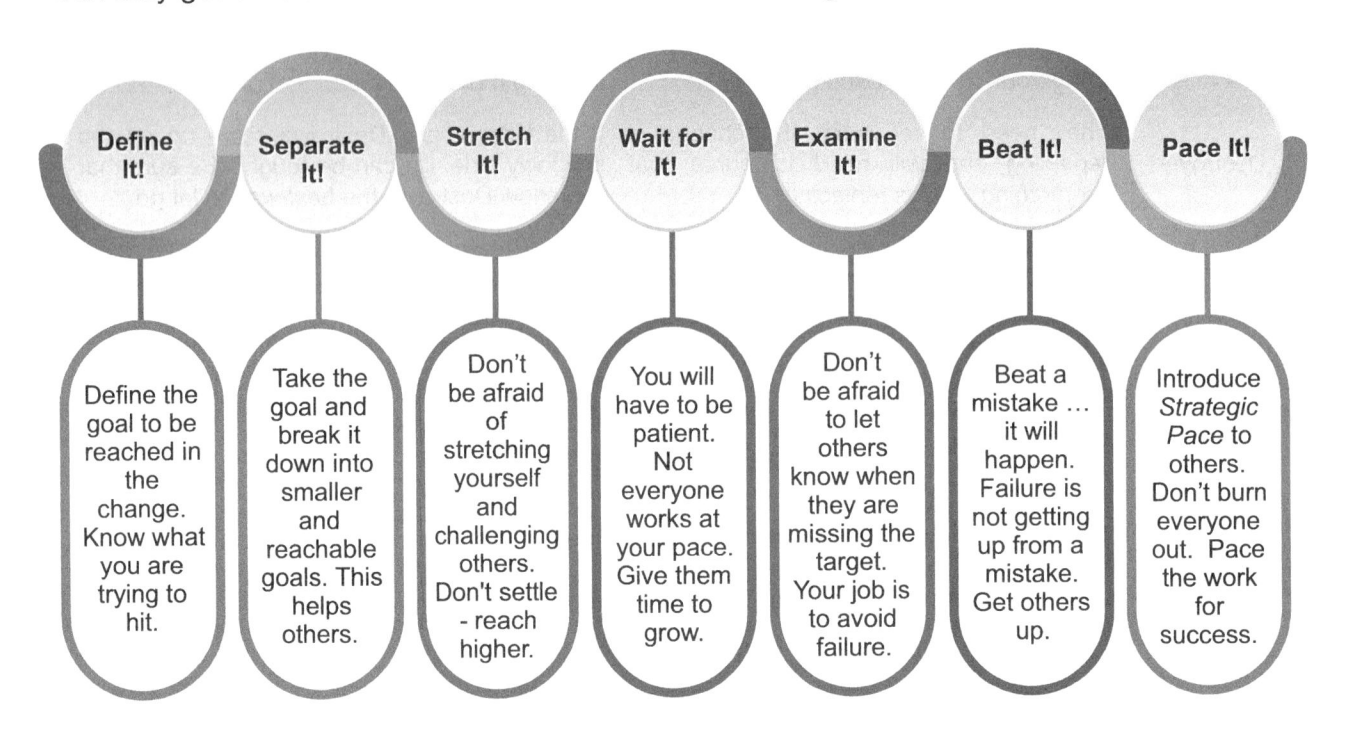

Define It!	Separate It!	Stretch It!	Wait for It!	Examine It!	Beat It!	Pace It!
Define the goal to be reached in the change. Know what you are trying to hit.	Take the goal and break it down into smaller and reachable goals. This helps others.	Don't be afraid of stretching yourself and challenging others. Don't settle - reach higher.	You will have to be patient. Not everyone works at your pace. Give them time to grow.	Don't be afraid to let others know when they are missing the target. Your job is to avoid failure.	Beat a mistake … it will happen. Failure is not getting up from a mistake. Get others up.	Introduce *Strategic Pace* to others. Don't burn everyone out. Pace the work for success.

Conclusion - an Email to the Warrior

Dear Warrior,

Okay, so you can outwork and outperform everyone. Thank you for that. You set the pace for us all. If we didn't have your work ethic and drive, most of our changes will fall flat. You push us all to get better. We have one suggestion, however. Can you find a way to make sure we don't all burn out before the change(s) takes place? Your pace of work is as exhausting as it is exciting and inspiring. We all don't have your drive. We know that might come as a strange thing, but we really can't keep up sometimes. At times it looks like you are so concentrated on the product and getting it done, that you forget we are people with flaws and, dare we say it, weaknesses. We know weakness is not an option to a Warrior. We have heard you say, "Pain is weakness leaving the body." That is a quaint saying, but in reality, pain can also tell us something is wrong. We are not saying every time we *cry* we have to stop to take a rest. But when you see tears, it may be that we are injured, not weak. Just saying!!

Thanks again … the other 11 archetypes.

Warrior Warning: Passionately Learn *Strategic Abandonment*

It can be gathered from all that has been stated about the Warrior, they don't like to fail. Warriors have a saying: "Winner's never quit, and quitters never win!" (Famous NFL football coach, Vince Lombardi). Most people have parents who would never let them quit something. Their saying was, "Start what you finish, and finish what you start." Let's face it, most people probably never took a class on *How to Quit*. We simply don't do *quit* well. This might be why we struggle with the Destroyer archetype. The concept of letting go of something sounds like quitting. That is why Warriors struggle. They simply don't like to quit. This is where change can be tough for the Warrior. If they are in favor of the change, they may not be able to quit if the change is not working. If they do not favor the change, it may be because someone is asking them to quit a status quo they find successful.

Quitting is an Option

To help a Warrior learn to quit something, we can reframe the term *quit* and identify it as **Strategic Abandonment**. Warriors don't like to quit, but they love to do *strategy*. Strategic Abandonment is the ability to identify what is not working and how to stop doing it so that you are not wasting energy. To learn how to do Strategic Abandonment, you have to combine three other archetypes: Destroyer, Lover and Sage. This guidebook is not a treatise on Strategic Abandonment, but we can't address change without talking about assisting the Warrior in how to quit something, and we can't discuss how to quit without reframing the term in a way that the Warrior can approach it. A Warrior who wants to excel has to be strategic in their approach to work. When pushing for the best, you can't afford to have any wasted motion. Here is how a Warrior, striving for **Excellence,** must partner with Destroyer, Lover and Sage to learn that quitting is an option, if it is done strategically.

DESTROYER	LOVER	SAGE
A partnership with the Destroyer means listening to a voice that is calculating and looks for waste. It is tough for a Warrior to believe they might be doing something wasteful. In partner with the Destroyer archetype, the Warrior will look for areas in their performance that might be redundant, fatigued, and/or antiquated. Asking deliberate questions about waste in a performance plan can benefit the Warrior by increasing success. Have others evaluate the success.	A partnership with the Lover might seem odd in context of Strategic Abandonment. However, the Lover provides the aspect of the passion behind the Warrior's performance. When the Warrior identifies their passion, they are better equipped to abandon something that is not in their passion world. The Destroyer might say something isn't worthy, but the Lover is the lens to determine if it is or not. Warriors should quit doing as much outside their passion as possible. They will be more successful if they can stay in their passion world.	The partnership with the Sage gives the Warrior the knowledge they need to make better decisions. Often the Warrior can practice automaticity: Doing something over and over in autopilot because it continues to be successful. When the Warrior listens to the voice of the Sage, they study their performance activities and learn what might be wasteful and no longer profitable. The Sage archetype teaches the Warrior. As the Warrior learns, they see what they need to quit.

Warrior's Audition Checklist
(You think you are equipped for the Warrior's part in the Drama of Change?)

The following activities give the Warrior energy:	Never	Seldom	Sometimes	Often	Always
I get energy from competition:	☐	☐	☐	☐	☐
I get energy from reaching a hard sought goal:	☐	☐	☐	☐	☐
I get energy pushing teams to reach their best:	☐	☐	☐	☐	☐
I get energy from games:	☐	☐	☐	☐	☐
I get energy from recalling past accomplishments:	☐	☐	☐	☐	☐
I get energy collecting memorabilia of wins:	☐	☐	☐	☐	☐

- ☐ I like to win at games
- ☑ I work out on the weekends
- ☐ I like vacations with activities
- ☐ I desire to win arguments

What Role Do You Play In Change?   The Archetypes and the Change Process

Secrets for a Successful Callback for a *Warrior* Role

❖ You have a history of setting and reaching goals.

❖ You spend time on the weekend and holidays competing.

❖ You would be willing to learn how to motivate others to reach their best.

❖ Your resume looks like a scorecard of accomplishments.

❖ You have a trophy or award you earned stashed away someplace.

❖ You read books about winners.

ACT II - THE STRUCTURAL ARCHETYPES
SCENE TWO - *RULER* CENTER STAGE

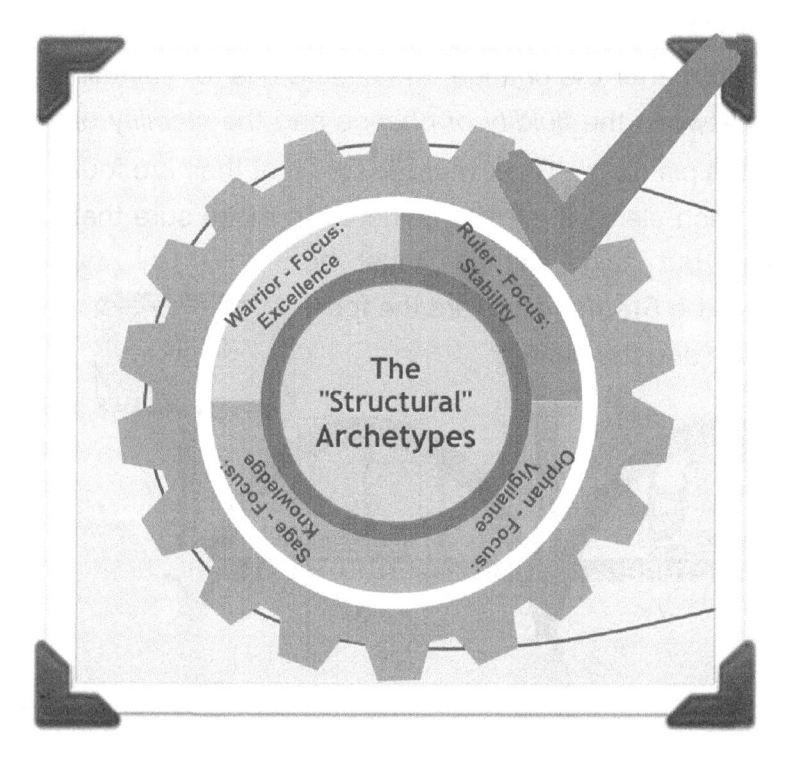

CHANGE **PUNCH CARD**

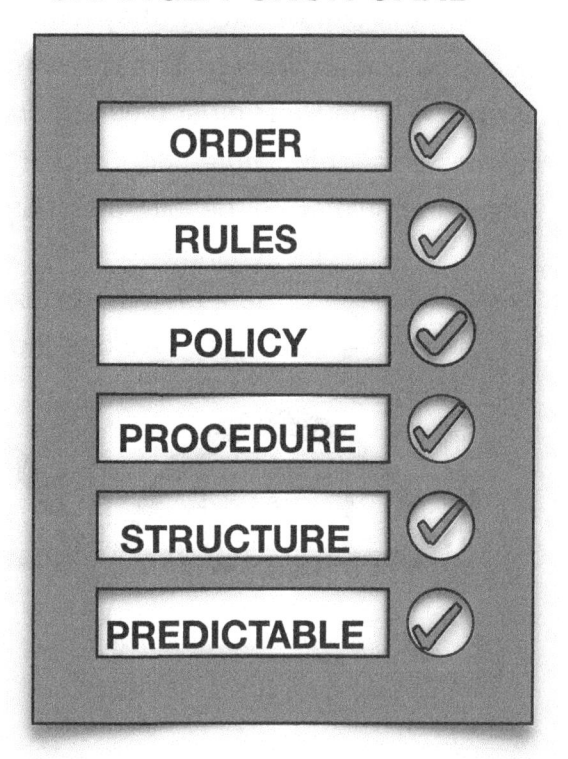

- ORDER ✓
- RULES ✓
- POLICY ✓
- PROCEDURE ✓
- STRUCTURE ✓
- PREDICTABLE ✓

When it comes to change, the Ruler has one thing on their mind: **Stability**! They want to make sure there is order, structure and guidelines so that the drama of change does not crash the current culture. We NEED the Ruler archetype as a strong voice in the change process. When Seeker comes up with the idea for change, they are not typically thinking of **Stability**. This is why we say that the Seeker, "Colors outside the lines." Anything *outside the lines* puts fear into the heart of the Ruler. To the Ruler, *nothing should be outside the lines*.

It is the Ruler that ensures our drama of change can survive. Every *change* must, at some point, conform to a stable process and be guided by procedures and policies. The Ruler is the archetype that changes *innovation* to *efficiency*. That is not a bad thing. The Ruler archetype can, actually, mistake *efficiency* for *innovation*. There is a difference. In the drama of change, it does not have to be one or the other. It can be a both/and rather than an either/or. We can have BOTH innovation AND efficiency. IF, however, there is to be efficiency, it will be at the hands of the Ruler. The Ruler can shape the change as it takes place with predictable and necessary structure that it lacks in the early stages of the idea. Like a small baby who starts to stand up, the Ruler turns the wobble into a walk and, eventually, into a run. The baby can't move to adulthood until they can be stable. So, too, change can't become status quo until **Stability** takes place at the work of the Ruler. The Ruler's ability to provide

Stability is necessary for any strong culture. In fact, **Stability** is what makes a culture strong. The **Stability** of a culture is both its greatest strength and its weakness. The fact that the culture doesn't change is what makes it the unique culture it is. The fact that the culture doesn't change makes change dramatic. Hence the drama of change. In order for the Ruler to keep the culture strong, they must find a way to get the proposed change to continue to keep the culture **Stable**. This is their role. No matter the change, the culture has to maintain **Stability**. The Ruler must create a *bridge* between the *fluidity of change* and the *stability of the organizational culture*. For **Stability** to take place, the Ruler must assure that their are four elements maintained, despite the change. Each element can be adjusted to make sure that the change reaches fruition, but each element must be present for the organization to be **Stable**. Here are the four elements to bridge the change and the culture:

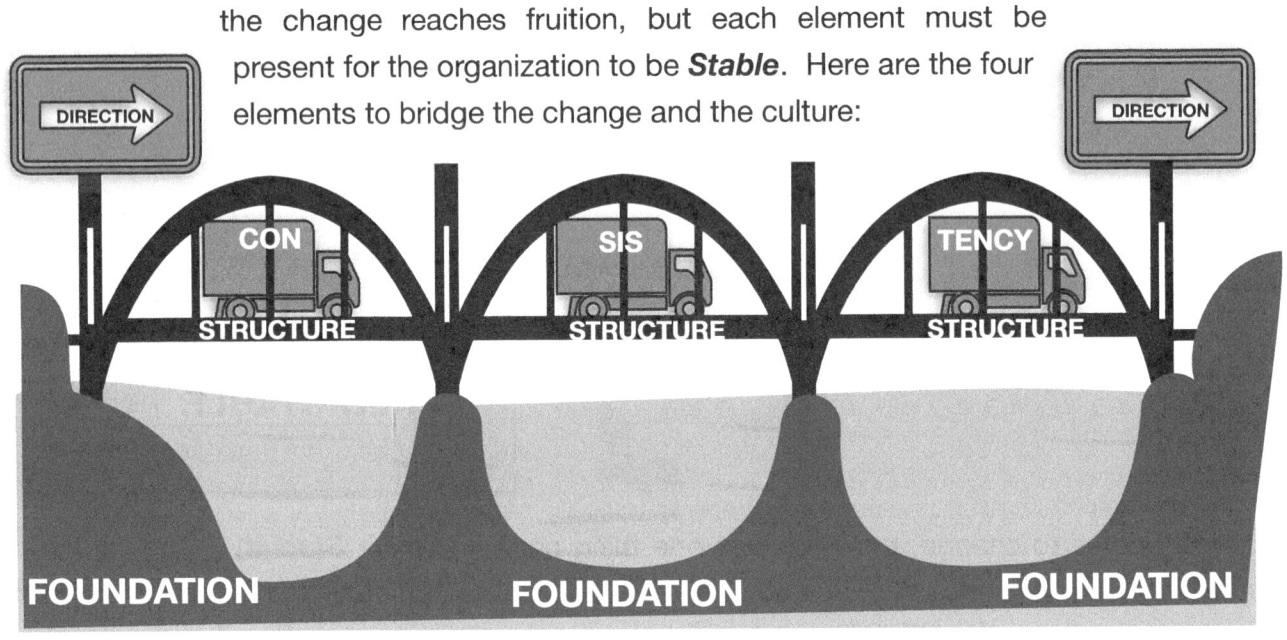

	FOUNDATION	STRUCTURE	DIRECTION	CONSISTENCY
DESCRIPTOR	BELIEFS	POLICIES	MISSION STATEMENT	ACCOUNTABILITY
MEANING	Every organization has to know what it believes. These are the mores it will NOT leave - no matter the change(s).	These are the procedures, policies and rules that keep the organization on track to fulfill its beliefs - no matter the change(s).	This is where the organization intends for its beliefs to take it - no matter the change(s).	This is the ability to apply the beliefs across all departments and for all personnel - no matter the change(s).
EXPLANATION (for the purpose of this work in the context of change)	Beliefs are not values. Values are how you practice your beliefs. Beliefs are truths that *typically* don't change (not easily). Values can change, but beliefs tend to remain the same. The Ruler should insist on guarding the beliefs and working them out in the values. Lovers can hold tight to these as well.	Policies, procedures and rules change as new information and change comes along. They must adjust to the change to make the change work. The Ruler (and Lover) can hold on to these. A key for the Ruler is to adjust the policies, procedures and rules to meet the demands of the culture and the change.	To make sure the organization is stable, the Ruler stands guard over the direction of the organization. The mission of the organization can change, but not without a real understanding of why and how it is done.	The Ruler assures that the beliefs, policies and mission are practiced with fidelity with everyone throughout the organization. The **Stability** of the organization is sabotaged when *some* are allowed to circumvent the mores, policies and mission.

The Ruler's Script in the Change Drama

The Ruler's script in the drama of change includes three scripts:

Ruler Script #1 - Center Stage

As an example of the above, consider a change mentioned earlier going through the educational industry. There is a long standing *belief* in education that teachers are employed to help children learn. However, with new research the belief has morphed into a new belief. The new belief is that *all* children can learn. This might sound odd, but it has become an important distinction in the past years. Students who have unique challenges were often viewed as though they had limits to their learning. Today's research shows this to be far from the truth. They might learn in a different manner and need different tools, but they can keep learning. They can keep growing. This change in belief (based upon new research) has changed the *structure* of today's classroom. This change in the classroom has changed the *mission* for each child. The *mission* has morphed with this change. The struggle for the Ruler in this example is the consistency as the new belief meets the new structure and the new structure meets the morphed mission and the morphed mission meets each teacher in the school. Holding each teacher responsible for this new belief is a dramatic change. But it is an example of the Ruler keeping the **Stability** of the organization intact in the drama of change.

Below are some specific steps the Ruler can take in each of these elements to make the change process find a sense of **Stability**. Here is your script.

FOUNDATION	Make sure everyone knows what the organization believes. This can be especially difficult when new personnel are added. It is typically assumed that members of an organization know the beliefs. That can be a dangerous assumption.	Make sure the beliefs are reviewed and re-evaluated on a regular basis. If it was something true, that typically prevents personnel to accept it is NO LONGER true. But with new information and new research, a belief can be changed or at least adjusted.	Allow beliefs to be challenged by the proposed change. A belief might better guide the change and allow the Creator to develop the change with a sure foundation. The desire with the foundation is NOT to prevent change but to blend and/or bend the change into the beliefs.
STRUCTURE	Most personnel of an organization will fight rules, policies and procedures. It is within the nature of man to do so. That doesn't diminish their need. It does, however, regulate how we use and apply them. Be ready for the resistance. People are safer with them … they just may not know it, or they may not want to acknowledge it.	Sometimes rules, policies and procedures outlive the belief they were attempting to protect and carry out. Don't hang on to outdated policies, rules, procedures and/or processes. They might have been needed at one time but have since outlived the belief. Evaluate them regularly, and don't allow any to become *untouchable*.	Don't fight change simply because it initially looks like it will damage the structure. This is the role of the Ruler. Your skill set is to look at the change and figure out a way to incorporate it into the current structure or to adjust the structure to the change. Don't make the Creator/Seeker do it. They don't have your skills.
DIRECTION	Does everyone know the mission? Has the mission made it beyond the statement on the wall of the entrance to the organization. Mission statements are fine, but they have to make it to the practical side of the entire organization. Can you draw a line from your mission statement to every task of the organization?	The mission can change. This might be the broadest distinction the Ruler makes during change. When change comes, it can change or alter the mission. The Ruler must assist the organization in this process. Everyone in the organization has to know the mission and how the proposed change might change this direction.	Don't allow a threat in the mission to derail any change. Instead, the Ruler has a role to blend the change and the mission to each other. Perhaps the mission has matured from the past. Perhaps the change will morph into something different that allows the mission to morph along with it. The Ruler's role is to make this happen.
CONSISTENCY	Is there anyone in the organization out of bounds when it comes to foundation, structure and/or direction? Regretfully, the individuals who hold the Ruler role can be those who think they are beyond the reach of these elements of stability. Don't be that way!	To make sure everyone is accountable, make sure accountability is defined. What does it look like to hold someone accountable? Does it look the same for everyone? Does it look the same for every situation? If it is different, is that okay?	When change(s) is proposed, consistency can be cloudy and muddy. The waters get churned and consistency can look different as it finds balance. The Ruler's role is to alert everyone to this and patiently work the team through the mud.

Ruler Script #2 - Moving Off Stage

Rulers are not the main thing in change. But they are the archetype that makes sure the main thing remains the main thing: The mission of the organization is at the center. The Ruler's role in the change process is to make sure the change does not derail the **Stability** of the organization. But be careful you don't attempt to do this via legislative acts. If you keep in mind that you want to help everyone succeed and that your desire for **Stability** might look different to the other archetypes, you can use their skills to keep the organization foundation, structure, mission and consistency clear. The Ruler role can be a very powerful figure in an organization. Don't use it to make things the way YOU want, but the way you keep **Stability** relevant.

The success of the change will depend upon how you work with and utilize the skills and the roles of each of the archetypes. They have their own ideas and will want to contribute to the change. Because the Ruler can be so powerful, this might be easier said than done. Once the change process actually starts to move forward, your desire might be to just *legislate*. Granted, to make sure the change keeps the organization **Stable**, you might want to get everyone to *conform* to *your way* of thinking. It might be better, however, to think of supporting the other archetypes and utilizing and incorporating their unique skills, rather than telling them what to do.

The Ruler must make sure we maintain **Stability** by using the other archetypes. Here is your moving off stage script.

Ruler's script to interact with the other archetypes

Archetype	Possible objections they may have with the change	Goal Association Work (See Addendum #4)
Seeker	They may want to take the organization into a new direction. This isn't always bad and, in fact, necessary at times.	The Ruler will have to hold the Seeker responsible to the belief and mission of the organization. They will tend to forget.
Lover	They may want to hang on to the status quo. They may value the wrong thing, but, nevertheless, they see change as dangerous to their status quo.	The Ruler and the Lover can fall into the same trap: You will want to hang on to things (but for different reasons). Make sure you know the reason you might hold on in the midst of change if it is necessary. Learn to *morph*.
Destroyer	They need to see what the change is replacing and will need to agree that "something" needs replacing.	The Destroyer can help you see what policy, procedure, rule, or process is out of date and no longer profitable. Form a partnership.
Creator	They can't always see the real practical application or design of the change. They need to know the vision has something tangible behind it.	As the Creator constructs, be along side to see what they are thinking. Keep the *why* of the organization in front of them. They might get so lost in their creation they forget the mission.
Warrior	They might reject the change if they think it will fail. They will want someone to show them that the change is successful or has the ability to be successful.	The Warriors push for excellence puts them in your camp, as excellence can only be maintained by the structure you provide. Make sure you don't use them to force *your way*.
Caregiver	They might reject the change because of all the work that will be put on the plates of the workers to accomplish the change.	Here is the challenge: The Caregiver might twist the policy to help someone. Teach them the belief. Mores can govern them.
Innocent	They might reject the change because they either don't see the need (naïveté) behind it or because they think it will be a hopeless pursuit.	The Innocent needs to know that any hope for organizational longevity is tied directly to your work. Their naïveté of beliefs can run the mission into very mirky waters. Teach them.
Orphan	They might reject the change because of failure to solve some of the problems the change will create when implemented.	This is another voice that can help you. The Orphan can spot challenges to the structure you put in place. Listen and learn from them.
Magician	They might reject the change if they think the change lacks any ability to see transformation. They will be your least resistor if they see "change" as good for anyone or any organization.	The Magician tends to buck the rules. They constantly want to transform from the inside, and they fight the *conforming* by structure. They need to know the beliefs and structure. It will protect them if they can see they will support them rather than fight their mission.
Sage	They might reject change because they see the change as foolish and lacking substance or because it has little research (and it probably does because it is a new idea).	The Sage is another partner to the Ruler. The Sage will know the significance of past beliefs, structures, and the mission. But they can think of themselves as outside of those elements.
Jester	They might reject the change because they think the change will be boring, too much work (that will steal the joy of the current work), or because they see the change as too complicated (the Sage will make it so).	The Jester's need for enjoyment can often see them reject policies, procedures and rules. They see these things as confining. Show them that enjoyment *for everyone* can only come through support of the structure. Help them see that without structure enjoyment is diminished.

Ruler Script #3 - Backstage

The Ruler must make sure that during the implementation process the **Stability** of the organization is maintained. This means that as they allow the archetypes to speak into the change, they can keep the organization solvent and moving forward with fidelity. They will get a better change if they listen to the other archetypes during the drama of change. The biggest question backstage for the Ruler is, "Can I allow the other archetypes to have a structure different than mine and still keep the organization stable?"

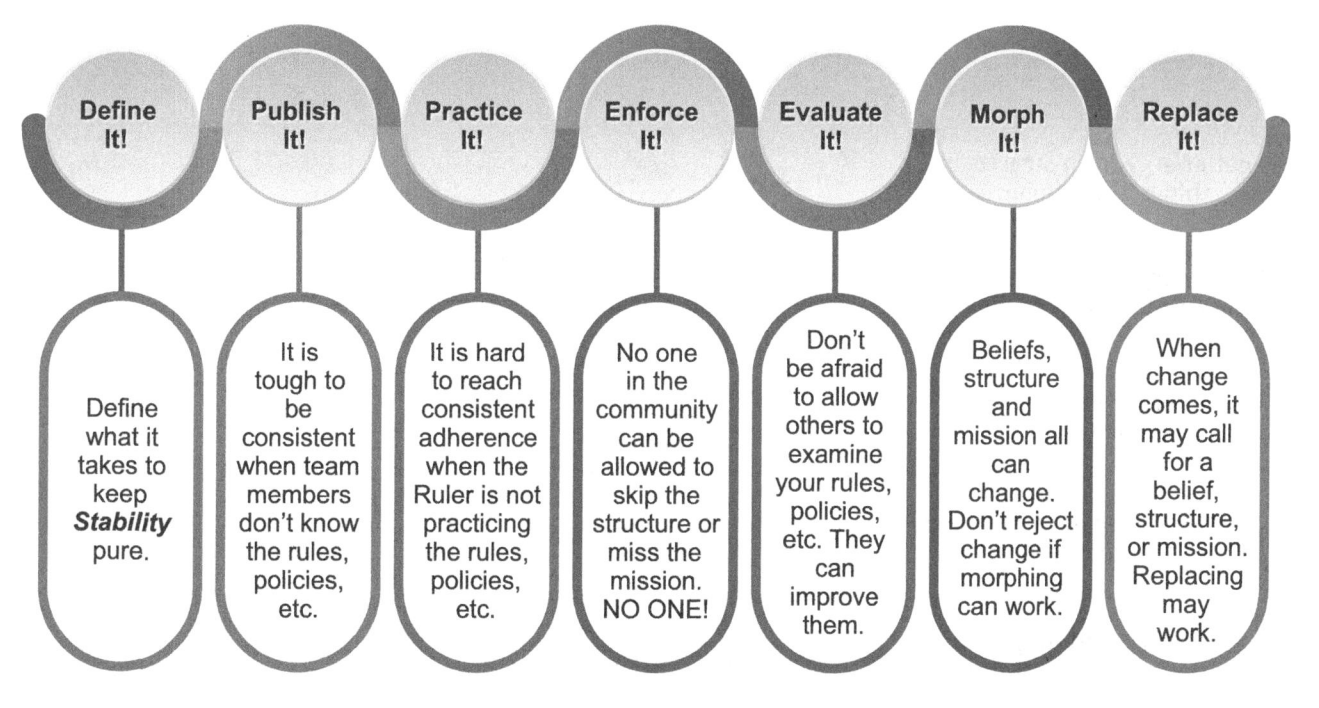

Define It!	Publish It!	Practice It!	Enforce It!	Evaluate It!	Morph It!	Replace It!
Define what it takes to keep **Stability** pure.	It is tough to be consistent when team members don't know the rules, policies, etc.	It is hard to reach consistent adherence when the Ruler is not practicing the rules, policies, etc.	No one in the community can be allowed to skip the structure or miss the mission. NO ONE!	Don't be afraid to allow others to examine your rules, policies, etc. They can improve them.	Beliefs, structure and mission all can change. Don't reject change if morphing can work.	When change comes, it may call for a belief, structure, or mission. Replacing may work.

Conclusion - an Email to the Ruler

Dear Ruler,

Okay, to be honest, we find your structure confining and limiting. Really, you are the child who kept telling us all, "Mom and dad are SO going to find out ... I'm going to tell them!" You do know that kid was often not liked, right? You tend to crush our parties (Jester wanted that stated), and you make it hard to color outside the lines (do you know who wanted that stated?). You are often seen by us all as a real downer. When you get too close to the Warrior, we are actually fearful.

However, the truth of it all is we need you. We would all sink without you. Please don't stop regulating us. Without our beliefs, we will sink into the abyss of the meaningless. Without the structure of policies, procedures, rules and processes, we would run off the road and over the cliff. We know this. Without a clear mission, our identity is lost. We would be two-faced. And without holding us all consistent, we would fight among ourselves. So, keep us all on track ... just make sure you stay within your own rules as well. Thanks again ... the other 11 archetypes.

Ruler's Audition Checklist
(You think you are equipped for the Ruler part in the Drama of Change?)

The following activities give the Ruler energy:	Never	Seldom	Sometimes	Often	Always
I get energy from RULES:	☐	☐	☐	☐	☐
I get energy from structuring things ... anything:	☐	☐	☐	☐	☐
I get energy seeing people kept safe by policy:	☐	☐	☐	☐	☐
I get energy when others ask what the policy is:	☐	☐	☐	☐	☐
I get energy being asked to be in charge of something:	☐	☐	☐	☐	☐
I get energy outlining and designing steps to take:	☐	☐	☐	☐	☐

- ☐ I read the owners manual
- ☑ I like to set standards
- ☐ I organize vacations
- ☐ I win by the rules

Secrets for a Successful Callback for a *Ruler* Role

- You have a history of setting and reaching goals.

- You spend time on the weekend and holidays competing.

- You would be willing to learn how to motivate others to reach their best.

- Your resume looks like a scorecard of accomplishments.

- You have a trophy or award you earned stashed away someplace.

- You read books about winners.

ACT II - THE STRUCTURAL ARCHETYPES
SCENE THREE - <u>*ORPHAN*</u> CENTER STAGE

(NOTE: The descriptor *Orphan* has been changed to *Realist*.
Please see Addendum #2 as to why this author is using the *Orphan* descriptor.)

CHANGE PUNCH CARD

The Orphan archetype, during the change process, is our watchdog. They are focused on **Vigilance**. The Orphan's desire is to make sure that everyone sees the dangers in the change. Obviously, with that mindset, the Orphan is highly active during change. At first glance, we might not enjoy someone investing their entire energy to spot problems. We have a phrase in our lexicon for this image: *Debbie Downer*. This is a difficult role for some to play. In the *shadow* side of the archetype, however, it seems to be a very exciting role for a select few. There are some who can't wait to point out what will go wrong and what is wrong with a change initiative. The Orphan, in the *shadow* side, who is simply practicing **Vigilance**, can sound like a sour note in a symphony of change.

The Orphan should not be viewed in the *Debbie Downer* image, however. This is a very important archetype voice in the change drama. Imagine the Orphan voice in the strength side of the archetype. If someone isn't watching for dangerous aspects of the change, then what? If no one is willing to speak up about the possible challenges in the change, what then? If someone doesn't cry out about a possible iceberg ahead that could cause a shipwreck, what would happen? Can you spell T-I-T-A-N-I-C?

The real problem with the Orphan archetype is not that they see danger. The real issue with the Orphan voice during change is how the voice sounds as the Orphan expresses their warning. The warning of the Orphan can often come across like a bad warning sign, when in reality they simply want to be heard. The key for the Orphan is not *what* they are saying, but *how* they are saying it. The archetype that shouts danger might want to be willing to listen to some dangerous truths about their voice and how others might view it. Here are six warnings that, if the Orphan hears them, can improve the success in their role.

Be Warned: The way you use your voice can cause people to *tolerate* it and not actually hear what you are saying.

Be Warned: You often give a bleak forecast for future events. It may be tough for others to hear your warning as a result.

Be Warned: Yelling, "Fire, fire," mostly causes people to run and not actually stay to put out the fire.

Be Warned: You often speak using mostly "exclamation points" and might fair better using questions to get others to see your view.

Be Warned: If you are going to tell people where lightning is going to strike, also tell them a solution and where to go for protection.

Be Warned: People will embrace someone who lets them know where there is danger IF they are not also dangerous in their delivery.

Not Just an Orphan Challenge

The issue of the delivery of the Orphan voice does not fall solely at the feet of the Orphan. They can be rough in delivery, but they don't start out that way. The first foray into the potential issues typically starts out as a simple comment. When their comment is ignored, they might mention it again to more than one team member. When those team members give little regard to their thought pattern, they might find another Orphan to hear their concerns. Now they have an audience. Together, they may speak a little louder and with many more exclamation points. Soon, left unheard, they will begin to sound like those fingers on a chalkboard. It all started, however, with a simple comment left unheard. The team might do well to listen to some warnings as well. Here are three warnings the team should hear:

Be Warned: The team has to stop *ignoring* the early warnings of the Orphan. They don't always want to come across negative. They often start in a small voice and, often, only increase the volume when they garner limited or no response.

Be Warned: The team should avoid *marginalizing* the Orphan. It is easy to simply create space between the team and the Orphan, rather than hear their warnings. An immature team can allow the Orphan to speak and then simply continue on the path they were headed (again, think of the Titanic).

Be Warned: The team has to stop *punishing* the Orphan. We punish them by characterizing them with negative terms (Negative Neal); by shouting them down; by ignoring their voice; by moving them to another department; by not promoting them; etc.

The Orphan's Script in the Change Drama

The Orphan's script in the drama of change includes three scripts:

Orphan Script #1 - Center Stage

The key for the Orphan during the drama of change is to be able to deliver a warning about what they see as dangerous to the organization. There are three techniques the Orphan should master to develop their delivery method of their warning. Here is a script for each technique that the Orphan can develop to practice *Vigilance*:

LEARN TO ASK GREAT QUESTIONS		
Asking questions can be much more profitable than making statements. During the process of spotting a flaw, danger or a suspicious aspect of the change, such as talking with exclamation points, can alienate team members. Asking questions can open minds. Be careful not to be sarcastic. Be sure not to be the Sage-Orphan (where you know more than anyone else in the room and they *simply don't get it*).		
FIVE TYPES OF QUESTIONS TO USE		
What it would be called:	How it would be described:	What it may sound like:
1). A **DIG DEEPER** QUESTION	A question that wants to find out more about the change.	"Could you tell me more on how this might work? Could you help me understand this aspect of the change in a deeper manner?"
2). A **COMPARE IT TO A KNOWN** THING QUESTION	A question that wants to compare the change to something already working.	"Could you walk me through how this relates to what we are currently doing? How does this new change work with this aspect of our process?"
3). A **THIS COULD HAPPEN** QUESTION	A question that proposes a scenario with *high predictability* and *data driven* support.	"Can you walk me through these numbers again? Do you see any issue with how this applies to last quarter's number?"
4). A **THIS MIGHT HAPPEN** QUESTION	A question that proposes a hypothesis. You have little support, but your intuition says it *could* happen.	"Let's dream a little; what would happen with this change if these factors actually happened?"
5). AN **ALTERNATIVE** QUESTION	A question that proposes an alternative path.	"Would this proposed change still meet your goals if we took this direction with it? Could we add this to the change?"

BE SOLUTION ORIENTED - OFFER A SOLUTION(S)

Perhaps the weightiest complaint registered toward the Orphan voice is that they always see the wrong but seldom offer an answer to solve the problem(s) they pointed out. It is easy to see the problem, play the victim of the drama of change and/or speak up to complain, and then shrink to solve the problem. Until the Orphan voice is held accountable to also provide solutions, they will have a hard time being heard.

FIVE TYPES OF SOLUTIONS TO PROVIDE

What it would be called:	How it would be described:	What it may sound like:
1). A **WE SOLVED THIS BEFORE** SOLUTION	This is a solution based upon a historical record. Even though a change may be new, there are often tried and true repetitive solutions to new challenges.	"I know we are in a new change initiative, but do you think that solution we used a few years back might still work to solve this potential problem?"
2). A **SIMPLE** SOLUTION	This is a common sense solution that others are missing because they simply didn't see the problem, and this solution is obvious to all.	"I hate to point out the obvious, but here is a problem with the change, but could this be a simple solution?"
3). A **CHANGE TO IMPROVE** SOLUTION	A solution that would significantly change, but improve the initiative being changed. This is often hard to suggest because it might take the change in a new direction.	"I see what we are tying to do here, but I am wondering if a way to solve a problem with this change might be to actually, slightly alter the direction by changing one of the major premise of the change?"
4). A **THIS HAS HOLES IN IT TOO** SOLUTION	A solution that is not, on its own, totally safe either. This is a solution that the Orphan offers to solicit other Orphan voices.	"I can see the problem, but I am also struggling with a good solution. I have a solution, but can you point out the holes in my solution as well?"
5). A **MANY OPTIONS** SOLUTION	This solution offers a mix of solutions that could be considered by the team. It shows the Orphan is NOT simply trying to block something but is also trying to assist in the success of the change.	"I see a danger in this change initiative, but I think there are several solutions that could be incorporated to assure we don't crash. I am not tied to anyone in particular but wonder if I could offer some alternatives?"

CREATE A PROPER PLATFORM FOR ORPHAN WORK

No, a suggestion box does not qualify. There needs to be a legitimate place and method the Orphan voice can be heard and even sought out. To place the entire burden for speaking up on the Orphan is not just unfair, it is ineffective. Placing the burden on the Orphan to speak when they see something dangerous or suspect is the reason we characterize them in a negative fashion. The Orphan must know how to approach the Ruler, the Warrior, the Creator and the other members of the change team to speak their voice.

FIVE TYPES OF PLATFORMS TO DEVELOP

What it would be called:	*How it would be described:*	*What it may sound like:*
1). A **LET ME ASK** PLATFORM	When the change is introduced to the team, those leading the change invite the Orphan voice early and often to speak up during the drama of change.	"I know you will have a number of areas of concern as this change is rolled out. We are hoping your eyes will be open, and you CAN speak up."
2). A **SCHEDULED** PLATFORM	A time and a place are put on the calendar to gather the Orphan voice concerns.	"Ruler has scheduled this change to roll out in six steps. At the end of each step, we are going to need the Orphan voice to alert us to what happened. Gather your thoughts as we go, and we will address them together after each step."
3). AN **ORPHAN SUB-TEAM** PLATFORM	A team is created that will play the Orphan role for the entire change drama. This is what an in-house *quality control* team is all about.	"As this change is rolled out, we have asked these team members to play a key role to watch for problems. They will be speaking up at meetings to assure we don't crash the bus."
4). AN **OUTSIDE REVIEW** PLATFORM	The organization hires an outside voice to look for dangers as the change initiative is rolled out.	"You will notice a new face among us as we role out this change. We have asked "x" to keep an eye on the work and to point out to us any potential issues and blind spots we might be missing."
5). A **MIXED TEAM** PLATFORM	Representatives from a variety of departments or sub-teams are put together to represent the interests of their respective departments.	"We have a culture group that is going to watch this change and see how it interacts with our culture. Their job will be to speak up and report any dangers we might be missing."

Orphan Script #2 - Moving Off Stage

Orphans are not the main thing in change. But they are the archetype that makes sure we don't crash the bus on our way to where the change is taking us. Your role in the change process is to make sure the change does not hurt us now and in the future by having a sense of **Vigilance**. You have to be careful, however, that you don't marginalize your work by how you do your work. Sometimes, it is easy for you to see the holes in something, and you may wonder why others don't see what you see. Simply put, others simply do not have a sense of **Vigilance** for the organization. It doesn't mean they don't care, but it does show your role is highly important.

The success of the change will depend upon how you also work with and utilize the skills and the roles of each of the archetypes. They have their own ideas and will want to contribute to the change. Because the Orphan can *sound* negative, this might be easier said than done. Once the change process actually starts to move forward, your desire might be to just *complain*, *shout*, or even *scream*. Granted, to be **Vigilant** you might have to speak louder because they are not listening. It might be better, however, to think of bringing the other archetypes into your **Vigilant** process, rather than thinking you are the lone voice of danger.

The Orphan must make sure the **Vigilance** needed to keep us safe is shared by the other archetypes. Here is your moving off stage script.

Orphan's script to interact with the other archetypes

Archetype	Possible objections they may have with the change	Goal Association Work (See Addendum #4)
Seeker	They may want to take the organization into a new direction. This isn't always bad and, in fact, necessary at times.	It is important that you listen early and often to the Seeker's ideas. You might tend to believe they are so far fetched no one will catch on.
Lover	They may want to hang on to the status quo. They may value the wrong thing, but, nevertheless, they see change as dangerous to their status quo.	Be careful you don't hang onto a Lover's value and criticize an idea simply on their thoughts. Remember, the value they hold had some holes at one time as well. Examine it all!!
Destroyer	They need to see what the change is replacing and will need to agree that "something" needs replacing.	Your partnership with the Destroyer can be powerful. You can help them see what is dangerous; they can show you how to let it go.
Creator	They can't always see the real practical application or design of the change. They need to know the vision has something tangible behind it.	The Creator will be the first to marginalize you. Make sure you maintain a positive relationship with them by using great questions and developing a way to speak up as they create.
Warrior	They might reject the change if they think it will fail. They will want someone to show them that the change is successful or has the ability to be successful.	The Warrior can falsely think you are just not a team player and even lazy. Make sure you use great language with them, and show them how a danger can cause underperformance.
Caregiver	They might reject the change because of all the work that will be put on the plates of the workers to accomplish the change.	They might see you as a complainer. They might, however, help you complain. Work with them to show how you are helping others as you point out dangers.
Innocent	They might reject the change because they either don't see the need (naïveté) behind it or because they think it will be a hopeless pursuit.	Innocent can really balance your work. They can be the perfect source to help you find solutions when all you see is problems. Don't reject their naïveté. Blend it into the solutions.
Ruler	They might reject the change because they don't see structurally how the change will work. They will want to policy and procedure any change.	As Ruler structures, they might not always see the dangers of the change. You can help them with their quest of stability, if you show them that the danger can hurt their stable world.
Magician	They might reject the change if they think the change lacks any ability to see transformation. They will be your least resistor if they see "change" as good for anyone or any organization.	The Magician seldom sees the dangers you see. If they do, they see them not as obstacles but as opportunities for transformation. They, like Innocent, can be the perfect fit to help with solutions to problems.
Sage	They might reject change because they see the change as foolish and lacking substance or because it has little research (and it probably does because it is a new idea).	Here is another great partner. The Sage will offer some great knowledge as to why things will work or not. But be careful the two of you don't become the in-house *know-it-alls*.
Jester	They might reject the change because they think the change will be boring, too much work (that will steal the joy of the current work), or because they see the change as too complicated (the Sage will make it so).	The Jester does not like to put road blocks up if it looks like it might make things stressful and uninviting. Your work with them might seem insignificant, but you must find a way to show them that correcting a potential problem can allow enjoyment to take place, not stop it.

Orphan Script #3 - Backstage

The Orphan must make sure that during the implementation process **Vigilance** for the safety of the organization is maintained. This means that as they allow the archetypes to speak into the change, they can keep the organization alerted to possible dangers and problems most don't see. They will get a better change if they listen to the other archetypes during the drama of change. The biggest question backstage for the Orphan is, "Can I point out the danger without members of the team rejecting the message because of how I say it?"

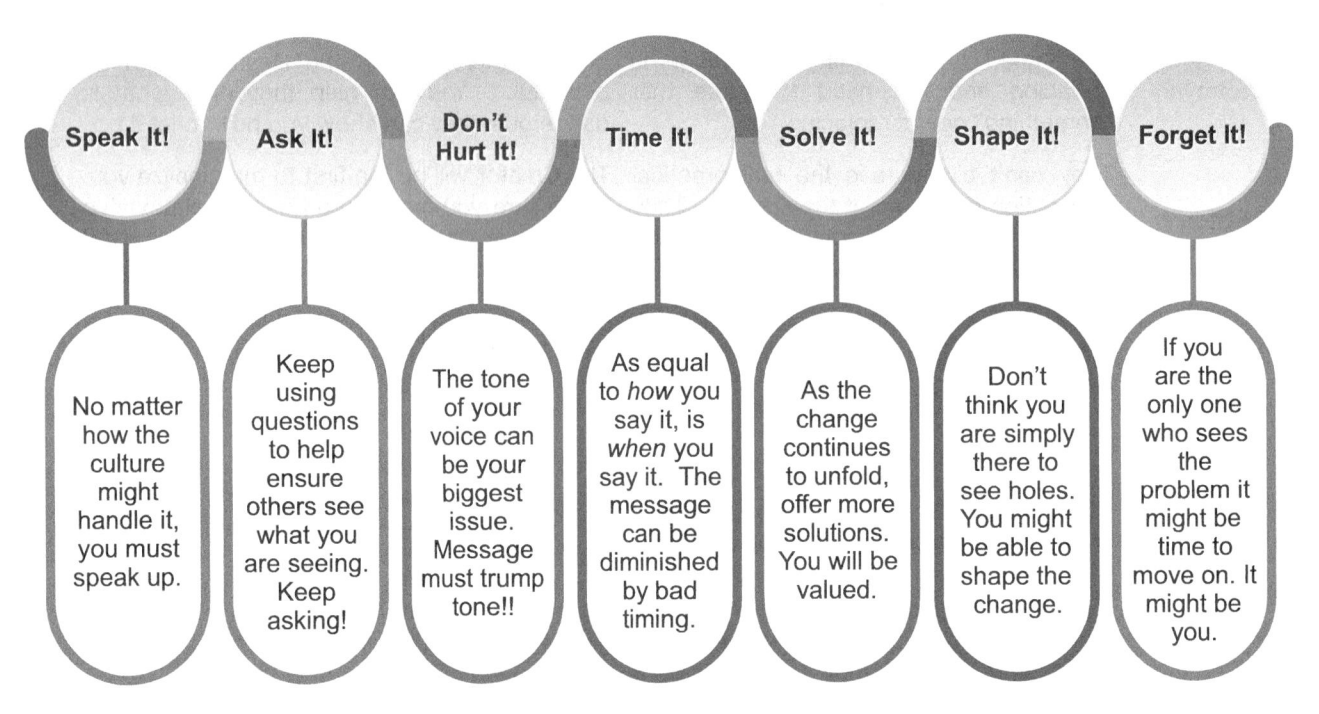

Speak It!	Ask It!	Don't Hurt It!	Time It!	Solve It!	Shape It!	Forget It!
No matter how the culture might handle it, you must speak up.	Keep using questions to help ensure others see what you are seeing. Keep asking!	The tone of your voice can be your biggest issue. Message must trump tone!!	As equal to *how* you say it, is *when* you say it. The message can be diminished by bad timing.	As the change continues to unfold, offer more solutions. You will be valued.	Don't think you are simply there to see holes. You might be able to shape the change.	If you are the only one who sees the problem it might be time to move on. It might be you.

Conclusion - an Email to the Orphan

Dear Orphan,

Okay we get it ... you have a very watchful eye. We also know that if we listened to you, we would have avoided that mistake last week, last month or last year. We do see that hindsight is 20/20. But if we are honest, you did warn us. It might be hard for us to hear, but we need you to point out these potential problems.

However, can we ask that you use a different approach? This constantly being negative can wear on us. We might be wrong, but your constantly seeing danger can be hard to hear. We would like to see you join with us in seeing a new thing. We all know there will be holes to fill as change is rolled out. But if you can approach your role with a little more positive speech, we might actually hear you. But if we hear you, make sure you realize the downside of that ... you won't be able to say, "I told you so," as much. We are good with that if you are.

Thanks again ... the other 11 archetypes.

Orphan's Audition Checklist
(You think you are equipped for the Orphan's part in the Drama of Change?)

The following activities give the Orphan energy:	Never	Seldom	Sometimes	Often	Always
I get energy from spotting dangers others miss:	☐	☐	☐	☐	☐
I get energy from speaking up about problems:	☐	☐	☐	☐	☐
I get energy when people hear the danger and fix it:	☐	☐	☐	☐	☐
I get energy when others are kept safe by my warnings:	☐	☐	☐	☐	☐
I get energy when others ask me to look over projects:	☐	☐	☐	☐	☐
I get energy in safe environments:	☐	☐	☐	☐	☐

- ☐ I read the safety manuals
- ☑ I like to play it safe
- ☐ I tend to see problems fast
- ☐ I like safe vacations

What Role Do You Play In Change?   The Archetypes and the Change Process

Secrets for a Successful Callback for a *Orphan* Role

❖ You have a history of seeing dangers before others.

❖ You would be willing to check and double check the project.

❖ You would be willing to learn how to show others and teach others how to maintain safe working conditions.

❖ You like movies and stories about whistle blowers or underdogs.

❖ You attend conferences about difficult problems to solve.

ACT II - THE STRUCTURAL ARCHETYPES
SCENE FOUR - *SAGE* CENTER STAGE

CHANGE PUNCH CARD

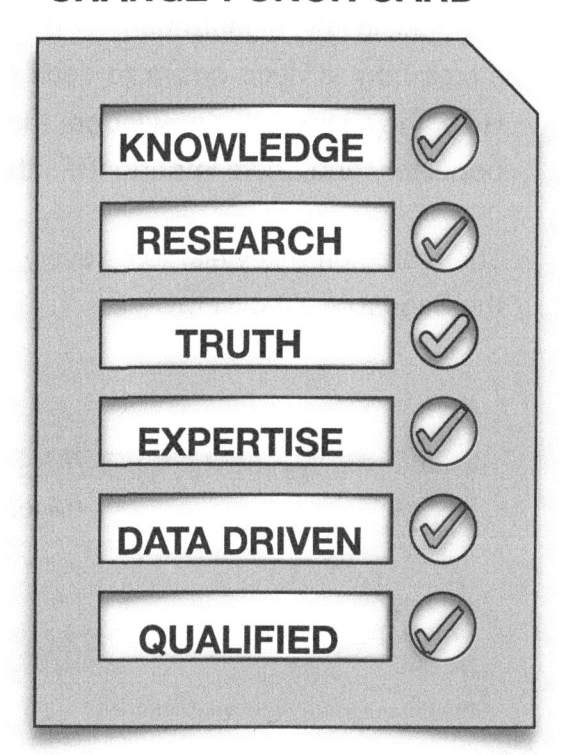

- KNOWLEDGE ✓
- RESEARCH ✓
- TRUTH ✓
- EXPERTISE ✓
- DATA DRIVEN ✓
- QUALIFIED ✓

The archetype of the Sage and change have an interesting and intriguing relationship.

- How do you think the Sage would approach a proposed change?
- What would they do first?
- Where would the initial steps take them?
- As the change unfolds, where does the Sage want to go with their role?
- Where might the Sage hinder a change initiative?
- Does the Sage interact well with all the other archetypes, especially the Seeker?

You get the point? The Sage role in the drama of change is seeking **Knowledge**. This is where a new idea and the change process are captivating to the Sage. Their dance begins with a struggle, because a new idea is, by nature, limited in **Knowledge**. As the Seeker begins to think, mostly outside the box (and the box is full of **Knowledge**), they produce an idea that has no or limited research. New ideas might not even have a pattern of truth behind them (at least apparent to others). The Sage role will feel comfortable when they KNOW things. If they don't KNOW, they ask a lot of questions. (Note: Remembering the last chapter, asking questions was a way to improve the Orphan voice. So, you can see where a Sage can often be accused of operating in the Orphan's domain. The difference is that the

Sage is asking questions to build a lexicon for the change. The Orphan is asking questions to expose possible difficulties in the change.)

We might, by mistake, think that the Sage role is played by the oldest or more mature team member in the organization. However, that would be a false assumption. The Sage role stems from a deep desire to seek **Knowledge**, and that can live inside any team member. How they express **Knowledge** they already posses can change with maturity, seniority, popularity and, more importantly, other aspects of the Sage's archetypes and personality.

There are some key elements every Sage must know (pun intended) to make sure they utilize the Sage role effectively.

The **Know-It-All Syndrome**: It is important that the Sage doesn't *show off* their knowledge. It can be tempting to want to demonstrate what you know all the time, if not most of the time. If you are valued for what you know, you will have the urge or need to feel valued and seek to share.

The **I'm the Smartest Guy in the Room Syndrome**: This is different than being the know-it-all, because it is one thing to think you are smart and know things and quite another to think others aren't and don't. When people think you think they are not smart, you cease to be considered so yourself!

The **I'm the Star of Jeopardy Syndrome**: This is different than the above two, as this syndrome for the Sage is about knowing trivia and not actually demonstrating any depth. In this syndrome, the Sage offers disconnecting facts and unrelated truths. They may appear that they know but are impractical.

The Important Role: Evolving-Knowledge in the Drama of Change

The Sage is vital in change, since it provides the ongoing **Knowledge** base we need to make sure we are progressing and growing during the change process. When change begins to happen, we cannot be content with the same level of **Knowledge** from day-to-day. We must be growing. Here are key elements to consider as the Sage role is played out in the change process. As you can see from the diagram, the key work in the drama of change (based upon

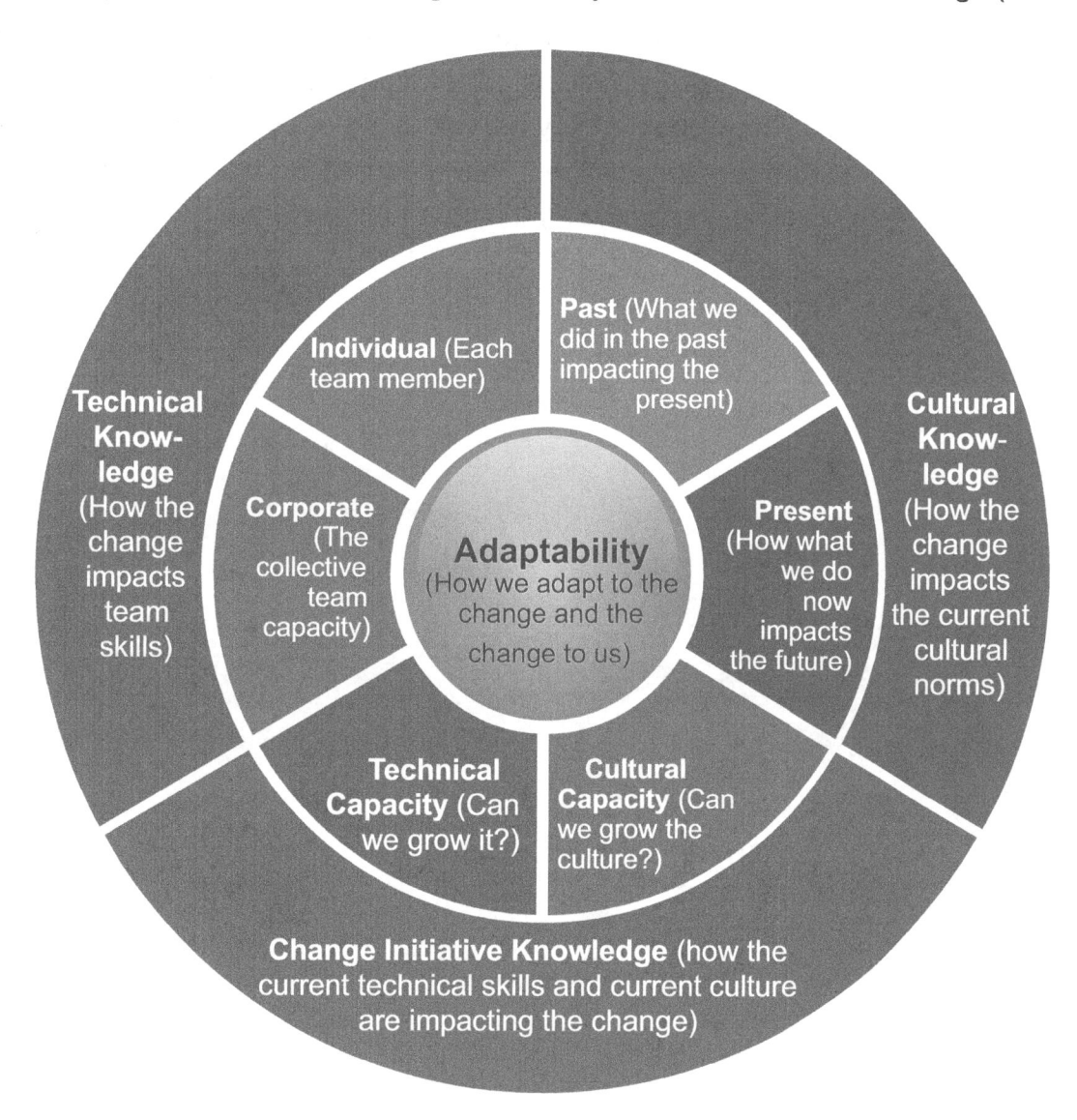

Diagram

- **Technical Knowledge** (How the change impacts team skills)
- **Cultural Knowledge** (How the change impacts the current cultural norms)
- **Change Initiative Knowledge** (how the current technical skills and current culture are impacting the change)
- **Individual** (Each team member)
- **Corporate** (The collective team capacity)
- **Technical Capacity** (Can we grow it?)
- **Cultural Capacity** (Can we grow the culture?)
- **Past** (What we did in the past impacting the present)
- **Present** (How what we do now impacts the future)
- **Adaptability** (How we adapt to the change and the change to us)

the role of the Sage) is Adaptability: The ability for everyone to adapt to the change and the change to adapt to everyone working the change. The Sage has a different definition for success than the Warrior archetype. The Sage sees success as a way for the past and present **Knowledge** to adapt to the change and, in return, what we know about the evolving change as it unfolds, to adapt to **Knowledge**. The role of the Sage is to make sure all of the **Knowledge** interrelates with each other, and we don't *ignorantly* move in a way that lacks logical sense to them.

The Sage's Script in the Change Drama

The Sage's script in the drama of change includes three scripts:

Sage Script #1 - Center Stage

The key for the Sage during the drama of change is to be able to track new data to identify and establish new truths as the change unfolds. The Sage does not want to move forward with suspicious or sketchy **Knowledge**. They are not afraid of change and the absence of data surrounding the foundation of the change ... however, they do fear the change unfolding if no one is gathering, collecting and analyzing the data to either broaden or establish a new **Knowledge** lexicon.

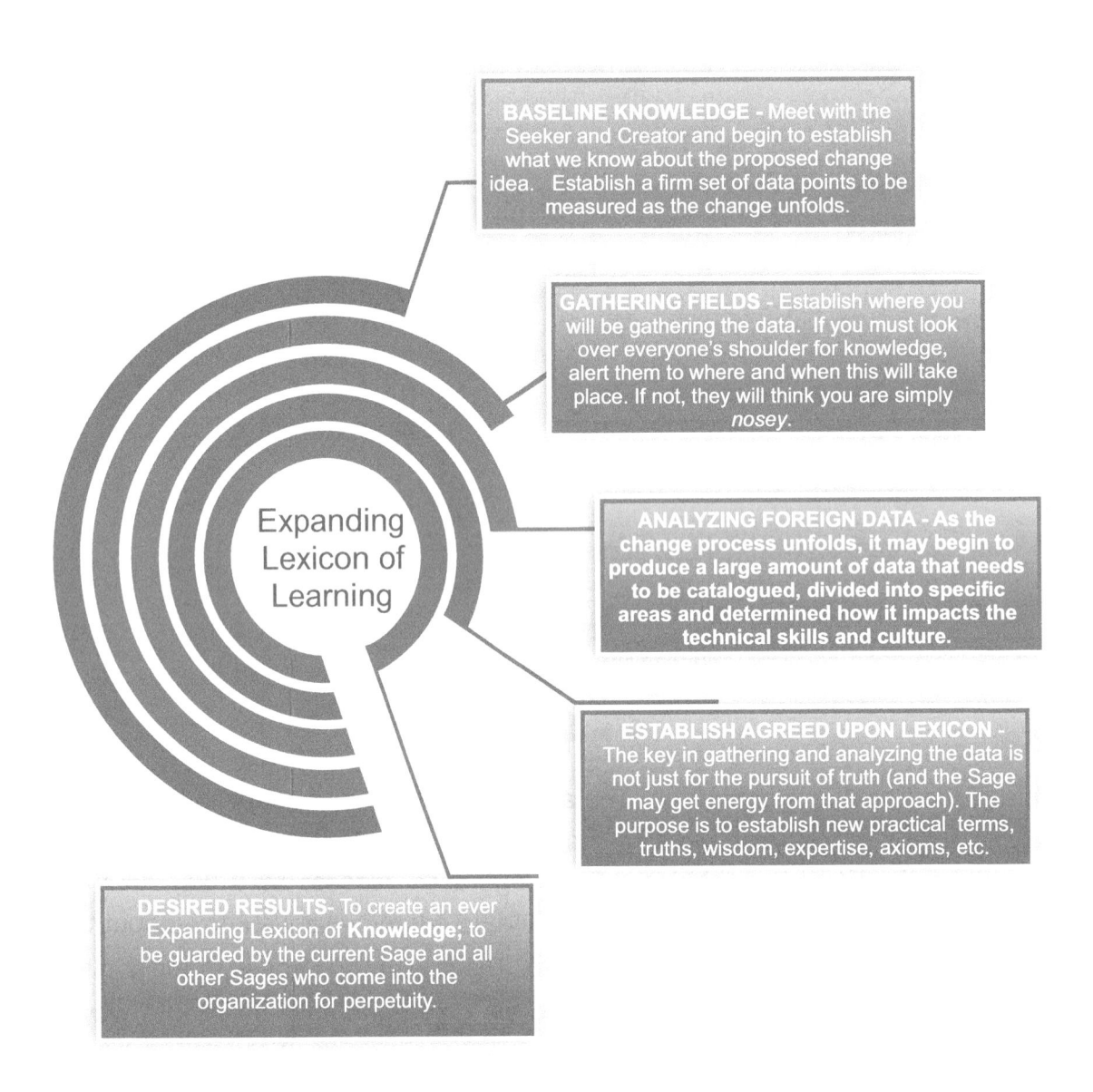

Expanding Lexicon of Learning

- **BASELINE KNOWLEDGE** - Meet with the Seeker and Creator and begin to establish what we know about the proposed change idea. Establish a firm set of data points to be measured as the change unfolds.

- **GATHERING FIELDS** - Establish where you will be gathering the data. If you must look over everyone's shoulder for knowledge, alert them to where and when this will take place. If not, they will think you are simply *nosey*.

- **ANALYZING FOREIGN DATA** - As the change process unfolds, it may begin to produce a large amount of data that needs to be catalogued, divided into specific areas and determined how it impacts the technical skills and culture.

- **ESTABLISH AGREED UPON LEXICON** - The key in gathering and analyzing the data is not just for the pursuit of truth (and the Sage may get energy from that approach). The purpose is to establish new practical terms, truths, wisdom, expertise, axioms, etc.

- **DESIRED RESULTS** - To create an ever Expanding Lexicon of **Knowledge**; to be guarded by the current Sage and all other Sages who come into the organization for perpetuity.

Sage Script #2 - Moving Off Stage

The Sage is not the main thing in the drama of change. But they are the archetype that makes sure we learn our lesson as we go and into the future. Your role in the change process is to make sure that both the organization and change initiative grow in **Knowledge.** We all have to be careful that during change:

1. We don't become foolish - based upon foolish data or false narratives from the data.
2. We grow in what we know about the organization, adapting the change to our culture.
3. The workers carrying out the change are adapting.
4. The change itself is adapting.

A new idea doesn't always have the **Knowledge** we need initially. As it morphs into what it will become, the Sage must use the other archetypes to gather as much **Knowledge** as possible.

The success of the proposed change will depend upon how the Sage, too, works with and utilizes the skills and the roles of each of the archetypes. They have their own ideas and will want to contribute to the change. Because the Sage can be so curious, this might be easier said than done. Once the change process actually starts to move forward, the desire of the Sage might be to just *speak up* about what they know. The sage must also learn during the change process. There is much more to learn in life, and the Sage must employ the other archetypes to teach them, as well as being taught by them.

The Sage must make sure the **Knowledge** needed to keep the organization is gathered by the other archetypes. Here is your script.

Sage's script to interact with the other archetypes

Archetype	Possible objections they may have with the change	Goal Association Work (See Addendum #4)
Seeker	They may want to take the organization into a new direction. This isn't always bad and, in fact, necessary at times.	As stated earlier, make sure you know early what the Seeker is thinking. Don't think simply because you don't know it, the idea is wrong.
Lover	They may want to hang on to the status quo. They may value the wrong thing, but, nevertheless, they see change as dangerous to their status quo.	The Lover has historical knowledge you can learn and should know. Find out how to incorporate what they know about the past, and incorporate it into the proposed change.
Destroyer	They need to see what the change is replacing and will need to agree that "something" needs replacing.	Use your established lexicon, and the one you are building, to help the Destroyer with discerning what to leave and what to toss.
Creator	They can't always see the real practical application or design of the change. They need to know the vision has something tangible behind it.	As the Creator creates, learn what they are thinking. Incorporate your knowledge with them, and learn their thoughts. Use the new knowledge to change the change.
Warrior	They might reject the change if they think it will fail. They will want someone to show them that the change is successful or has the ability to be successful.	The Warrior can use your knowledge base to show the team how to strive for excellence. But you each have a different view of success. The Warrior can help you find purpose for your expanding lexicon. They make you practical.
Caregiver	They might reject the change because of all the work that will be put on the plates of the workers to accomplish the change.	Knowledge and new-knowing is important to the Caregiver only if it is practical and useful to help others on their journey. They, like the Warrior, can make your work very practical.
Innocent	They might reject the change because they either don't see the need (naïveté) behind it or because they think it will be a hopeless pursuit.	The Innocent can be naive because they are ignorant of the knowledge you possess. Feed them with a constant stream of knowledge, and they can grow and be less blindsided.
Orphan	They might reject the change because of failure to solve some of the problems the change will create when implemented.	In one sense, Orphan is like a distant cousin to you. They have a different purpose but a similar road: To educate those around you.
Ruler	They might reject the change because they don't see structurally how the change will work. They will want to policy and procedure any change.	The Ruler can be stuck in their own ways in regard to what stability looks like. They might scoff at your new knowledge if they don't see a practical way to structure it. They will help in the analyzing stage by structuring the data.
Magician	They might reject the change if they think the change lacks any ability to see transformation. They will be your least resistor if they see "change" as good for anyone or any organization.	The way a Magician thinks about knowledge is that the new axiom has to find a way to convert the person they are working with into the change they desire. They can help the Sage make their knowledge have a purpose.
Jester	They might reject the change because they think the change will be boring, too much work (that will steal the joy of the current work), or because they see the change as too complicated (the Sage will make it so).	The Jester may be your balance in life, but they are no fan of the stuffed shirt approach you can often take. They will be quick to point out when you are acting pompous or greater than others ... they just might tell you to your face. They want to learn, but in a fun way.

Sage Script #3 - Backstage

The Sage must make sure that during the implementation process **Knowledge** is expanding for the organization and the individuals in the organization. This means that as they allow the archetypes to speak into the change, they can keep the organization alerted to a growing lexicon and new truths being discovered. They will get a better change if they listen to the other archetypes during the drama of change. The biggest question backstage for the Sage should not be, "When and where can I show these fools what I know?" But rather, it should be, "Can we all learn something here, and make it practical so the change succeeds?"

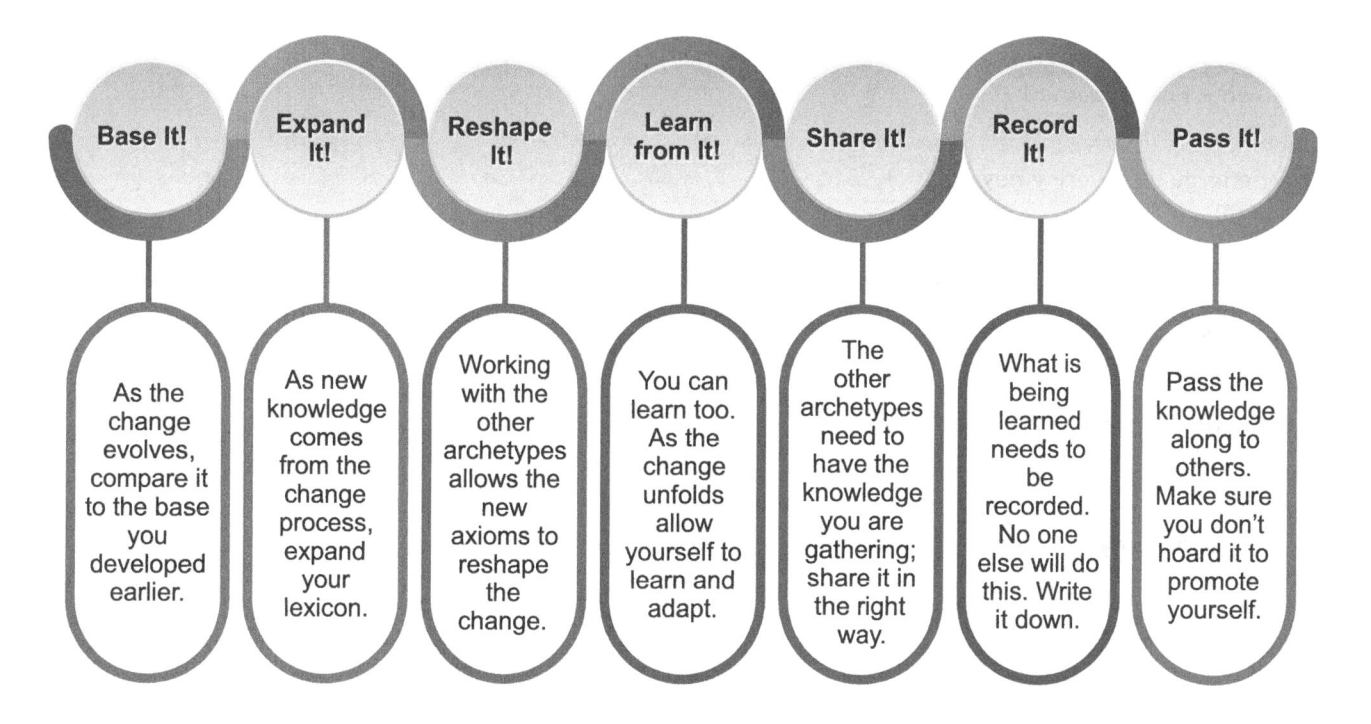

Base It!	Expand It!	Reshape It!	Learn from It!	Share It!	Record It!	Pass It!
As the change evolves, compare it to the base you developed earlier.	As new knowledge comes from the change process, expand your lexicon.	Working with the other archetypes allows the new axioms to reshape the change.	You can learn too. As the change unfolds allow yourself to learn and adapt.	The other archetypes need to have the knowledge you are gathering; share it in the right way.	What is being learned needs to be recorded. No one else will do this. Write it down.	Pass the knowledge along to others. Make sure you don't hoard it to promote yourself.

Dear Sage,

Okay, we know you are the smartest one in the room. You were probably voted the most likely to become a professor. But to be honest, we all wonder if you can tie your own shoes. Your continuous providing unrelated facts and trivia gets old after awhile.

However, if you could give us new **Knowledge** in a practical way that actually connects to our change, we would value you more. This change process is teaching us all new things, but we have no one to put it into a legible and categorical lexicon. We do need to learn from this, and it would be regretful to go through the entire process without learning what there is to learn. So, teach us. Just don't sound like that old college professor … we all skipped his class you know. Not because he didn't know anything, he just refused to know us.

Thanks again … the other 11 archetypes.

Sage's Audition Checklist
(You think you are equipped for the Sage's part in the Drama of Change?)

The following activities give the Sage energy:	Never	Seldom	Sometimes	Often	Always
I get energy from learning new things:	☐	☐	☐	☐	☐
I get energy teaching others what I have learned:	☐	☐	☐	☐	☐
I get energy discovering new concepts:	☐	☐	☐	☐	☐
I get energy from expressing knowledge in a new way:	☐	☐	☐	☐	☐
I get energy when I hear a deep speaker:	☐	☐	☐	☐	☐
I get energy studying complex problems:	☐	☐	☐	☐	☐

- ☐ I read
- ☑ I like to read quotes
- ☐ I do word puzzles
- ☐ I like historical vacations

Secrets for a Successful Callback for a *Sage* Role

❖ You have a reputation for being smart.

❖ You would be willing to learn anything.

❖ You have a desire to get more and more education.

❖ You get frustrated by simple people or people who act foolishly.

❖ You have degrees framed on your wall.

❖ You read a variety of different books.

The Warrior-Ruler-Orphan-Sage Dynamic

The drama of change can create many challenges as an idea moves from the incubation stage to the implementation stage. During the incubation stage, the idea needs to develop and the archetypes of Seeker-Lover-Destroyer-Creator get numerous opportunities to stretch each other and challenge each other. Once through this development, we have four more archetypes that have similar dynamics during the implementation stage. Warrior-Ruler-Orphan-Sage are key archetypes to avoid what author, *Michael Fullen,* calls the *implementation dip*. The diagram below shows us what these four do in their efforts to diminish the dip caused by any new initiative.

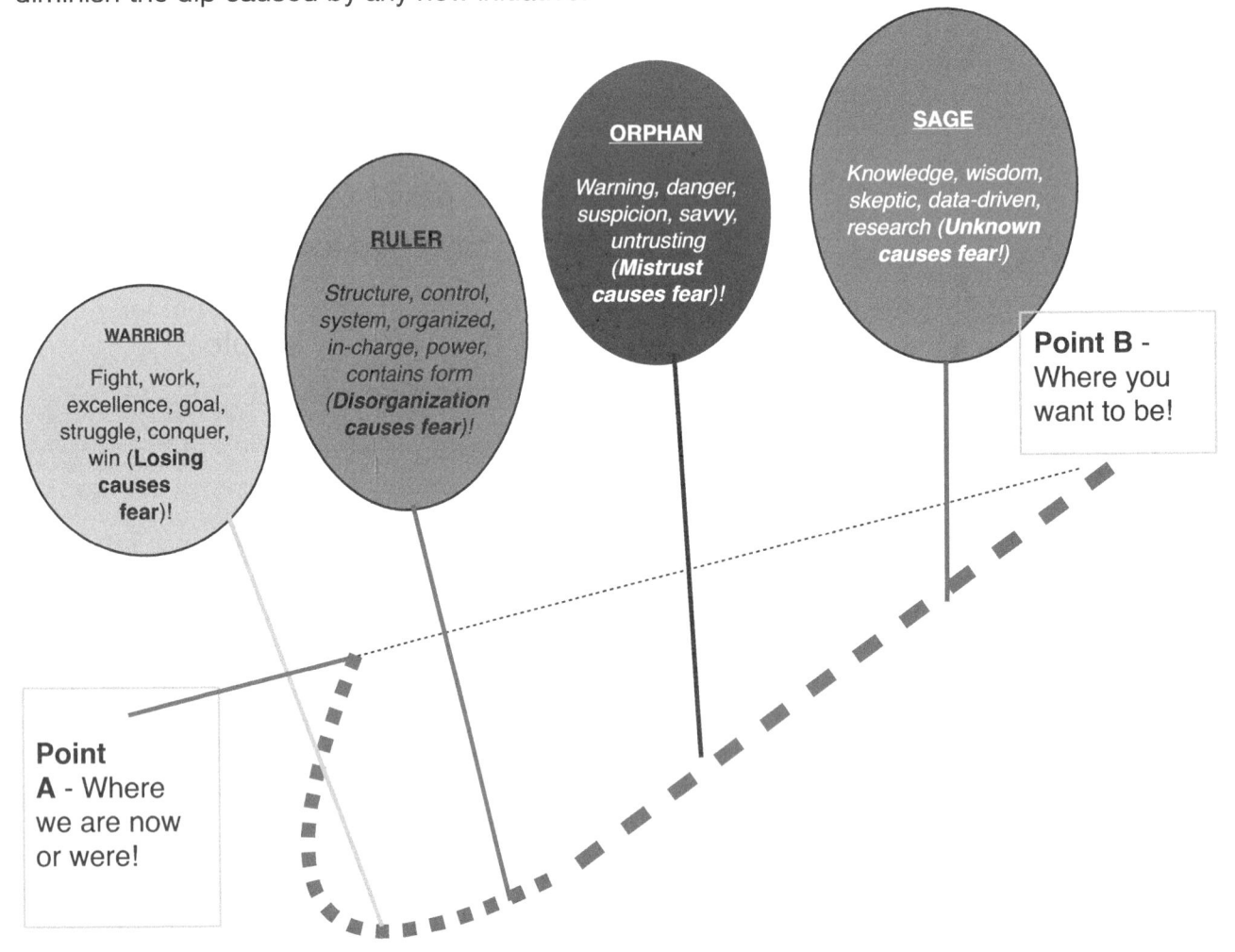

WARRIOR
Fight, work, excellence, goal, struggle, conquer, win (**Losing causes fear**)!

RULER
Structure, control, system, organized, in-charge, power, contains form (***Disorganization causes fear***)!

ORPHAN
Warning, danger, suspicion, savvy, untrusting (***Mistrust causes fear***)!

SAGE
Knowledge, wisdom, skeptic, data-driven, research (***Unknown causes fear!***)

Point A - Where we are now or were!

Point B - Where you want to be!

Implementation Dip - What is the implementation dip? Michael Fullen (2001), in his book *Leading in a Culture of Change*, defines the implementation dip as the following:

"...*a dip in performance and confidence as one encounters an innovation that requires new skills and new understandings*" (p. 40).

Optional Definition: When the actual performance after a change is implemented does not equal the perceived or desired performance (as stated by Warrior).

What Role Do You Play In Change?   The Archetypes and the Change Process

As the implementation of any change initiative moves forward, there will be a dip in performance. According to Fullen, there will be a dip. We must plan on it during any change initiative. The Warrior-Ruler-Orphan-Sage dynamic, however, can diminish this dip by providing the necessary **Structure**. This is why they are referred to as the **Structural** Archetypes. The fact that there will be a dip in performance in the implementation of any change is not the debate. The debate is whether the drama of change will be taken care of by these four as they play their roles in the drama of change. They each play a vital role in the change story. They are needed to avoid a dip so deep that the team stops performing and drops the change before it really has a chance to forge ahead.

Now that we have seen that the Developmental Archetype Dynamic (Seeker-Lover-Destroyer-Creator) will get the new idea ready for the change drama, the Structural Archetype Dynamic (Warrior-Ruler-Orphan-Sage) will give the change the strength it needs to move forward and find success; we now need to investigate how we keep everyone on board by looking deeper into the Attitudinal Archetype Dynamic (Caregiver-Magician-Innocent-Jester).

THE CHANGE STORY

- Three Acts -

Act I - The Developmental Archetypes

Scene 1 - The Seeker

Scene 2 - The Lover

Scene 3 - The Destroyer

Scene 4 - The Creator

Act II - The Structural Archetypes

Scene 1 - The Warrior

Scene 2 - The Ruler

Scene 3 - The Orphan

Scene 4 - The Sage

Act III - The Attitudinal Archetypes

Scene 1 - The Caregiver

Scene 2 - The Magician

Scene 3 - The Innocent

Scene 4 - The Jester

ACT III - THE ATTITUDINAL ARCHETYPES

Act I of the change drama ended with The Developmental Archetypes (Seeker-Lover-Destroyer-Creator) all working together to incubate a change idea to the fullest. In Act II we saw how The Structural Archetypes (Warrior-Ruler-Orphan-Sage) can take an idea from the incubation phase to the implementation stage. We find, however, during the implementation stage as the change drama unfolds, that this is the time that the most pressure falls on the members of the organization. In Act III, therefore, we introduce The Attitudinal Archetypes.

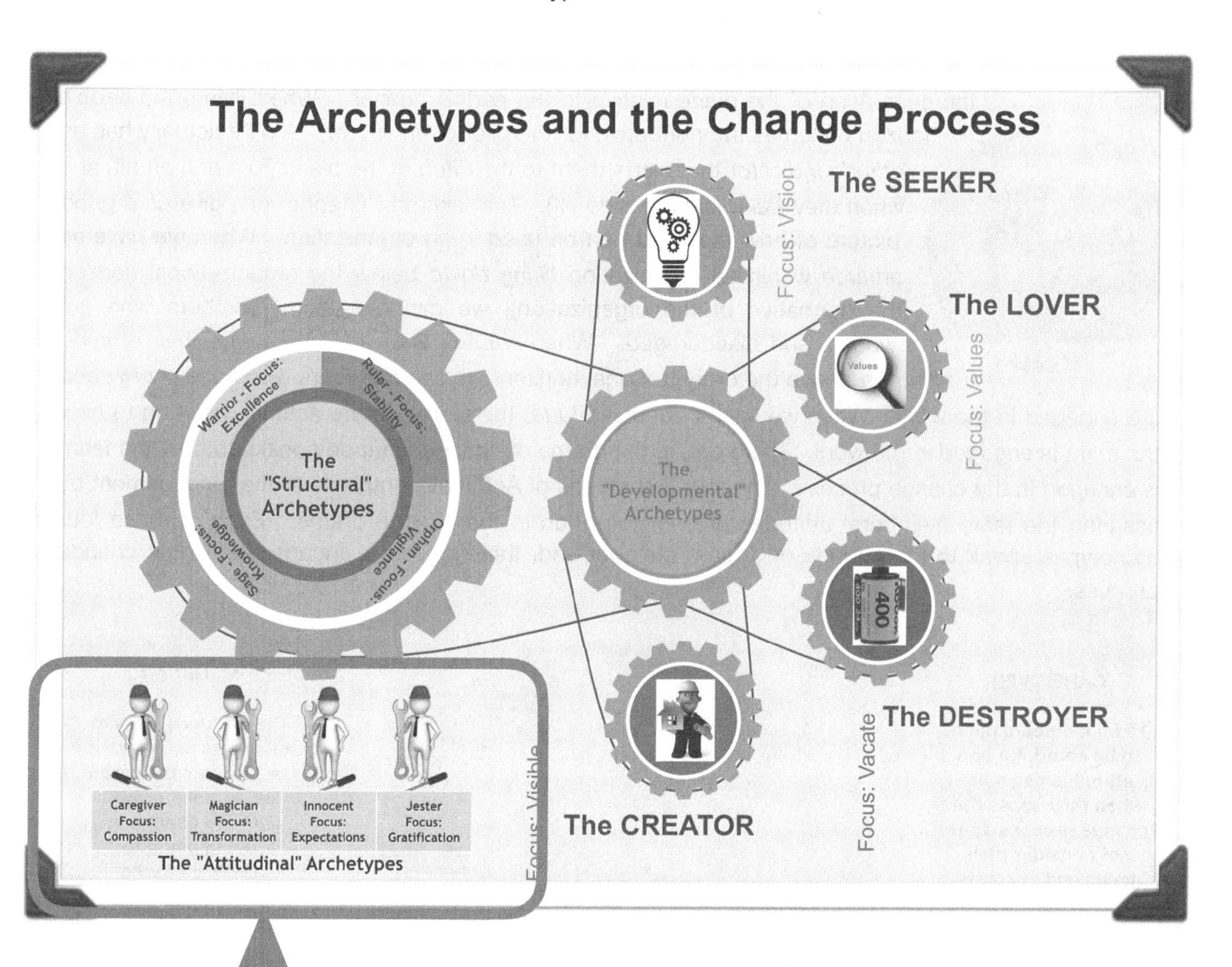

The Archetypes and the Change Process

- The SEEKER — Focus: Vision
- The LOVER — Focus: Values
- The DESTROYER — Focus: Vacate
- The CREATOR — Focus: Visible

The "Structural" Archetypes:
- Warrior - Focus: Excellence
- Ruler - Focus: Stability
- Orphan - Focus: Vigilance
- Sage - Focus: Knowledge

The "Attitudinal" Archetypes:
- Caregiver — Focus: Compassion
- Magician — Focus: Transformation
- Innocent — Focus: Expectations
- Jester — Focus: Gratification

Act III will demonstrate the need for the Caregiver, Magician, Innocent, and Jester archetypes. The drama of change can produce a variety of stress points on everyone in the organization. It can severely impact the morale of the team and, by extension, therefore, the performance and production of the team. In Act III we will learn how to incorporate these four archetypes into our change drama. They are vital to keep members engaged and onboard.

WHY DOES ATTITUDE MATTER?

Before we look at each of the four archetypes in this act, we must answer the question as to why does attitude matter? Why is it so important to the change drama? Can't we just do our jobs and not worry so much about the morale of the team? Isn't this all just mushy *heart* stuff? Change is *head* stuff, and if the head says the change is good for production, why should we let attitude slow us down? If someone has a *bad* attitude, why not just exit them and find someone else to take their place?

The word *attitude* is a 17th century word coming from the world of art. It was a technical term, and it stated that the *posture of the body supposed to imply some mental state*. In an aircraft, the *attitude* is the orientation of the plane relative to the earth's horizon. When flying, the earth's horizon becomes the normative for the pilot of an aircraft. A pilot actually has an *Attitude Indicator* that alerts them to the *Pitch* of the plane (fore and aft tilt) and when they *Bank* (side-to-side tilt). That aircraft metaphor can give us a good picture of how the word can be used in an organization. When we have an *attitude* within an organization *tilting down* below the organizational horizon (the normative of the organization), we can see team members who are downcast and discouraged. When we see team members with their attitude *tilting up* above the organizational horizon, we see members who have energy and are engaged in the work. When we speak about *Attitude,* therefore, we are actually referring to how the team is *engaged* in the work. Therefore, in the drama of change, *attitude* speaks to how the team is *engaged* in the change process. The four archetypes of Act III all contribute to that engagement by assuring the team members' attitudes are not forgotten in the change drama. Each of these four archetypes speak to the attitude of a team member and, therefore, their engagement in the change process.

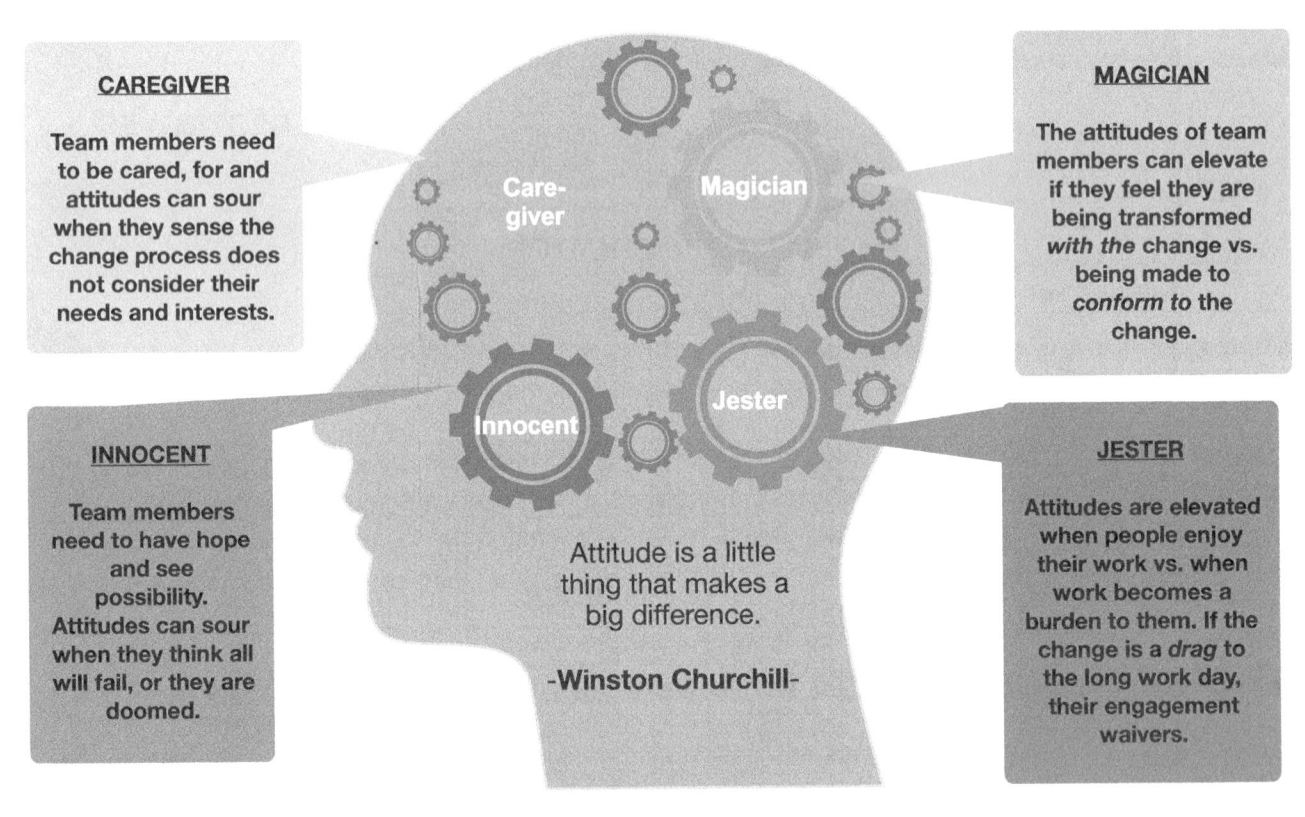

CAREGIVER

Team members need to be cared, for and attitudes can sour when they sense the change process does not consider their needs and interests.

MAGICIAN

The attitudes of team members can elevate if they feel they are being transformed *with the* change vs. being made to *conform to* the change.

INNOCENT

Team members need to have hope and see possibility. Attitudes can sour when they think all will fail, or they are doomed.

JESTER

Attitudes are elevated when people enjoy their work vs. when work becomes a burden to them. If the change is a *drag* to the long work day, their engagement waivers.

Attitude is a little thing that makes a big difference.

-Winston Churchill-

ACT III - THE ATTITUDINAL ARCHETYPES
SCENE ONE - *CAREGIVER* CENTER STAGE

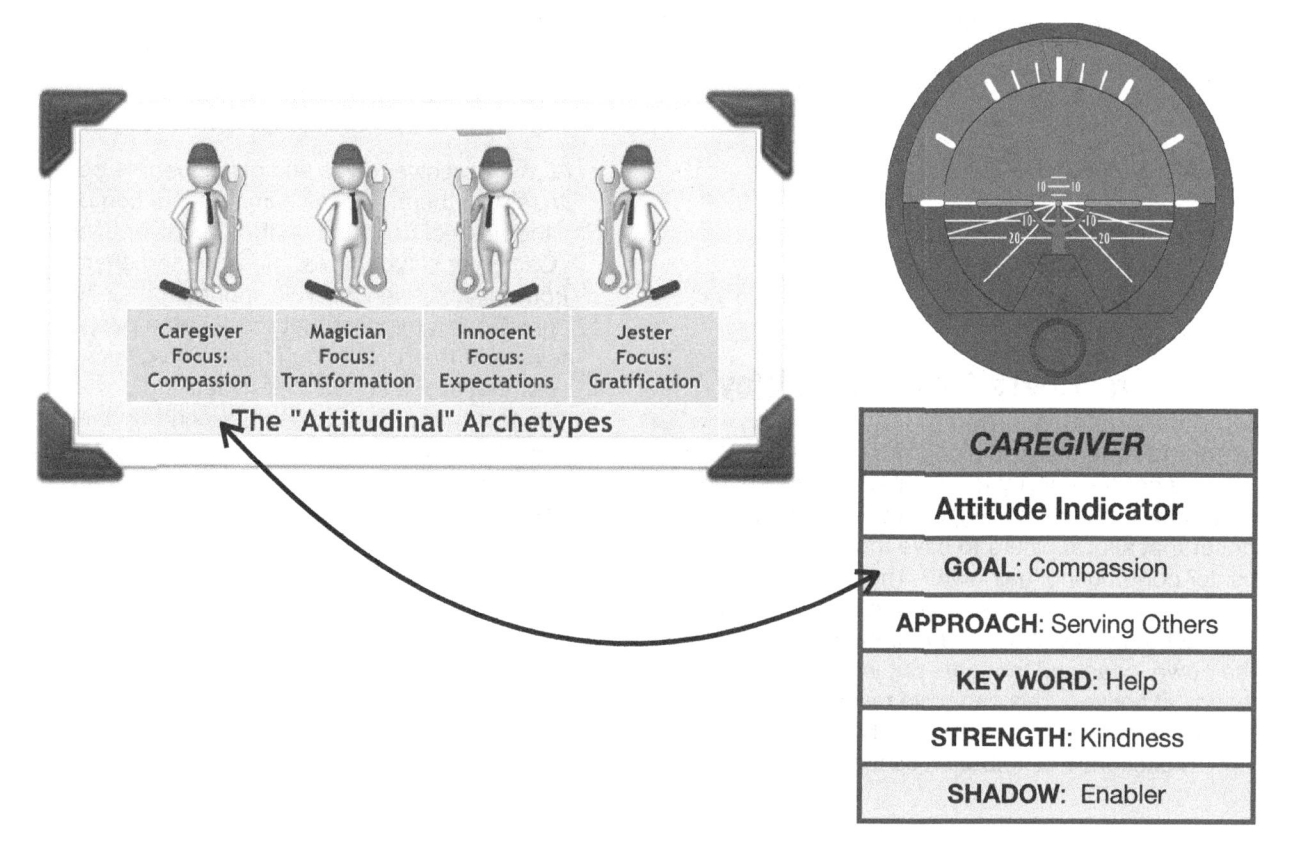

The "Attitudinal" Archetypes

Caregiver	Magician	Innocent	Jester
Focus: Compassion	Focus: Transformation	Focus: Expectations	Focus: Gratification

CAREGIVER
Attitude Indicator
- **GOAL**: Compassion
- **APPROACH**: Serving Others
- **KEY WORD**: Help
- **STRENGTH**: Kindness
- **SHADOW**: Enabler

The beauty of the Caregiver is their unending kindness. They simply want to help everyone - as often as possible. They get great energy from being a helpmate to others and serving them. The Caregiver's attitude and goal for the change process is **Compassion**. If they believe the change is working in a **Compassionate** manner, they can be the strongest allies for the change drama. If, in contrast, they believe the drama of change is simply being harsh and ignoring the needs of mankind within the organization, they can be the strongest opponents to the change initiative.

The Caregiver needs to know that the previous archetypes already mentioned have not just the *change initiative* in mind, but also the people who are making the change work. This doesn't mean the Caregiver doesn't have an opinion about the change idea itself. Like each of the archetypes, the Caregiver has a view of the change. They can accept it or resist the change on the merit of the change. However, because they get so much energy from serving others and helping others reach their goals, they can quickly rally around the goal when they evaluate the change initiative as beneficial to those they work with, work for and work around.

The Caregiver world is one of self-sacrifice. They often give so much they neglect themselves, however. This is where the pattern of poor performance can begin to deteriorate the very purpose they want to accomplish. As they neglect their own work, or own bodies in some cases, they become less useful and less productive to the team. When they overextend themselves, they can become very bitter towards those they work with and the work itself. Suddenly, their **Compassion** can turn to cruelty, kindness to meanness and charity to tyranny. No Caregiver would admit to those last statements, but observers of their approach to life might be willing to produce evidence to support that narrative. Caregiver can provide **Compassion** as long as one of four familiar phrases don't stop them first. Before the Caregiver can practice real **Compassion**, they have to evaluate these four internal mindsets:

People Need Me!

As the Caregiver gives and gives, people begin to rely on them. These same people come to the point of counting on the Caregiver. The Caregiver can get great pleasure and energy from this experience. This imprint in their lives produces a mindset that these same people now *need* them. Although most Caregivers are not the least bit interested in seeking power, the fact that others come to depend on them gives them a sense of power in the workplace. This power is based upon a belief that they have actually created in their own minds and the minds of others: You need me!

Letting Others Have Their Way

Caregivers have great opinions and great ideas. The issue is not their ability to contribute to the change drama with their knowledge, but that they have a mindset that allows others to have their way before they consider contributing their own. The truth of the matter is that they get more energy and value from helping others get their way about change, than they do having their own ideas and thoughts put into action via the change initiative. This can build resentment as their voice is silenced; not by others, but by their own imprint that makes their contribution second to everyone.

Everyone is More Important than Me

The Caregiver has typically played this role for many years before they discover both the strength and the shadow of the archetype. The first born child who is asked repeatedly to care for the younger siblings has learned their role in the family structure: To care for others. The wife, who is married to an overly dominate spouse, have learned that their job is to care for someone. These imprints are typically engrained in repeated behaviors that has caused the Caregiver to believe they are born to serve others, and others are more important than they are in the change process. They simply believe they are second to all.

Helping is What Makes Me Valued

There is nothing like being valued in the workplace. Some team members go weeks, months and years trying to discover how to be valued in an organization. The Caregiver seems to find it faster than most. The *Employee of the Week*, *Month*, or *Year* comes easy for the Caregiver archetype. The truth is that caregiving is very valuable. The issue is not to *stop* caregiving, but to realize there are many other ways to show you're valued. Helping can make you valuable, but it is not the **ONLY** thing that makes you so.

CHANGING A CAREGIVER'S MINDSET IMPRINTS

CHANGE WHERE YOU FIND VALUE

Study your organization, and look for what the organization values. Yes, they will value people who **help** others. But they also value other aspects of service. You can serve the organization in a lot of ways. Make a list of what you see the leadership values. Develop those same attributes, and change *how you* are valued vs. just being valued.

CHANGE YOUR HIERARCHY OF IMPORTANCE

First, recognize you are important for many reasons. But you have to uncover some of the past imprints. Your childhood, family dynamic, and your roles outside of work can contribute to your hierarchy. Everyone in the organization has importance and your role in the present is not defined by the past. Discover and unlearn past imprints.

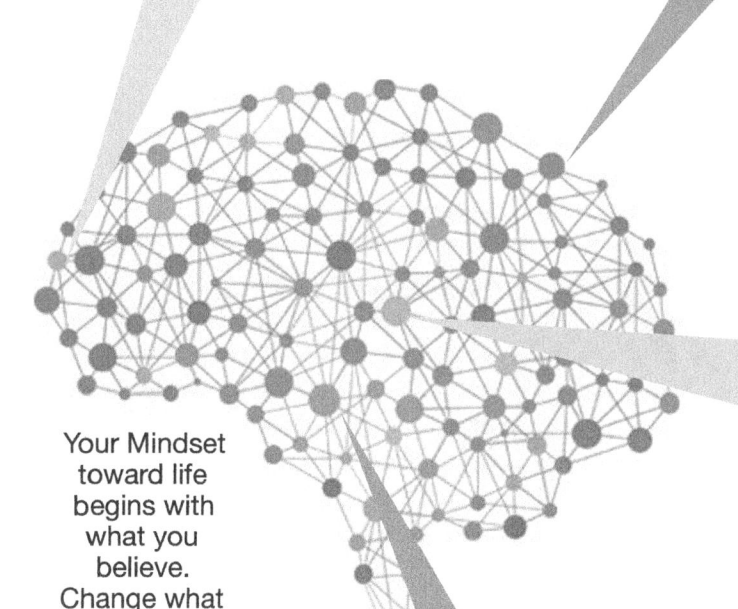

CHANGE WHAT YOU THINK OF YOUR OWN OPINIONS

It is sometimes easier to just let others have their way and think your way is not i valid, than it is discovering it is REALLY NOT valid. The issue here is that offering your thoughts is more important than if they are accepted as right. Your thoughts can be a small chisel that moves the ideas of others in slightly different directions. You don't have to be right, but if you speak up to your ideas it might help.

Your Mindset toward life begins with what you believe. Change what you believe, and you will change your mindset.

CHANGE *WHY* PEOPLE NEED YOU

It is nice to be needed. But if you created the need because you are enabling others to simply rely on you, is that really being needed? If others CAN do it, but they LET you do it, are you really needed? Begin to contribute to the organization in areas that you are REALLY the only one who can do it. That means they will need you. Look for ways to reinvent yourself, and develop skills that others don't have in the organization.

What Role Do You Play In Change? **The Archetypes and the Change Process** Page 125

The Caregiver's Script in the Change Drama

The Caregiver's script in the drama of change includes three scripts:

Caregiver Script #1 - Center Stage

The value of the Caregiver is to help the other archetypes reach their fullest potential. This is a natural manner for the Caregiver. This is their expression of **Compassion** to the organization. They not only want to show **Compassion** themselves, but they want the organization to be **Compassionate**. For the Caregiver to find real value in the organization, they need to find a way to develop a culture around change where the change drama doesn't consume team members, but the change can actually be an avenue for **Compassion**. This does not just happen. There must be intent to make sure **Compassion** happens within any organization. Here are six options the Caregiver can demonstrate to create Compassion and to show their own value in the change drama:

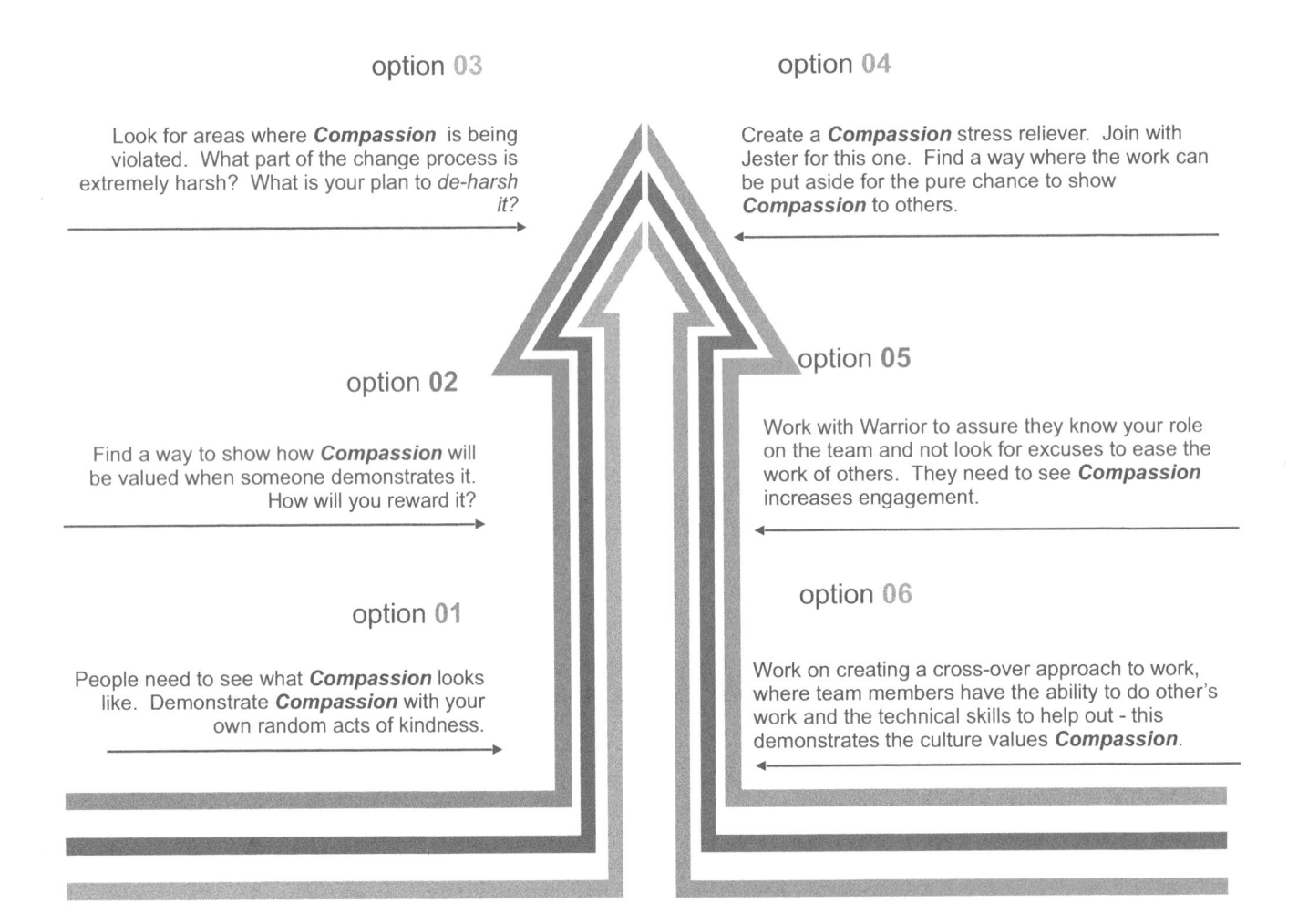

option 03
Look for areas where **Compassion** is being violated. What part of the change process is extremely harsh? What is your plan to *de-harsh it?*

option 04
Create a **Compassion** stress reliever. Join with Jester for this one. Find a way where the work can be put aside for the pure chance to show **Compassion** to others.

option 02
Find a way to show how **Compassion** will be valued when someone demonstrates it. How will you reward it?

option 05
Work with Warrior to assure they know your role on the team and not look for excuses to ease the work of others. They need to see **Compassion** increases engagement.

option 01
People need to see what **Compassion** looks like. Demonstrate **Compassion** with your own random acts of kindness.

option 06
Work on creating a cross-over approach to work, where team members have the ability to do other's work and the technical skills to help out - this demonstrates the culture values **Compassion**.

Caregiver Script #2 - Moving Off Stage

The Caregiver is not the main thing in the drama of change. The Caregiver is, however, the one person who will have as their primary thought, the team members who are making the change work. As they move away from creating a place of **Compassion**, however, they need to work in a way that sustains the **Compassion**. The change drama will tax team members and the very culture of the organization. When the team gets stuck and the change is expressly stressful, the Caregiver's work will be highly needed and valuable.

The success of the proposed change will depend upon how the Caregiver, too, can work with and utilize the skills and the roles of each of the other archetypes. They have their own ideas and will want to contribute to the change. Because the Caregiver can be so sensitive, they might see *how the work is being done* as more important than *getting the work done*. Once the change process actually starts to move forward, your desire to focus on the *way* and the *who* of the work will have to be balanced by the *what* of the work. You must, therefore, balance your work with the roles of the other archetypes.

The Caregiver must make sure that **Compassion** is fostered in the organization. To do so, they must keep the other archetypes engaged in helping and giving, while allowing them to fulfill their roles. Here is your moving off stage script.

Caregiver's script to interact with the other archetypes

Archetype	Possible objections they may have with the change	Goal Association Work (See Addendum #4)
Seeker	They may want to take the organization into a new direction. This isn't always bad and, in fact, necessary at times.	Engage with the Seeker and discover how the new idea can produce something beneficial to the team. You must engage them early.
Lover	They may want to hang on to the status quo. They may value the wrong thing, but, nevertheless, they see change as dangerous to their status quo.	The Lover can be your source of energy. They have a similar desire for Compassion. But they might objectify the very people you are trying to help. Watch this, and speak out.
Destroyer	They need to see what the change is replacing and will need to agree that "something" needs replacing.	The Destroyer can be harsh with letting go and hurt the very team members you care about. Show them the people behind the letting go.
Creator	They can't always see the real practical application or design of the change. They need to know the vision has something tangible behind it.	Like the Seeker, you need to engage early and often with the Creator. They often don't see the people that will do the work. Ask questions that get them to see the faces.
Warrior	They might reject the change if they think it will fail. They will want someone to show them that the change is successful or has the ability to be successful.	The Warrior wants performance. They need to know that esprit de corps is one of the best motivators for engagement. Show them your drive for compassion is a fuel not a fence.
Innocent	They might reject the change because they either don't see the need (naïveté) behind it or because they think it will be a hopeless pursuit.	As Innocent offers hope to the team, you can compliment that, and show them the actual act of hope via kindness. Partner with the Innocent to show what hope looks and feels like.
Orphan	They might reject the change because of failure to solve some of the problems the change will create when implemented.	The Orphan is, at times, untrusting. It takes trust to reach out to help. You might have to repair this trust issue to get them to help.
Ruler	They might reject the change because they don't see structurally how the change will work. They will want to policy and procedure any change.	The Ruler will want to legislate kindness. They may want to set up a structure for it that appears cold. But structure is good. It can make the kindness consistent.
Magician	They might reject the change if they think the change lacks any ability to see transformation. They will be your least resistor if they see "change" as good for anyone or any organization.	The Magician is another ally for you. However, they often see your caring as a tool to get people to transform the way they see transformation happening. Make sure they see that your caring is genuine and not a tool.
Sage	They might reject change because they see the change as foolish and lacking substance or because it has little research (and it probably does because it is a new idea).	The Sage might not readily engage in this concept of compassion via acts of kindness, unless they see some historical data correlating it to performance. Gather the data.
Jester	They might reject the change because they think the change will be boring, too much work (that will steal the joy of the current work), or because they see the change as too complicated (the Sage will make it so).	Jester likes you, typically. To the Jester you are an avenue of enjoyment. You want to help others. They might, however, turn your helping into immature games that are resented by other archetypes (like the Sage, Warrior, and Ruler). Make sure they see you're genuine.

Caregiver Script #3 - Backstage

The Caregiver must make sure that during the implementation process **Compassion** is expanding in the organization and within the individuals of the organization. This means that as they allow the archetypes to speak into the change, they can keep the organization alerted to the need to keep the people in perspective with the work product. They will get a better change if they listen to the other archetypes during the drama of change. The biggest question backstage for the Caregiver should not be, "How can I help everyone, so they aren't overburdened?" But rather, it should be, "How can I help everyone use their tools to produce a **Compassionate** organization?" (Because **Compassion** produces engagement and engagement produces work effort, which produces product.)

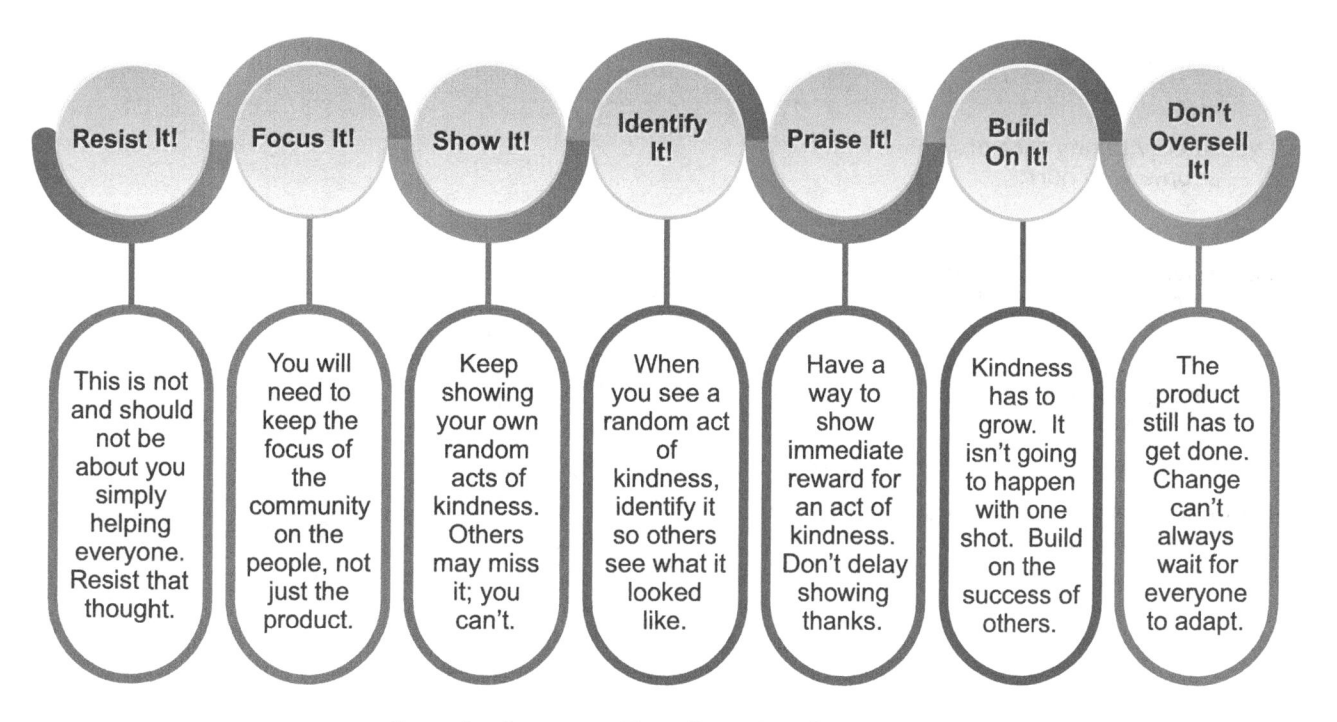

Resist It!	Focus It!	Show It!	Identify It!	Praise It!	Build On It!	Don't Oversell It!
This is not and should not be about you simply helping everyone. Resist that thought.	You will need to keep the focus of the community on the people, not just the product.	Keep showing your own random acts of kindness. Others may miss it; you can't.	When you see a random act of kindness, identify it so others see what it looked like.	Have a way to show immediate reward for an act of kindness. Don't delay showing thanks.	Kindness has to grow. It isn't going to happen with one shot. Build on the success of others.	The product still has to get done. Change can't always wait for everyone to adapt.

Conclusion - an Email to the Caregiver

Dear Caregiver,

How many times have we voted you *Employee of the* _____? We know you are nominated every time. Thanks for that. You are consistent. Thanks for getting us coffee. Thanks for getting us a new shirt when we spill our coffee. Thanks for not telling Ruler, who would stop us from having coffee. You are simply the best person to have in our corner.

We do realize, however, that what we are about to say will probably mean you will stop doing most of our work. But it has to be said. We can do this stuff. We want you to focus on making sure **Compassion** never stops. But teach us how to fish; don't just give us a fish (that was a metaphor). Teach us how to be kind as we watch you care for us. But we can do it. We just need to know how. Thanks again … the other 11 archetypes.

Caregiver's Audition Checklist
(You think you are equipped for the Caregiver's part in the Drama of Change?)

The following activities give the Caregiver energy:	Never	Seldom	Sometimes	Often	Always
I get energy from HELPING:	☐	☐	☐	☐	☐
I get energy from seeing others help others:	☐	☐	☐	☐	☐
I get energy taking care of people who hurt:	☐	☐	☐	☐	☐
I get energy when others have an easy day by my efforts:	☐	☐	☐	☐	☐
I get energy serving the less fortunate:	☐	☐	☐	☐	☐
I get energy remembering past times we all helped:	☐	☐	☐	☐	☐

- ☐ I volunteer on weekends
- ☑ I like stories about helping
- ☐ I help others on vacation
- ☐ I don't mind others winning

Secrets for a Successful Callback for a *Caregiver* Role

- Your weekends can be spent at a soup kitchen.

- You are first-born and raised your siblings.

- You would be able to do cross-over training to do someone else's job.

- Your history of work shows employee of the year awards.

- You have a trophy or award you earned stashed away someplace.

- You read *Tuesdays with Morrie* ... three times.

ACT III - THE ATTITUDINAL ARCHETYPES
SCENE TWO - *MAGICIAN* CENTER STAGE

The term Magician can conjure up some different, and perhaps, unusual meanings. The less flattering terms might be trickster or showman or con artist. In reality, the Magician archetype is about **Transformation**. The better picture that associates the term Magician with the archetype's role is the *change* that takes place for a magician in a magic act. There are several elements to a magic act, but mostly there is an unexplained change, a

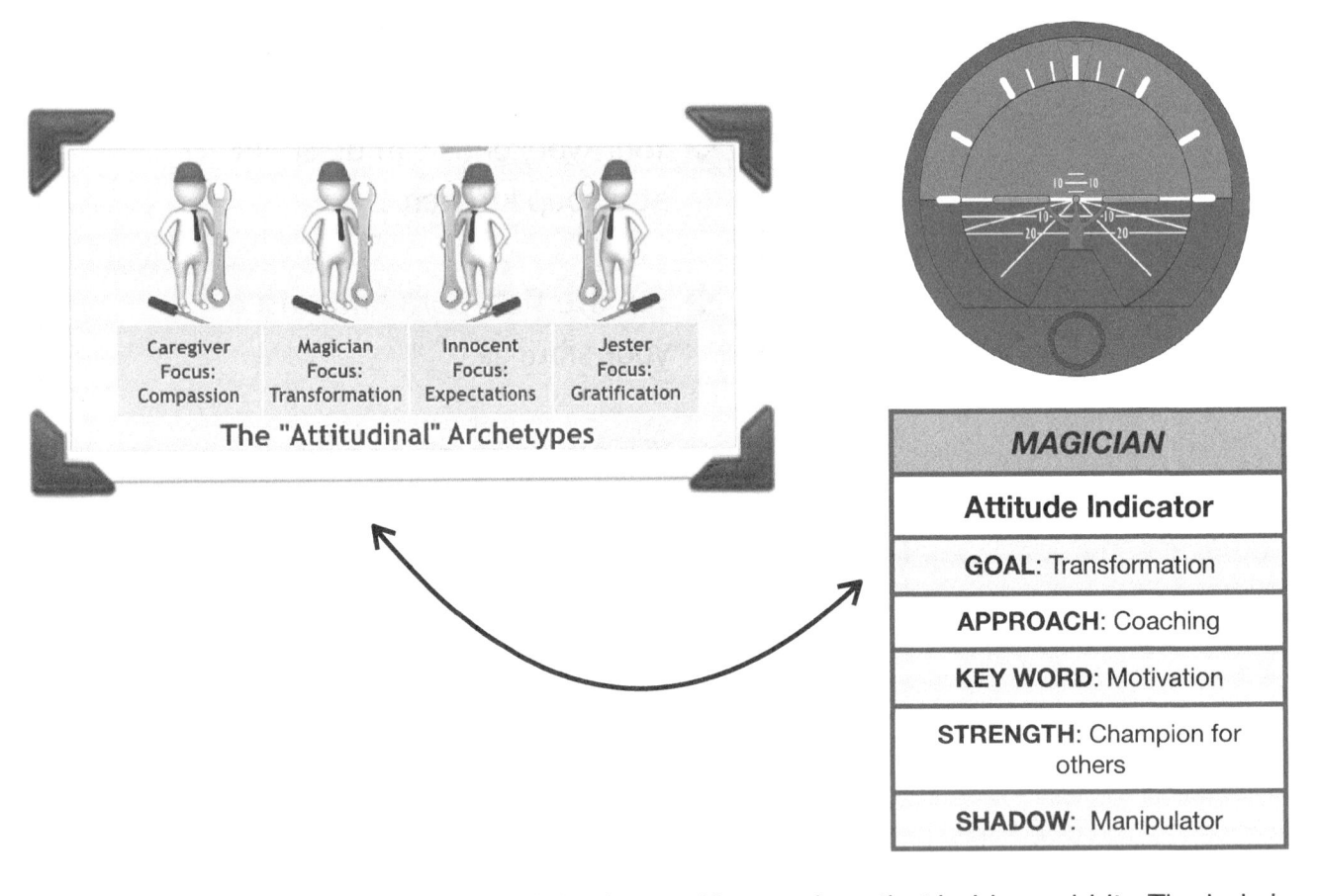

MAGICIAN
Attitude Indicator
GOAL: Transformation
APPROACH: Coaching
KEY WORD: Motivation
STRENGTH: Champion for others
SHADOW: Manipulator

Transformation. The hat isn't a hat; it is changed into a place that holds a rabbit. The lady in the box or cage is changed to a leopard or lion. The Magician can take a simple deck of cards and produce an illusion that the King of Clubs was changed to the Queen of Diamonds.

In the drama of change, the Magician is right at home. They see change as a natural act that should be happening in the lives of people and/or the ethos of the organization. The Magician is often the catalyst for change. They are not the Seeker, but the path of the two often cross. The Magician, however, doesn't need a new idea to create change. They can create change simply by …! Well, there is the problem … simply by *what*? Every Magician has their own bag of tricks. They can certainly use the Seeker's new idea. That works for them. They like new things to exact change. But they don't need a Seeker. They can use the tried and true values of the Lover to start change. They can incorporate the passion of the Lover with the performance driven Warrior and create an entirely new concoction or elixir that, once swallowed, will cause every subject in the kingdom to *change*. That is the way of the Magician. Obviously, there can be some holes in the Magician's approach. Rather than walking around trying to "poof" people (using secret arts, potions, and/or panacea), Magicians need to **Transform** their own act around several areas. Before they can benefit the drama of change, they need to:

1). Quit trying to change people because you think they need to be changed. Yes, you have a keen eye for change. Your intuition is amazing. However, not everyone needs to change, and not everyone needs to change the way you think. If you use the coaching method (see below), you will see that others will actually benefit from your skills.

2). Your intuition CAN BE wrong. Yes, you can look into a crystal ball and see amazing things. But you need to do the research into the lives of those you are working with to know what makes them tick. Your gut is not always right ... well, it is right most of the time. But when you are wrong (and you are wrong), it can be so bad. These are real people.

Changing people is not magic ... it is not done in three easy wishes.

3). Get some depth to your tricks. As you work your *magic* and see change, it will be easy to rely on old tricks that worked in one location. But they may not work in another location. Develop depth and better ways to adapt to your new audience. What plays in New York won't play in Nebraska. You have to develop deeper meanings.

4). Identify and articulate the principles, truths and guidelines you employ to create change in organizations and individuals. There is no doubt you can create change. Just because you know how to do it, doesn't make it valid. Others need concrete tools. They need to see the truth behind the theory. Yes, a Magician never shows how the trick is done, but this isn't really magic; this is the lives of people and the welfare of organizations. Identify the tools.

The Magician can provide a great service to any organization going through change. The key for them, however, is to have a better intent with their approach to working with the team and/or individuals. There are a number of terms that can be used to change the Magician's intent, but perhaps the best is the word *Coach*. The word *coach* comes from the sixteenth century, where they made a *buggy* in a town in Hungary and called it a *kocsi*. The object of the *coach* (buggy) was to pick someone up at point "A" and take them to point "B." You can imagine wealthy parents instructing their *coachmen* to take their young children to school and then after school to some sporting playing field. These *coachmen* would be standing on the side of the playing field doing all the things contained in the words below. This etymology is where we probably get our use of the term *coach* today. A *coach* today probably doesn't pick up a young athlete and take them to where the athlete wants to go. The *coach* today probably takes the athlete where the *coach* wants them to be. But if we return to the original meaning, we may have found the perfect term for the Magician in regard to their role in the drama of change. Any Magician can improve their ability to create **Transformation** if they can master the concept of the sixteenth century *coach*. During the drama of change, the Magician should pick team members up where THEY are, and take them where THEY want to go. The Magician process of **Transformation** during change should look similar to the following script for the Magician.

What is the best word picture we could use to describe the role of the Magician?

Mentor Development Skill Practice Coaching Advising Instruction Education Training Potential Ability Knowledge

The Magician's Script in the Change Drama

The Magician's script in the drama of change includes three scripts:

Magician Script #1 - Center Stage

The Magician can find value in the organization as the drama of change unfolds, if they can find a way to assist the other archetypes in the process of **Transformation**. Change is **Transformation**. Here is a coaching script for the Magician to assist each archetype to reach their potential in the change process. Make sure, Magician, you strive to get them from THEIR point A to THEIR point B.

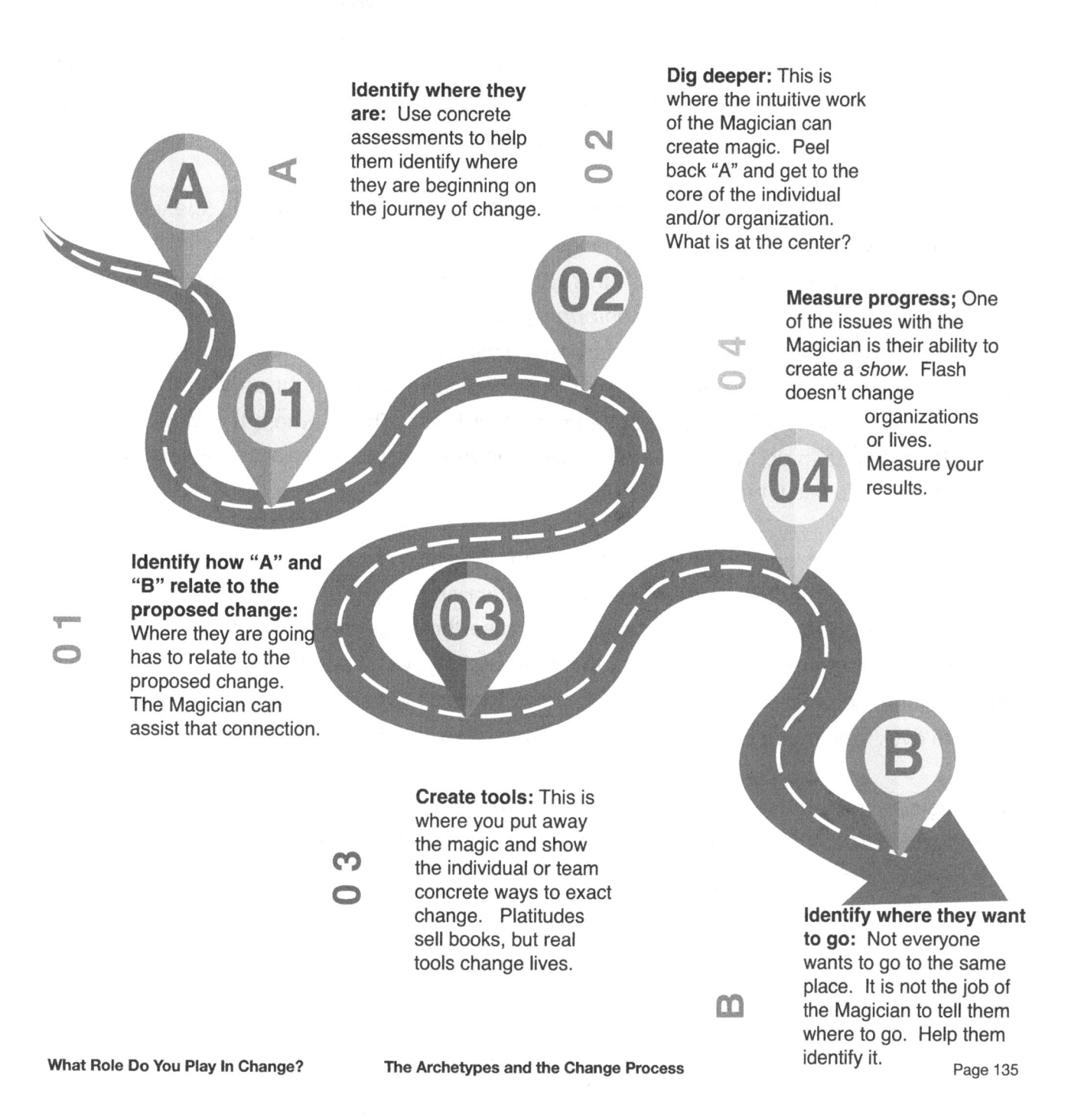

Identify where they are: Use concrete assessments to help them identify where they are beginning on the journey of change.

Dig deeper: This is where the intuitive work of the Magician can create magic. Peel back "A" and get to the core of the individual and/or organization. What is at the center?

Measure progress; One of the issues with the Magician is their ability to create a *show*. Flash doesn't change organizations or lives. Measure your results.

Identify how "A" and "B" relate to the proposed change: Where they are going has to relate to the proposed change. The Magician can assist that connection.

Create tools: This is where you put away the magic and show the individual or team concrete ways to exact change. Platitudes sell books, but real tools change lives.

Identify where they want to go: Not everyone wants to go to the same place. It is not the job of the Magician to tell them where to go. Help them identify it.

Magician Script #2 - Moving Off Stage

Like the other archetypes, the Magician is not the main thing in the drama of change. The Magician is, however, the role that can assist the other archetypes to find real **Transformation** in the drama of change. The difficulty with change is both the lasting *impact* and the *internal* aspect of the change on the people doing the work. We can often see change that is here today, but things return tomorrow the same as they were. Like clothing styles or popular paint colors for a room, they often come and go. People change to *conform*. They want to fit in. But that is not **Transformation**.

There is change that doesn't go back, at least not like it really was. This is change like from a horse to an automobile or from a written letter to email. You could go back, but probably will not. That is what we might call *reform*. The change was so much an improvement we won't go back. When people *reform*, they are not worried about fitting in; they are more worried about being left behind. But that is not **Transformation**.

But there is change that isn't simply outside our lives, but rather, it is *within* us (the term *within* is a key Magician word). This type of change impacts our mindsets and our belief structures. The changes in eating habits can reach this type of change. The way we treat our planet can be this type of change. This is not *conforming* or even *reforming*. This is **Transformation**. This is the level of change the Magician is working with in the drama of change. When people are **Transforming**, they are not trying to fit in or hoping to stay caught up with the masses. Instead, they are looking for dynamic change in their lives. This is where the Magician lives. The Ruler attempts to do this as well. However, the Ruler wants to legislate the change. The Magician wants to see it happen internally.

The success of the proposed change will depend upon how the Magician, too, can work with and utilize the skills and the roles of each of the other archetypes. They have their own ideas and will want to contribute to the change. Because the Magician can be manipulating, it is important that they partner with each of the other archetypes to prevent that from happening. Once the change process actually starts to move forward, your desire to see **Transformation** can take over. You must, therefore, balance your work with the roles of the other archetypes.

The Magician must make sure that **Transformation** happens within the organization. To do so, they must keep the other archetypes engaged, allowing them to fulfill their roles. Here is your moving off stage script.

Magician's script to interact with the other archetypes

Archetype	Possible objections they may have with the change	Goal Association Work (See Addendum #4)
Seeker	They may want to take the organization into a new direction. This isn't always bad and, in fact, necessary at times.	The Magician is good with the Seeker. As stated earlier, they have similar DNA. The Seeker can be motivated by the Magician.
Lover	They may want to hang on to the status quo. They may value the wrong thing, but, nevertheless, they see change as dangerous to their status quo.	The Magician can find a real anchor for their work in the Lover's values. Since Magicians can wander, the traditions offered by Lover can assist the Magician to establish work that is based upon values and not myths or theories.
Destroyer	They need to see what the change is replacing and will need to agree that "something" needs replacing.	The Destroyer's work is letting go. The Magician will need to help individuals let go to get real transformation. Partner up on this.
Creator	They can't always see the real practical application or design of the change. They need to know the vision has something tangible behind it.	As the Creator builds the tangible aspects of the proposed change, the Magician will need to return them back to non-tangible aspects for inward transformational change: Hard work.
Warrior	They might reject the change if they think it will fail. They will want someone to show them that the change is successful or has the ability to be successful.	The Warrior wants performance. The Magician has to show the Warrior that inward work needs to be done correctly to make sure the outward work is sustainable over time.
Caregiver	They might reject the change because of all the work that will be put on the plates of the workers to accomplish the change.	The Caregiver's desire to help others fits the Magician's work. However, their goals are different. Magician wants inward change; Caregiver wants to help them on their journey.
Innocent	They might reject the change because they either don't see the need (naïveté) behind it or because they think it will be a hopeless pursuit.	Innocent wants to inspire. What is more inspiring than real inward change? The connection between Magician and Innocent can produce some high level transformation.
Orphan	They might reject the change because of failure to solve some of the problems the change will create when implemented.	The Orphan can see right through a thin Magician. They can help you find depth. Let their criticism strengthen you and not stop you.
Ruler	They might reject the change because they don't see structurally how the change will work. They will want to policy and procedure any change.	The Ruler wants to change with outward rules. The Magician wants inward change without rules. Allow the Ruler to keep you safe from drifting and manipulating.
Sage	They might reject the change because they see the change as foolish and lacking substance or because it has little research (and it does ... if it is new).	The Sage, like the Orphan, can see your lack of depth. The Sage can help you grow and learn how to coach with more intent on learning and discovery.
Jester	They might reject the change because they think the change will be boring, too much work (that will steal the joy of the current work), or because they see the change as too complicated (the Sage will make it so).	The Jester and the Magician also share some DNA. The Jester wants enjoyment on the inside. They are less concerned about transformation, but they can relate to wanting the inside to change. The two can partner to show how transforming can be enjoyable.

Magician Script #3 - Backstage

The Magician must make sure that during the implementation process **Transformation** is happening in the organization and within the individuals of the organization. This means that as they allow the archetypes to speak into the change, they can keep the organization open to a change of mindsets and beliefs. They will get a better change if they listen to the other archetypes during the drama of change. The biggest question backstage for the Magician should not be, "How can I 'poof' everyone to my way of thinking?" But rather, it should be, "How can I provide specific tools to help each archetype get from point 'A' to point 'B'?"

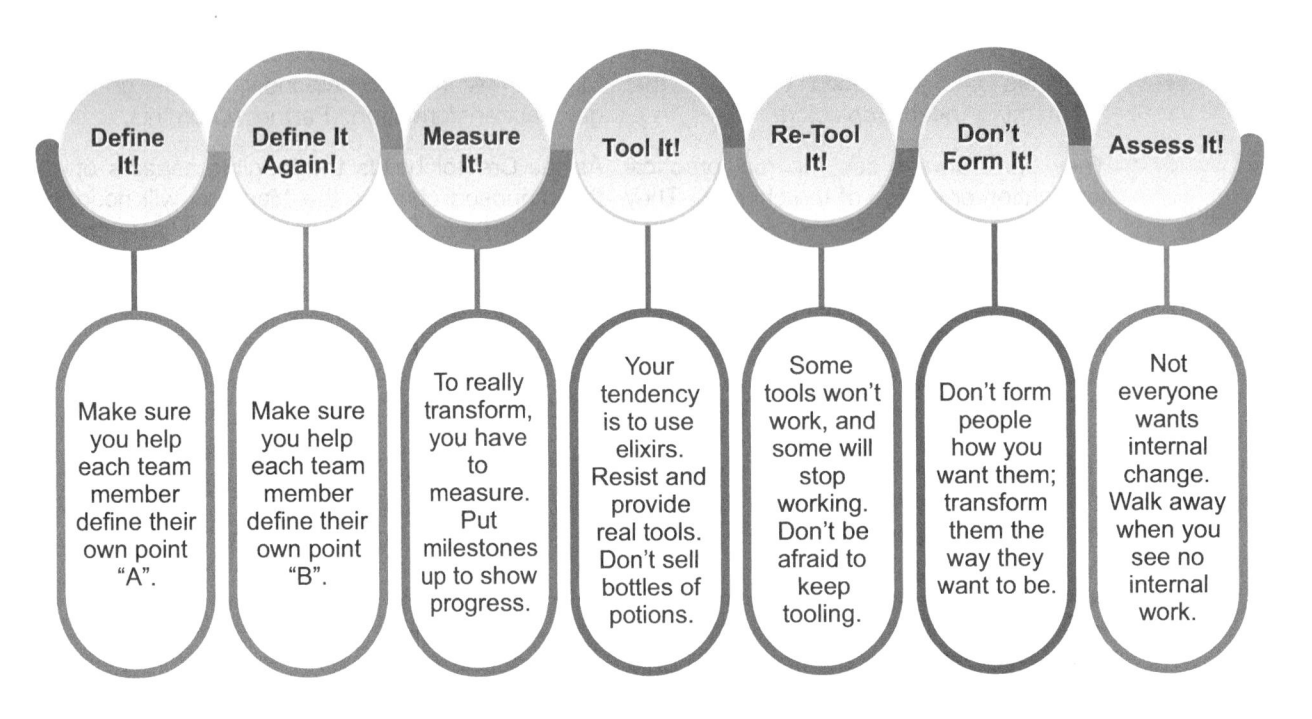

Define It!	Define It Again!	Measure It!	Tool It!	Re-Tool It!	Don't Form It!	Assess It!
Make sure you help each team member define their own point "A".	Make sure you help each team member define their own point "B".	To really transform, you have to measure. Put milestones up to show progress.	Your tendency is to use elixirs. Resist and provide real tools. Don't sell bottles of potions.	Some tools won't work, and some will stop working. Don't be afraid to keep tooling.	Don't form people how you want them; transform them the way they want to be.	Not everyone wants internal change. Walk away when you see no internal work.

Conclusion - an Email to the Magician

Dear Magician,

We want to thank you for the recent book you gave us all to read: *How to Become What I Want You to Be*. Subtle!! It isn't that we think we shouldn't change; we just resist changing into what you think we should become. It would be nice if you could accept us for what we are: Human and unchangeable.

Okay, so we know that last sentence can cause a fire to start in your transforming heart. Yes, we know we can change, but it is so, so hard. We do need to change. We do appreciate that you can help us get *there*. We just want to make sure that the *there* is *where* we want the *there* to be. Your *there* is not typically our *there*. We might have a different place to go.

Thanks again … the other 11 archetypes.

Magician's Audition Checklist
(You think you are equipped for the Magician's part in the Drama of Change?)

The following activities give the Magician energy:	Never	Seldom	Sometimes	Often	Always
I get energy from seeing someone transformed:	☐	☐	☐	☐	☐
I get energy when someone asks for help to change:	☐	☐	☐	☐	☐
I get energy studying how cultures work:	☐	☐	☐	☐	☐
I get energy when people say they can't change:	☐	☐	☐	☐	☐
I get energy learning about personalities:	☐	☐	☐	☐	☐
I get energy observing other people:	☐	☐	☐	☐	☐

- ☐ I read about change
- ☑ I like redemption stories
- ☐ I like life-changing events
- ☐ I want games to teach us

Secrets for a Successful Callback for a *Magician* Role

- You have a history of working with those who want a change.

- You attend conferences to learn about human behavior.

- You are willing to learn and study how organizations work.

- You get frustrated with people who won't change.

- You have memorabilia that shows you impacted someone's life.

- You are not afraid to look inside your own life.

ACT III - THE ATTITUDINAL ARCHETYPES
SCENE THREE - *INNOCENT* CENTER STAGE

(NOTE: The descriptor *Innocent* has been changed to *Idealist*. Please see Addendum #1 as to why this author is using the *Innocent* descriptor.)

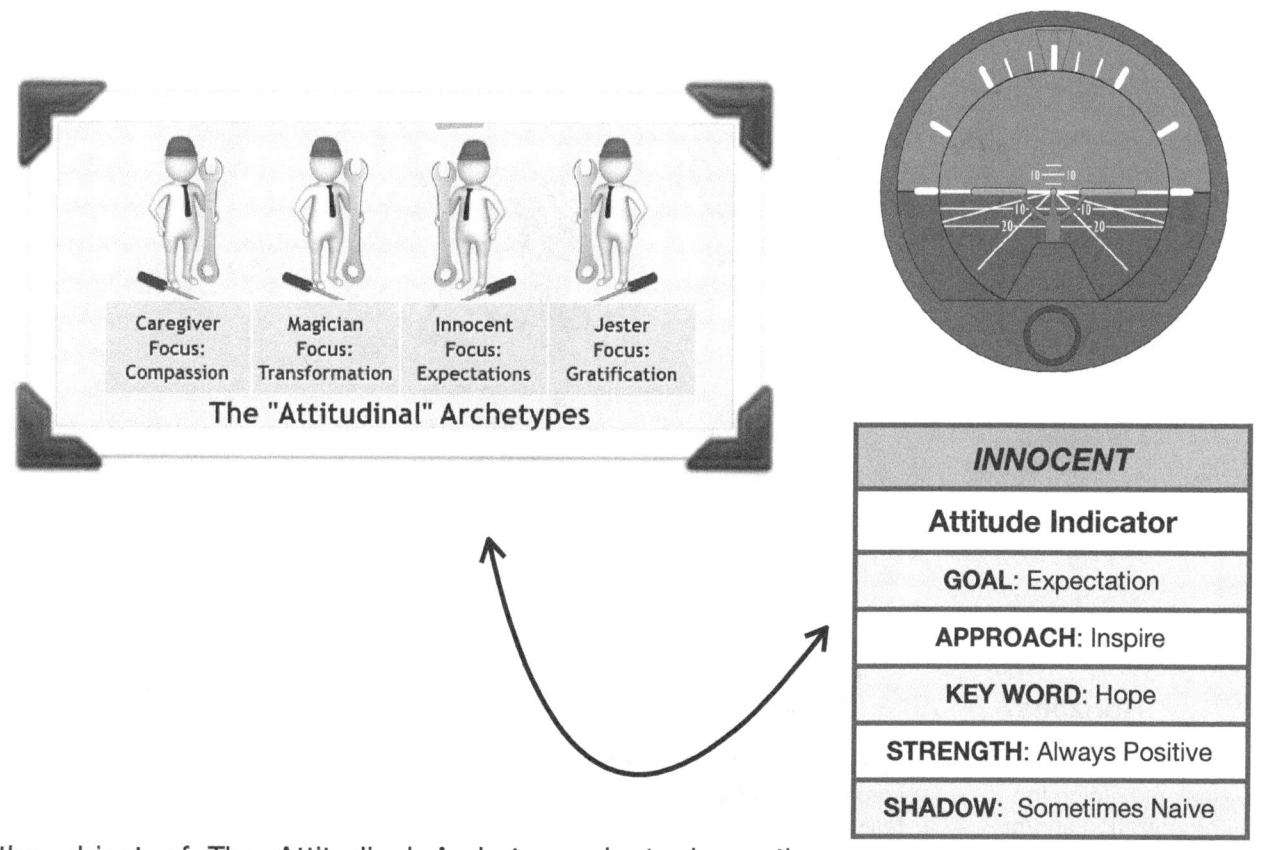

The "Attitudinal" Archetypes

Caregiver	Magician	Innocent	Jester
Focus: Compassion	Focus: Transformation	Focus: Expectations	Focus: Gratification

INNOCENT
Attitude Indicator
GOAL: Expectation
APPROACH: Inspire
KEY WORD: Hope
STRENGTH: Always Positive
SHADOW: Sometimes Naive

If the object of The Attitudinal Archetypes is to keep the members of the team positive during the drama of change, the Innocent archetype has a primary role as well. The Innocent strives to raise and/or maintain everyone's **Expectations** during the change process. As the Caregiver is keeping **Compassion** growing as the change drama unfolds and Magician is making sure the change demonstrates the **Transformation** everyone expects, hope can be lost. Change is hard. We use words like *cloudy* and *murky* and *slippery* to describe change because it is tough to navigate. We can often lose sight of the Promise Land predicted by the Seeker and Creator. When people lose hope, they soon perish into despair. Despair will, eventually, diminish production. When production is dismissed, the implementation dip, spoken of earlier, will cause most of the organization to give up on the change. The role of the Innocent is to manage these **Expectations**.

Before an Innocent can manage the **Expectations** of others, however, they have to manage their own. The Innocent must come to the realization that they have some challenges in governing their own thoughts about the blessings of the past, the goodness of the present and the possibilities of the future.

The Innocent is a master at preaching and inspiring others to have hope. This is a key word for them. Like the Caregiver offering Help and the Magician offering Transformation, the Innocent is all about offering Hope. There are four areas the Innocent must concentrate upon to make hope a reality for an organization or individual.

Horizons?

The Innocent has a key task of helping the organization and/or individual set horizons. *A horizon is where our hopes and dreams hit our limits and/or capacities.* But we have to see the horizon before we set our hope on reaching it. The Innocent plays a real part in identifying the horizon for the change initiative. Our hope, then, is built on our perception of reaching those horizons. Whether we think we can reach a horizon or can't is the complex role of the Innocent. When a change is introduced, the Innocent must step up to identify the possibility and the limits of the change. That is the horizon of change the Innocent must manage.

Opportunity?

The Innocent must make sure that the challenge facing the team during the drama of change is a real opportunity. Too many times the light at the end of the tunnel is the train. When the Innocent is working with the team, they must manage what is an opportunity and what is simply a mirage. Workers, during change, need to see that they have a chance for something great. The Innocent creates hope by making sure they can experience that sense of greatness through opportunity. But if the opportunity is only fantasy, their **Expectations** fail. Opportunity can expand horizons. Opportunity can increase the desire for greater capacity.

Promise?

You can't have hope without some type of promise. The Innocent must be careful how they deliver the **Expectation** promise. A group of people can go a long way on a promise. But to over promise or under deliver on a promise can sabotage the Innocent's desire to inspire. Saying this change can help us win might sound nice. But if we lose, the change is lost forever and the credibility of the Innocent is severely damaged. The Innocent might under promise and over deliver, but that still speaks to credibility. Managing promises is a major task for the Innocent.

Endurance?

When managing team **Expectations**, the Innocent has to make sure they know and understand the capacity of the team. The steadfastness of the team is a primary consideration in the management of their **Expectations**. A hopeful opportunity based upon a promise can only go as far as the team can endure working without a thing coming to fruition. Remember the change only presents what might happen. That is hope. If the team can't endure through the fog of change, they might not make it through the entire fluid process.

However, before the Innocent can set the HOPE for an organization or for an individual, they must work on three key areas of their own *Expectations* that can often hinder their work. These three are interrelated and tend to feed off each other and contribute to each other. Throttling one area can slow the other two and vice versa. Failing to control one can speed the other two as well.

Naïveté - There is no doubt that the Innocent WILL stick their head in the sand and simply not want to see the world the way it really is. This is why it makes great sense to change the descriptor to the Idealist. This can be a real issue when trying to inspire others with hope. You can't deny the facts and the real world issues around change to simply inspire. That is not inspiring … that is denying. The Innocent must not deny a problem exists, but rather (with the Orphan) identify the issues and dig deep to find the solutions that can solve the problem (something the Orphan does not do well).

Trusting All - The Innocent does not struggle with trusting other team members or the organization. In fact, that is the issue. They tend to trust easily. When change is introduced, they will seldom be the one asking the questions or looking for reasons to not trust (they leave that up to Orphan). This feeds their naïveté and vice versa. To offer real hope to the organization in the midst of change, the Innocent needs to build trust by having a healthy view of trusting everyone and all things.

Blindsided Optimism - The Innocent is often so optimistic they are blindsided. Just because while you walk into the street you are whistling *The Sun Will Come Out Tomorrow* from the play *Orphan Annie,* it doesn't mean you won't get hit by a bus. The Innocent has a hard time with the pessimist. But a healthy dose of pessimism can assist you in dealing with real world issues. If you are willing to see problems and not simply think the sun will always shine, you can stay dry in the storm. An umbrella is a good thing to have around in a storm, rather than simply believe it won't rain. The Innocent can't offer hope to others if it is raining outside, and they insist it is not. Don't be blindsided.

The Innocent's Script in the Change Drama

The Innocent's script in the drama of change includes three scripts:

Innocent Script #1 - Center Stage

The Innocent can add value to the drama of change by making sure **Expectations** are managed correctly. Too much hope or too little hope and you have a team falling into despair. Despair is the silent killer of team morale. Low morale depresses production. The Innocent has a direct role in keeping production high. But they have to identify, manage and corral team member's **Expectations** correctly. To do so, there is the Innocent at center stage in the drama of change. Their job is to keep the member's batteries fully charged with hope.

HORIZONS

ADJUST

SUBSTANCE

Make sure you have real hope and not empty promises. Work with Creator to know the real results of the change.

Set healthy horizons by aligning dreams with capacity. Meet with individuals to discover their goals in the change, and identify the skills they have to reach them.

STRESS

It is your job to manage the team's down days. Identify what they look like, and alert the team to your plan before it happens. Jester's here to help.

Horizons should not stay the same in a healthy organization. The Innocent should work at all times to adjust the **Expectations** to make sure new horizons are being reached.

100%   50%   60%   40%   20%   45%   80%

PROMISES

Since promises are the life blood of hope, make sure the promises are based upon the proven character of the person making the promise. If their character is weak, the promise is weak.

INSPIRE

The ability to inspire others is based upon your knowledge of what motivates specific people. You will need to learn the motivation appetite of members. What gives them energy? Help them identify that in their lives.

CELEBRATION

Managing **Expectations** includes when we *hit* them. It is your job to show the team when we reach a horizon and celebrate it.

Innocent Script #2 - Moving Off Stage

Again, like the others, the Innocent is not the main thing in the drama of change. The Innocent can, however, raise and keep everyone's **Expectations** in check during the drama of change. As change unfolds, the Innocent can see the taxing it takes on the team. Remember, the other archetypes are paying attention to roles. They are not managing expectations well. In fact, some of them might be contributing stress to the process. Warrior might be pushing for so much **Excellence** that the team is in high stress trying to meet the Warrior's **Expectations**. Ruler might also be so focused on **Stability** that the team is struggling to meet the **Expectations** of the new rules, policies and programs. The Innocent has a role to manage all the **Expectations** that are being created during the drama of change.

The success of the proposed change will depend upon how the Innocent, too, can work with and utilize the skills and the roles of each of the other archetypes. Especially realizing they all have different **Expectations**. They have their own ideas and will want to contribute to the conversation about **Expectations**. Because the Innocent can be naive at times, it is important that they form a strong allegiance with each of the other archetypes to *learn* from them what their **Expectations** might be to slow, and possibly prevent, the naïveté. Once the change process actually starts to move forward, your natural desire to manage **Expectations** will take over. You must, therefore, balance your work with the roles of the other archetypes.

The Innocent must make sure that **Expectations** are appropriate within the organization. To do so, they must keep the other archetypes engaged, allowing them to fulfill their roles. Here is your moving off stage script.

Innocent's script to interact with the other archetypes

Archetype	Possible objections they may have with the change	Goal Association Work (See Addendum #4)
Seeker	They may want to take the organization into a new direction. This isn't always bad and, in fact, necessary at times.	The Innocent needs to know right away what the Seeker hopes to accomplish. The best way to meet expectations? Identify them early.
Lover	They may want to hang on to the status quo. They may value the wrong thing, but, nevertheless, they see change as dangerous to their status quo.	The expectation of the Lover is to hold onto what they value. This will be a challenge if the actual values are changed. The Innocent needs to know if a value is changing or if it is a tool, method, or process used to reach the value.
Destroyer	They need to see what the change is replacing and will need to agree that "something" needs replacing.	The Destroyer expectation is to see addition by subtraction. They just need to know there is hope of something useless getting tossed out.
Creator	They can't always see the real practical application or design of the change. They need to know the vision has something tangible behind it.	As with the Seeker, the Innocent needs to meet with the Creator early in the process. Discover what the tangible product's expectation needs to be. Learn it to achieve it.
Warrior	They might reject the change if they think it will fail. They will want someone to show them that the change is successful or has the ability to be successful.	As the Warrior pushes for excellence, the Innocent will need to encourage others, even in their failures. There will be failures. Know how to bridge failures as growth opportunities.
Caregiver	They might reject the change because of all the work that will be put on the plates of the workers to accomplish the change.	The Caregiver can only reach their expectations if they know they are helping. Incorporate them into your work to help others reach their expectations.
Orphan	They might reject the change because of failure to solve some of the problems the change will create when implemented.	Orphans expect problems. Partner with them to alert you to when others are not meeting their expectations. They can be a support.
Ruler	They might reject the change because they don't see structurally how the change will work. They will want to policy and procedure any change.	Ruler can cause the most stress in expectation management. They want others to conform. Work with them to learn what that looks like and where there MIGHT be tighter constraints.
Magician	They might reject the change if they think the change lacks any ability to see transformation. They will be your least resistor if they see "change" as good for anyone or any organization.	The expectations of the Magician are the hardest to measure since they are internal. They often miss measuring results. So, your role will fit their need. They don't always want to have expectations measured, however.
Sage	They might reject the change because they see the change as foolish and lacking substance or because it has little research (and it does … if it is new).	The Sage also has difficult expectations to measure. They want to raise the knowledge level of the team. Help Sage create an assessment to measure the growing lexicon knowledge base.
Jester	They might reject the change because they think the change will be boring, too much work (that will steal the joy of the current work), or because they see the change as too complicated (the Sage will make it so).	The Jester's expectation is enjoyment. How do you measure enjoyment? Once you try to measure it, you will probably lose it. The Jester can help celebrate achievement, however. They can enjoy identifying achievement and finding ways to celebrate it.

Innocent Script #3 - Backstage

The Innocent must make sure that during the implementation process *Expectations* are being met within the organization and within the individuals of the organization. This means that as they allow the other archetypes to speak into the change, they can keep the organization reaching for the sky and touching it at some point. They will get a better change if they listen to the other archetypes during the drama of change. The biggest question backstage for the Innocent should not be, "I wonder why everyone just can't see the rainbow?" But rather, it should be, "How can I identify everyone's expectation(s) and help them reach it (them)?"

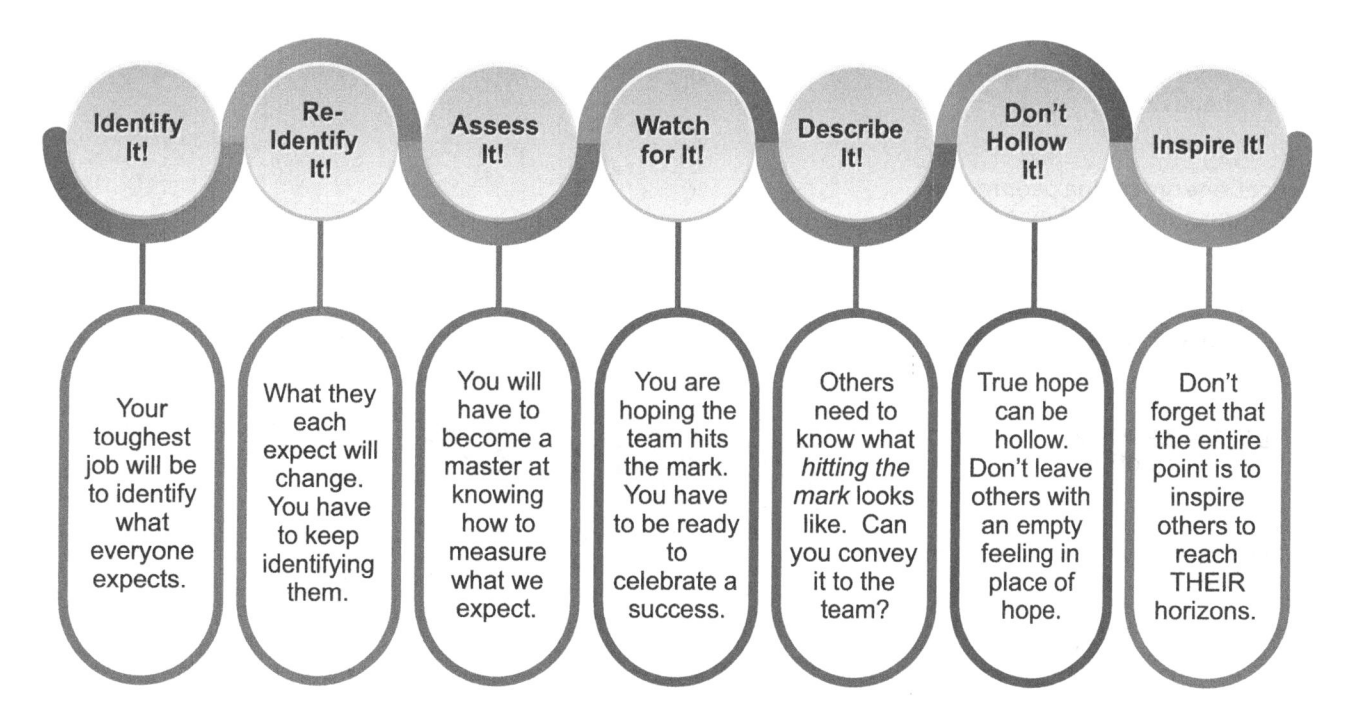

Identify It!	Re-Identify It!	Assess It!	Watch for It!	Describe It!	Don't Hollow It!	Inspire It!
Your toughest job will be to identify what everyone expects.	What they each expect will change. You have to keep identifying them.	You will have to become a master at knowing how to measure what we expect.	You are hoping the team hits the mark. You have to be ready to celebrate a success.	Others need to know what *hitting the mark* looks like. Can you convey it to the team?	True hope can be hollow. Don't leave others with an empty feeling in place of hope.	Don't forget that the entire point is to inspire others to reach THEIR horizons.

Conclusion - an Email to the Innocent

Dear Innocent,

No, you can't just sprinkle glitter on the change to make it work. Glitter, emojis, rainbows and sunshine are not real tools to produce hope. You do know this, right? We do appreciate that you are so optimistic. However, we often worry that you are going to be singing some song, failing to notice that you are about to walk off a cliff. Could we get you to get your head out of the clouds long enough to see that there is no silver lining?

We do need your constant encouragement and inspiration, however. On long, hard days we really appreciate that you didn't even notice and tell us you had a spectacular day. (We are not mocking here. We really meant that.) When we are at our lowest, it is nice to know that someone is trying to keep us all upbeat and inspired. Just give us real hope and not a mirage. Thanks again … the other 11 archetypes.

Innocent's Audition Checklist
(You think you are equipped for the Innocent's part in the Drama of Change?)

The following activities give the Innocent energy:	Never	Seldom	Sometimes	Often	Always
I get energy from fairytale endings:	☐	☐	☐	☐	☐
I get energy from positive behaviors:	☐	☐	☐	☐	☐
I get energy seeing people getting what they need:	☐	☐	☐	☐	☐
I get energy when others are encouraged:	☐	☐	☐	☐	☐
I get energy being asked to inspire others:	☐	☐	☐	☐	☐
I get energy seeing the good in people:	☐	☐	☐	☐	☐

- ☐ I read positive stories
- ☑ I like trips to fantasy places
- ☐ I easily trust people
- ☐ I truly want world peace

Secrets for a Successful Callback for an *Innocent* Role

- You struggle with people who are downers to the organization.

- You like Monday morning because it offers hope of a new week.

- You would be willing to learn how to motivate others.

- You look forward more than backward.

- You have an inspirational quote you favor and possibly posted on a wall.

- You read books with positive endings.

ACT III - THE ATTITUDINAL ARCHETYPES
SCENE FOUR - *JESTER* CENTER STAGE

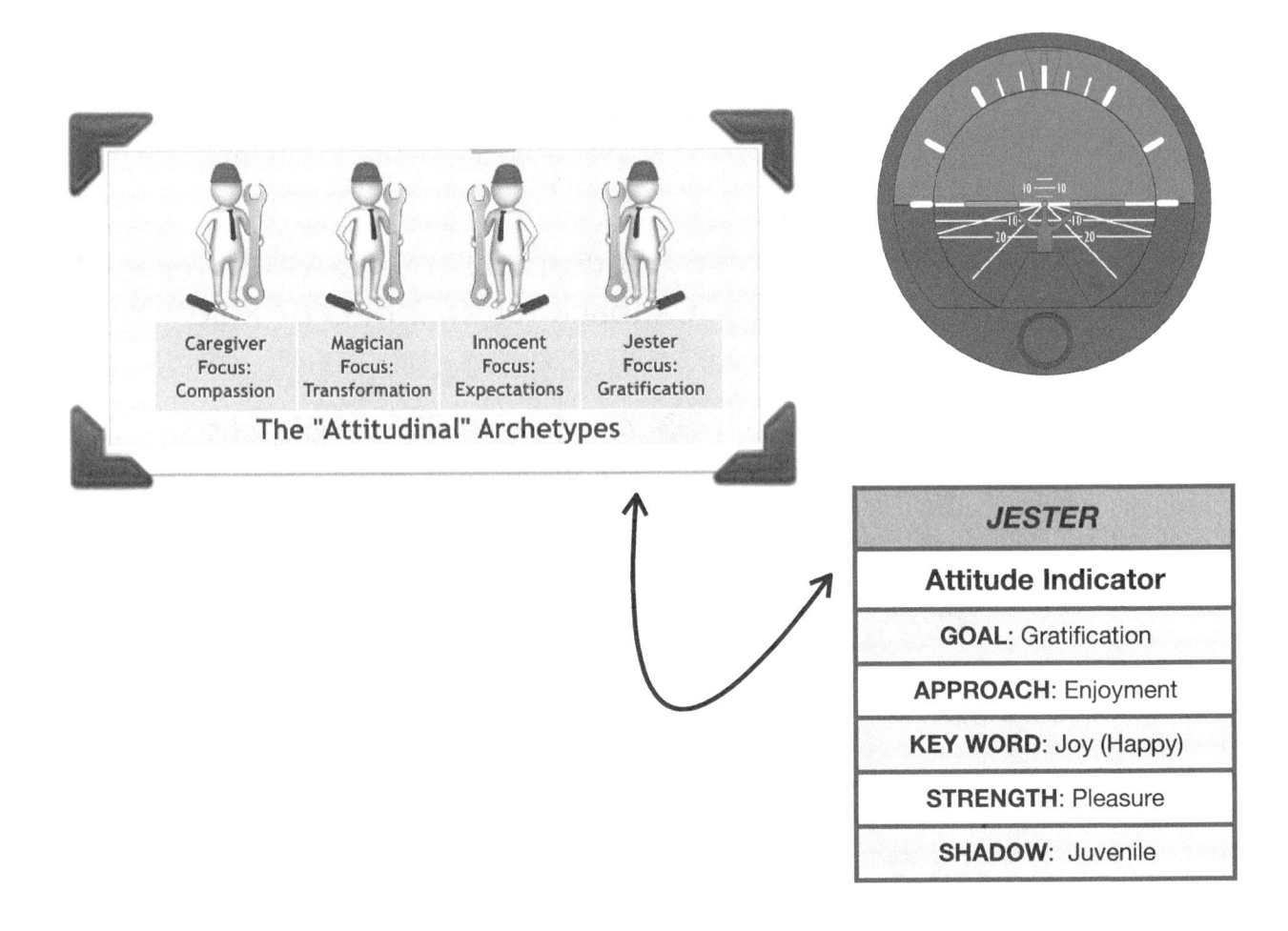

The "Attitudinal" Archetypes:

Caregiver	Magician	Innocent	Jester
Focus: Compassion	Focus: Transformation	Focus: Expectations	Focus: Gratification

JESTER
Attitude Indicator
GOAL: Gratification
APPROACH: Enjoyment
KEY WORD: Joy (Happy)
STRENGTH: Pleasure
SHADOW: Juvenile

The Attitudinal Archetypes are intended to keep the attitudes in check as we move through the drama of change. There is not always a positive and delightful attitude as change moves through an organization. The Caregiver's role enables the team to know that they are cared for and someone has **Compassion** for them. The Magician is constantly building up the attitudes of everyone by showing them there is **Transformation** taking place within them. There is nothing that motivates more than to know you are progressing and changing through the challenges of life. The Innocent role refuses to let any become discouraged, managing the various **Expectations** of each of the other archetypes as they reach for their own measure of success during change. However, there is one archetype left and the Jester may be the most pleasurable of all. That is because the Jester is focused exclusively on the team and organization reaching complete **Gratification** during the change process.

The Jester wants everyone to enjoy their jobs. It was probably the Jester archetype that said:

"Find a job you enjoy, and you will never work a day in your life."

No Warrior would probably say a phrase like that. Nor would a Ruler. Certainly an Orphan would not favor such an expression. The Jester looks for ways to find enjoyment in all that they do ... and in all that everyone else does. This is certainly the Jester's value and Achilles heel at the same time. They are constantly looking for **Gratification**, but they have a way *they* would like to define what it takes to be **Gratified**. Before we look intensely at their role, let's look at the concept of enjoyment, and try to define some particular elements the Jester may be trying to reach. Enjoyment has an elusive and highly personal definition attached to it. What gives the Warrior archetype enjoyment is different than the Orphan. The Warrior might find enjoyment in excelling through an obstacle course, while the Orphan might point out the dangers in the same adventure. The Sage finds enjoyment in learning a new thing and conveying that knowledge to others. However, the Ruler might get more enjoyment out of taking that knowledge and attaching some structure to it, thus making everyone safe.

Here are some elements of enjoyment and **Gratification** that might help us define the Jester role as they interact with the attitudes in the drama of change. This guidebook is not a treatise on the subject of **Gratification**, but we have to have some common understanding of it to move forward in our work.

Gratification is different than Happiness

The word *happy* comes from the little word *hap*, meaning *chance* or *good fortune*. **Gratification** can't come from happenstance. There has to be a purpose to **Gratification**; it isn't found in the chance encounters at work. In fact, in the drama of change, there would be even less chance for hap to happen.

Gratification has an element of Success

If you want to feel gratified, you will have to find some way to define what success looks like to you and when you reach it. Enjoyment typically comes when goals are reached. Goals can only be reached when they are defined. So, **Gratification** can ONLY be reached by intentional working on goals. If the Jester role is to be exercised in the best way, the Jester has to know what makes success possible for the other archetypes and help them reach it: basing it on intent - not chance!

Gratification has an element of Celebration

If you want to feel gratified, you will have to find some way to celebrate successes. This is probably what separates the Jester from the other archetypes so much. They all want success, but the Jester strives for the celebration. **Gratification** comes with an expression of outward emotions based upon an inward realization of the success. Try to stop that from happening in your life. Even a curmudgeon will smile if something happens inwardly. Celebration is a major component of **Gratification**.

What Role Do You Play In Change?   The Archetypes and the Change Process

The challenge for the Jester during the quest to find **Gratification** is to keep the celebration impactful and not wasteful, foolish, and/or juvenile.

JUVENILE HUMOR

The Jester can devalue their role in the drama of change by crossing the line into humor that is distasteful and possibly inappropriate. They won't see **Gratification** when they disparage humor.

OVERSELLING

The Jester so wants to enjoy life they can sell it all the time. It becomes so much of a tool for them to fit into the team, they can quickly become the *class-clown* and get treated and valued as such.

LACK GRAVITAS

When you always want to have fun, you can lack depth. Laughter doesn't compliment the scholar. In given situations, the Jester has to be heard. If they lead each thought with a joke, they may simply become the joke.

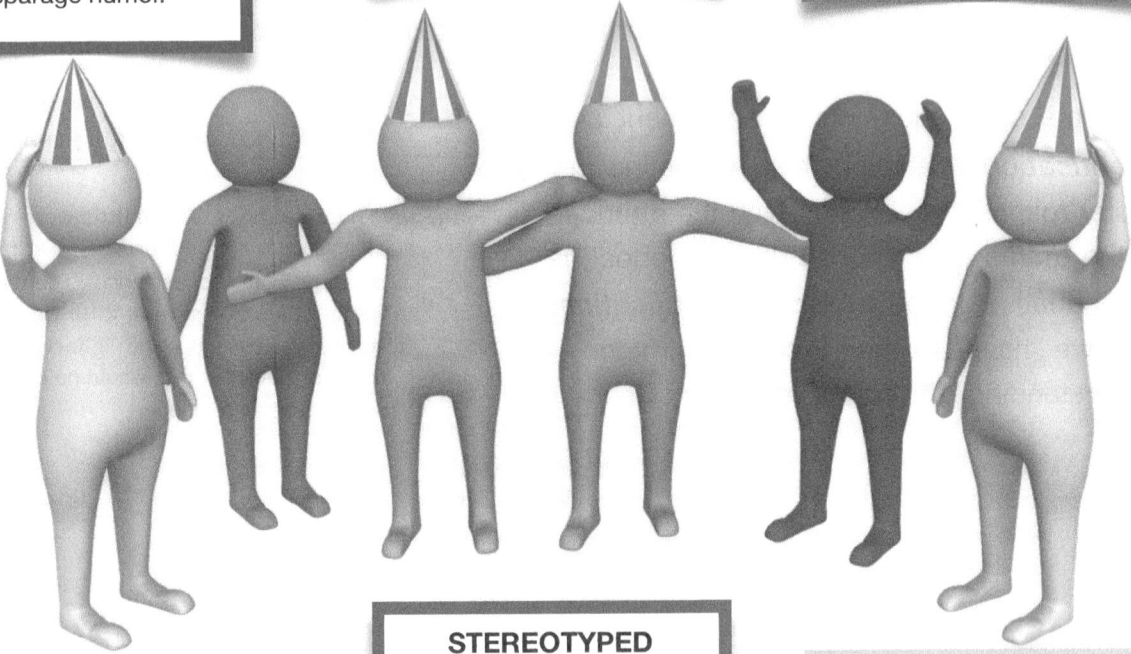

LACK WORK ETHIC

In their quest for fun and laughter, the Jester is often seen (especially by the Warrior and Ruler) as a lazy participant in the drama of change. Work is called *work* because it is work. The Jester can have a positive impact on change, if they can blend hard work with gracious humor. Lacking work, they may be just seen as lazy.

STEREOTYPED

The Jester can easily fall into a stereotype they will forever have to live down. Promotions can be diminished in both the reality of receiving them and the meaning when they are received. Without balance, the team will always view the Jester in the context of the *Jester*, and this prohibits them from leading and impacting others. The *shtick* becomes an image that sticks!!

DEVALUE LAUGHTER

The power of laughter in our society is a tool some might overlook. The Jester, on the other hand, might use it so much that the real power of laughter is devalued. When everything is humorous, then laughter can become devalued, and that is a loss to the organization. People need to laugh. Moderation is necessary even in **Gratification**.

The Jester's Script in the Change Drama

The Jester's script in the drama of change includes three scripts:

Jester Script #1 - Center Stage

The Jester's role in the drama of change is to make sure no one rains on the **Gratification** parade at work. The aspect of **Gratification** in the workplace has to be protected at all cost. Workers come to work to work, but that work must find a way to be enjoyable. When change is introduced, the enjoyment in the work process can be lost. Productivity has to get done, but if there is limited enjoyment, there will be limited production at work. Here is the Jester's script:

01 IDENTIFICATION

Gratification is only possible when you know the team member's definition of **Gratification**. If the Jester doesn't know what makes them find enjoyment, it is tough to help them find it. The Jester needs to, with intent, identify how each member defines enjoyment in their work. Once that happens, then the work of celebrating (the Jester's definition of **Gratification**) can really begin.

To do this type of work you will have to:
1. *Engage with team members.* You must get to know them.
2. *Educate yourself about motivational theory.* You must learn how to convert what you know into motivational tools.

02 CALIBRATION

Gratification is tough to measure. It has to be more than a feeling. Feelings are hard to measure. Meet with each team member and calibrate with them how you will measure their specific enjoyment; what does it look like?

03 EXPECTATIONS

Gratification has to be genuine. It can't be manufactured or imposed. It needs to be expected. Make sure you govern your own inward desires to not fact it.

04 VALIDATION

As a Jester, **Gratification** is your wheelhouse. You can often find many reasons and ways to party. Incorporate a plan to get input from others about how you look to celebrate. Don't just use your own intuitive feelings. Get others to validate when you think it is TIME!!

05 CELEBRATION

Gratification has a natural outflow in celebration. It might be a simple "high-five" with the team, or a real parade to show the appreciation everyone is feeling for other members of the team. Celebrations need to be:

1. *Measured*: Too much and it devalues the celebration; too little and it devalues the work.
2. *Distributive*: Make sure the celebrations are not always for the same things or same people.
3. *Appropriate*: Not everyone celebrates the same way. The celebration needs to be connected to #1 of this script.

Jester Script #2 - Moving Off Stage

The Jester can get a lot of attention because they are fun to be around. Like the other archetypes, however, they are not the main thing in the drama of change. The Jester is guarding the team to make sure they always find their work **Gratifying** during the drama of change. As change unfolds, the Jester, like the Innocent, can see the stress it puts on the team. Remember, the Jester has to be aware that the other archetypes are paying attention to their roles, and that can add more and more stress. Work can become boring, too serious and simply no fun. The team is so focused on the work, in the Jester's eyes, they forgot about life and living. The Jester has to make sure that the work keeps a high level of **Gratification** to make sure everyone is enjoying life. The Jester wants everyone to *want to come to work* and not simply *tolerate the work*.

Like the other archetypes, the Jester needs to remember that the success of the proposed change will depend upon how they, too, can work with and utilize the skills and the roles of each of the other archetypes. Especially realizing that all of them have a different way, they define **Gratification.** They have their own ideas of what celebration looks like. They may want to celebrate everything. To the Jester, life in general is a reason to celebrate ... their *I'm-bored-with-life* meter is super sensitive. So, it is important that the Jester knows how to engage with each of the other archetypes as they move off the center stage of the drama.

The Jester must make sure that **Gratification** is appropriate within the organization. To do so, they must keep the other archetypes engaged, allowing them to fulfill their roles. Here is your script.

	Orphan's script to interact with the other archetypes	
Archetype	**Possible objections they may have with the change**	**Goal Association Work (See Addendum #4)**
Seeker	They may want to take the organization into a new direction. This isn't always bad and, in fact, necessary at times.	The Seeker finds gratification in simple searching. The Jester's role will be to find ways they can *still* search as this idea unfolds.
Lover	They may want to hang on to the status quo. They may value the wrong thing, but, nevertheless, they see change as dangerous to their status quo.	The Lover finds gratification in holding onto something. The Jester's role will be to show them how the new idea/change can assist them to hold to past values they love.
Destroyer	They need to see what the change is replacing and will need to agree that "something" needs replacing.	The Destroyer finds gratification in letting go of something. The Jester's role is to show them what the change is going to replace.
Creator	They can't always see the real practical application or design of the change. They need to know the vision has something tangible behind it.	The Creator finds gratification by producing something tangible. The Jester's role is to show them how their creation is morphing and fitting into the culture and working.
Warrior	They might reject the change if they think it will fail. They will want someone to show them that the change is successful or has the ability to be successful.	The Warrior gets gratification from success and performance. The Jester's role is to show them how the change is succeeding and breaking new barriers and meeting new levels.
Caregiver	They might reject the change because of all the work that will be put on the plates of the workers to accomplish the change.	The Caregiver gets gratification from helping others. The Jester's role is to help them find ways they can help others without enabling.
Orphan	They might reject the change because of failure to solve some of the problems the change will create when implemented.	The Orphan gets gratification by spotting danger. The Jester's role is to help them learn to express that danger in a pleasant way.
Innocent	They might reject the change because they either don't see the need (naïveté) behind it or because they think it will be a hopeless pursuit.	The Innocent gets gratification from inspiring others. The Jester's role is to partner with the Innocent to find ways to show how celebration can inspire and produce hope.
Ruler	They might reject the change because they don't see structurally how the change will work. They will want to policy and procedure any change.	The Ruler gets gratification from stabilizing the organization. The Jester's role is to show them where their rules might be crushing or suppressing the joy, thus creating instability.
Magician	They might reject the change if they think the change lacks any ability to see transformation. They will be your least resistor if they see "change" as good for anyone or any organization.	The Magician gets gratification from seeing others transformed internally. The Jester's role is to incorporate their skill of celebration with the Magician's desire for transformation. The power of the two can transform others.
Sage	They might reject the change because they see the change as foolish and lacking substance or because it has little research (and it does ... if it is new).	The Sage gets gratification by learning and conveying that knowledge to others. The Jester's role is to learn from the Sage and to translate that knowledge into ways to celebrate and reach gratification for all members.

Jester Script #3 - Backstage

The Jester must make sure that during the implementation process **Gratification** is being met within the organization and within the individuals of the organization. This means that as they allow the other archetypes to speak into the change, they can keep the organization finding enjoyment and a reason to celebrate life. They will get a better change if they listen to the other archetypes during the drama of change. The biggest question backstage for the Jester should not be, "Why is this work so boring?" But rather, it should be, "How can I make sure everyone is enjoying their job as much as I am enjoying mine?"

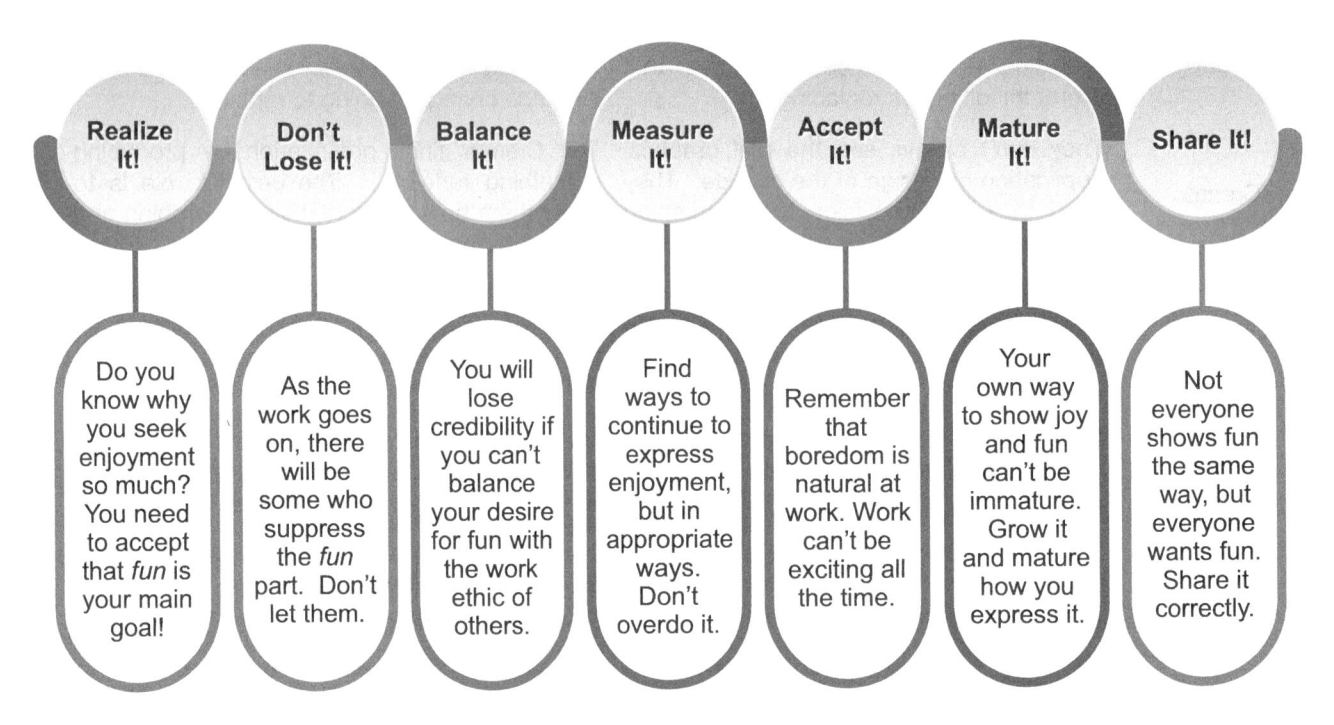

Realize It!	Don't Lose It!	Balance It!	Measure It!	Accept It!	Mature It!	Share It!
Do you know why you seek enjoyment so much? You need to accept that *fun* is your main goal!	As the work goes on, there will be some who suppress the *fun* part. Don't let them.	You will lose credibility if you can't balance your desire for fun with the work ethic of others.	Find ways to continue to express enjoyment, but in appropriate ways. Don't overdo it.	Remember that boredom is natural at work. Work can't be exciting all the time.	Your own way to show joy and fun can't be immature. Grow it and mature how you express it.	Not everyone shows fun the same way, but everyone wants fun. Share it correctly.

Conclusion - an Email to the Jester

Dear Jester,

We are so glad you are here. That trick you played on Henry from sales was epic. I think he will be plotting for years on how to get you back. Thanks for planning the party on Tuesday. Who has work parties on Tuesdays? Also, most of us still don't sit down without looking out for the whoopee cushion.

Seriously (you do *serious*, right?), however, we can't spend the whole time during meetings watching reruns of *The Office*. As much as a marathon of the last sitcom might sound exciting, we have much work to do. If you could keep it light and enjoyable without turning the place into a junior high locker room, that would be great. We need to know that this is not rocket science, and we are not curing cancer. But our work is serious, and your help to keep us lighthearted in it must be balanced with the fact that it is *work*. Thanks again … the other 11 archetypes.

Jester's Audition Checklist
(You think you are equipped for the Jester's part in the Drama of Change?)

The following activities give the Jester energy:	Never	Seldom	Sometimes	Often	Always
I get energy from enjoyment:	☐	☐	☐	☐	☐
I get energy from humor and a fun, relaxed atmosphere:	☐	☐	☐	☐	☐
I get energy knowing people are happy at work:	☐	☐	☐	☐	☐
I get energy when people tell funny stories about work:	☐	☐	☐	☐	☐
I get energy gathering workers together after work:	☐	☐	☐	☐	☐
I get energy making others laugh; and laughing:	☐	☐	☐	☐	☐

- ☐ I read comic books
- ☑ I have fun at everything
- ☐ I have fun on vacation
- ☐ I like games - their games

Secrets for a Successful Callback for a *Jester* Role

❖ You have a history of being fun to be around.

❖ You spend time on the weekends entertaining.

❖ You would be willing to visit those in the hospital to put a smile on their faces.

❖ You watch sitcoms and comics on television.

❖ You might have been voted class clown ... secretly you wanted to be called that.

❖ You still have memorabilia from your prom.

The Caregiver-Magician-Innocent-Jester Dynamic

As stated previously, the drama of change can create many challenges as an idea moves from the incubation stage to the implementation stage. In review, during the incubation stage the idea needs to develop, and the archetypes of Seeker-Lover-Destroyer-Creator get into numerous opportunities to stretch each other and challenge each other. As we have seen, once the implementation stage of the change begins, four more archetypes take over. The Warrior-Ruler-Orphan-Sage are key archetypes to avoid what *Fullen* calls the *implementation dip*. But the attitudes of the team within the organization can be significantly challenged. The Caregiver-Magician-Innocent-Jester dynamic continues to diminish the *dip* that *will* occur as any change takes place.

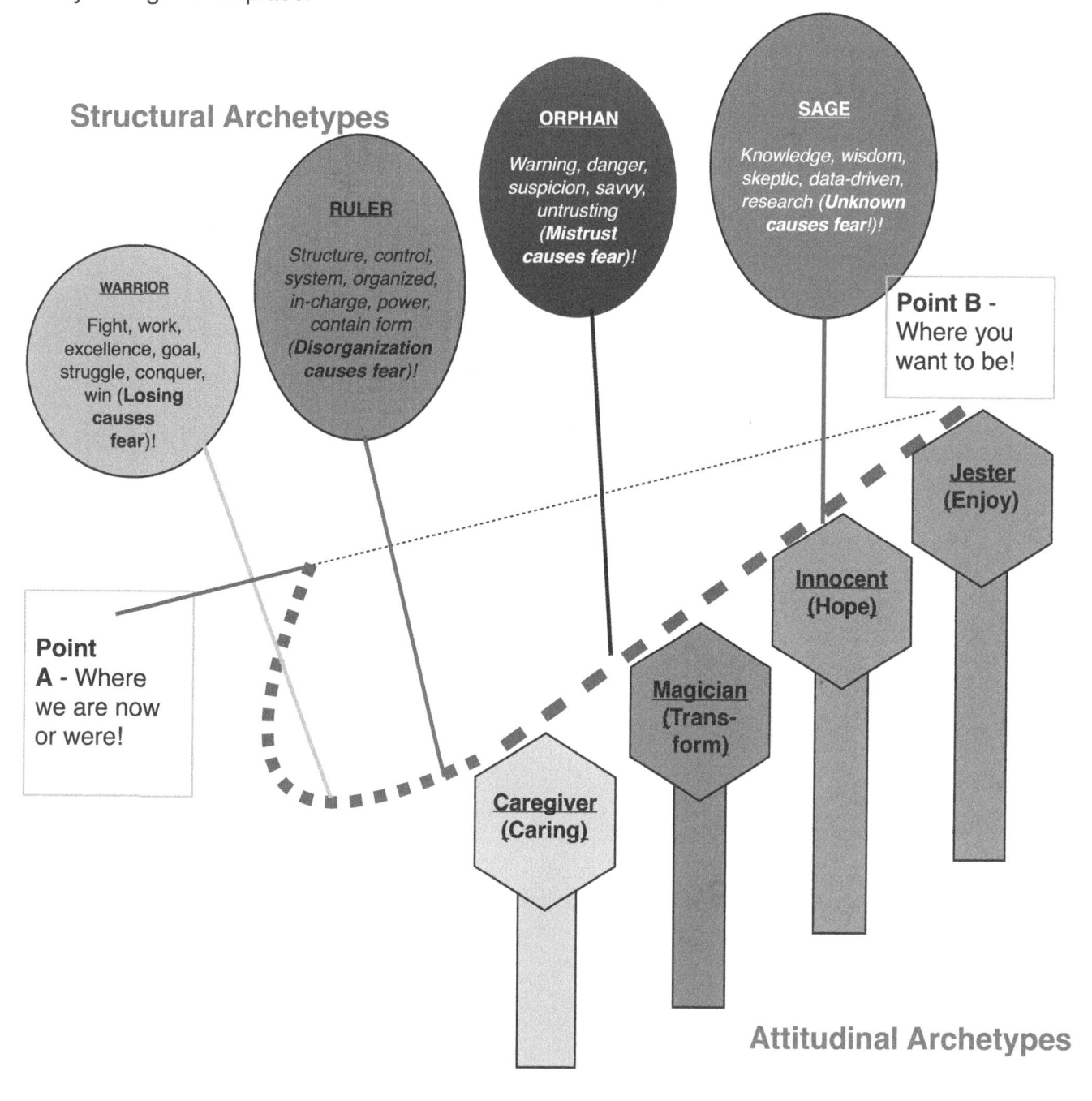

Structural Archetypes

WARRIOR — Fight, work, excellence, goal, struggle, conquer, win (**Losing causes fear**)!

RULER — Structure, control, system, organized, in-charge, power, contain form (**Disorganization causes fear**)!

ORPHAN — Warning, danger, suspicion, savvy, untrusting (**Mistrust causes fear**)!

SAGE — Knowledge, wisdom, skeptic, data-driven, research (**Unknown causes fear!**)!

Point A - Where we are now or were!

Point B - Where you want to be!

Attitudinal Archetypes

- **Caregiver** (Caring)
- **Magician** (Transform)
- **Innocent** (Hope)
- **Jester** (Enjoy)

What Role Do You Play In Change? — The Archetypes and the Change Process

As the implementation unfolds and moves through the change drama, The Attitudinal Archetypes support the change initiative by making sure the team pulling the weight of the change stays engaged because they are enjoying the work. The work certainly can get done without the work of these four archetypes (Caregiver-Magician-Innocent-Jester). But at what cost to the workers? A major flaw in the drama of change is the cost it takes on the morale of the organization. Change *can* get down without a focus on *caring*, *transformation*, *hope* and/or *enjoyment*. Just ask Warrior, Ruler, Orphan and/or Sage. The beauty of The Attitudinal Archetypes in the drama of change is that they help keep the staff that starts the change engaged, so that they can be the staff that completes the change. They, like The Structural Archetypes, can diminish the natural dip that occurs during the change process and will take and inspire and connect the staff to the work.

THE CHANGE STORY

- Three Acts -

Act I - The Developmental Archetypes

Scene 1 - The Seeker

Scene 2 - The Lover

Scene 3 - The Destroyer

Scene 4 - The Creator

Act II - The Structural Archetypes

Scene 1 - The Warrior

Scene 2 - The Ruler

Scene 3 - The Orphan

Scene 4 - The Sage

Act III - The Attitudinal Archetypes

Scene 1 - The Caregiver

Scene 2 - The Magician

Scene 3 - The Innocent

Scene 4 - The Jester

CONCLUSION(S)

CONCLUSION(S) - ARCHETYPE-CASTING

Any change is a story. As the change unfolds, the story unfolds. As the change is remembered, it is a story that is remembered and told and retold. Can you think about a change you have in your past? How would you tell the story? What role did you play?

In a drama production, there is a phrase known as *Typecasting*. When you *Typecast*, you put someone in the role you designed for them and for the way they typically act. The term *Against Type* is when you put someone in a role that is not staying with roles they typically play. Our challenge with the archetypes and their roles in the change drama can be complex. But there are two areas where we can gain control:

Proper Roles

Playing staff in their proper roles is essential to success in the drama of change. We would, obviously, like it when everyone had the capacity to play every role. But that is not generally the case. In reality, people are comfortable in the archetypes they have learned. Therefore, playing them in those comfortable roles can strengthen the organization during the drama of change. *Someone who is skilled in the Ruler archetype should be cast into the Ruler role*. That might seem as an obvious casting decision during the change drama, but it is often not. We often don't spend time thinking of our staff in terms of the archetypal roles they play. We simply look at their job tasks and move without properly casting them for their role in the change drama.

Filled Roles

This might sound as equally obvious, but making sure all the roles in the drama of change are filled is another important role in the casting stage. We all too often try to move forward making sure all the technical aspects of the change initiative are filled, but we often forget about, or simply don't consider, the tactical aspects of the change drama. Tactically, we want to make sure we have each of the archetypal roles filled. If we miss one, let's say the Orphan voice, we will often find three possibilities come to fruition: 1). The role goes unfilled, and we lose the voice completely (if it were the Orphan voice, we would lose Vigilance); 2). Someone unqualified to play the role plays it, and we miss the real nuance of the role (for example, the Ruler tries to play the Orphan); or 3). The role is played by someone in the shadowy side only.

CONCLUSION(S) - ARCHETYPE-CLOCK

As the story of change begins, there are certain aspects of the archetype roles that will have to be accomplished in order to see success. Below are 12 key steps a leader should consider to assure that, as the change story unfolds, you have placed your team in the best possible place to tell an extremely great story once the change is complete:

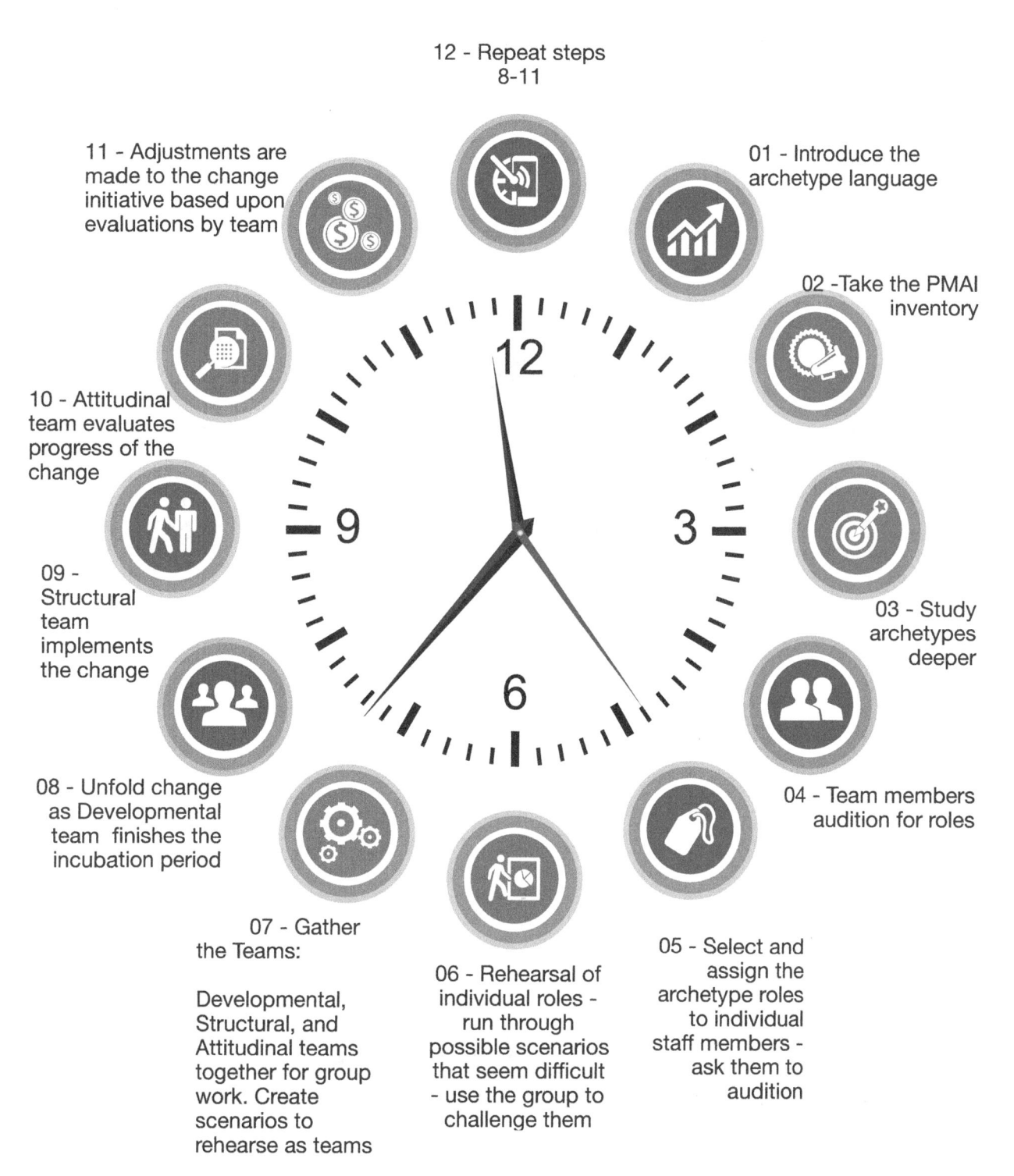

01 - Introduce the archetype language

02 - Take the PMAI inventory

03 - Study archetypes deeper

04 - Team members audition for roles

05 - Select and assign the archetype roles to individual staff members - ask them to audition

06 - Rehearsal of individual roles - run through possible scenarios that seem difficult - use the group to challenge them

07 - Gather the Teams: Developmental, Structural, and Attitudinal teams together for group work. Create scenarios to rehearse as teams

08 - Unfold change as Developmental team finishes the incubation period

09 - Structural team implements the change

10 - Attitudinal team evaluates progress of the change

11 - Adjustments are made to the change initiative based upon evaluations by team

12 - Repeat steps 8-11

What Role Do You Play In Change?   The Archetypes and the Change Process

CONCLUSION(S) - ARCHETYPE-EVALUATING TALENT (Part 1)

As the drama of change begins to take shape, team leadership will have to determine who will play what role (see steps 4 and 5 on the previous page). Having members of the team playing the correct archetype roles is fundamental to the success of the change. As *auditions* are held, what exactly are you looking for as a leader? In each chapter of the archetypes, there is plenty of fodder for what the leader may need to chew on to decide who should play what role. Below, in brief, is a question an organizational leader should ask each individual team member in regard to their ability to play the role of that particular archetype:

SEEKER: When have you generated an idea that others have had a chance to shape?

JESTER: Describe what a bad day looks like for you?

LOVER: Can you tell the difference between a value and a tool used to reach a value? Give us an example.

INNOCENT: When was the last time you were discouraged?

DESTROYER: What do you have in your life that you have struggled to let go?

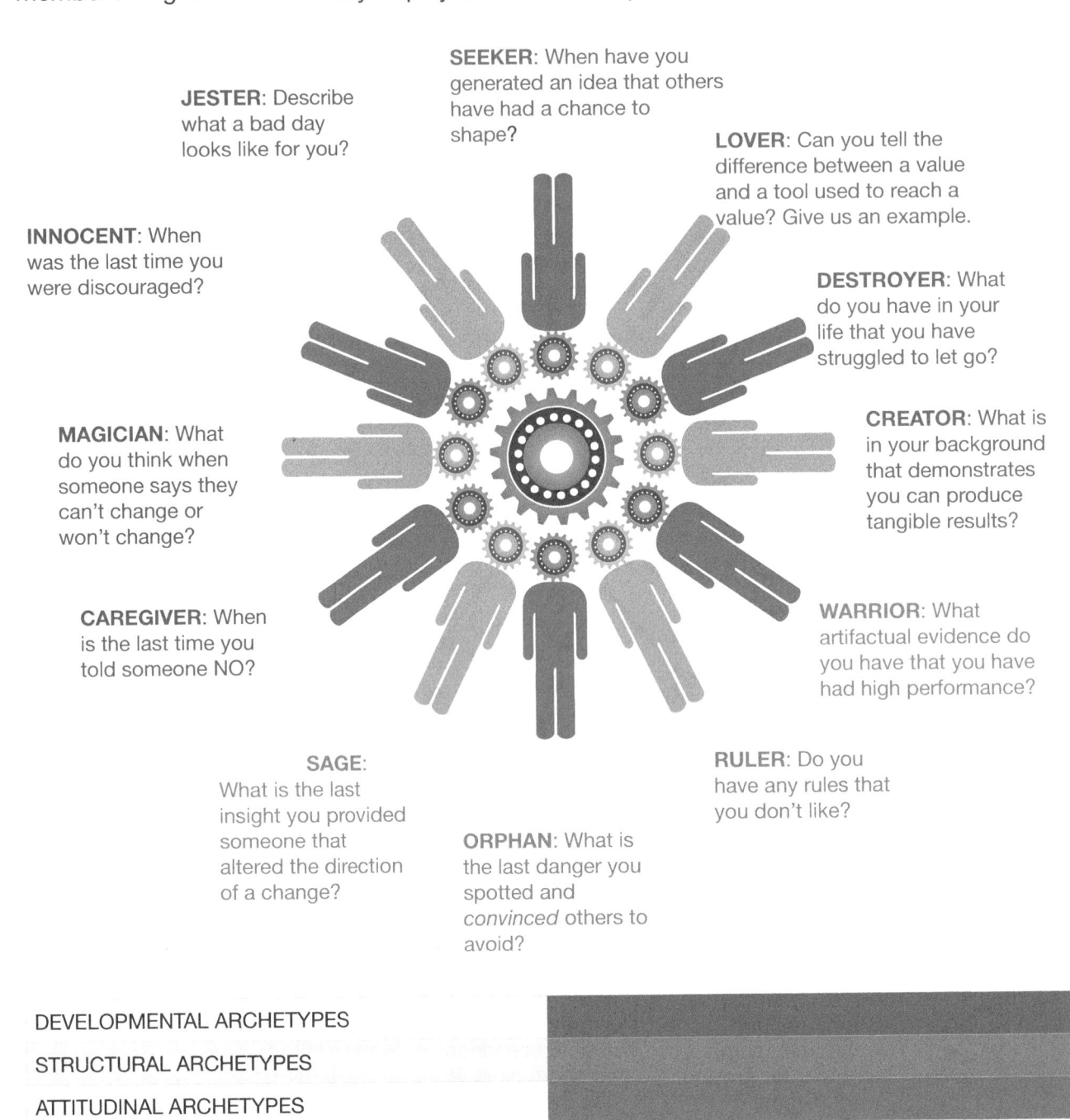

MAGICIAN: What do you think when someone says they can't change or won't change?

CREATOR: What is in your background that demonstrates you can produce tangible results?

CAREGIVER: When is the last time you told someone NO?

WARRIOR: What artifactual evidence do you have that you have had high performance?

SAGE: What is the last insight you provided someone that altered the direction of a change?

RULER: Do you have any rules that you don't like?

ORPHAN: What is the last danger you spotted and *convinced* others to avoid?

DEVELOPMENTAL ARCHETYPES
STRUCTURAL ARCHETYPES
ATTITUDINAL ARCHETYPES

CONCLUSION(S) - ARCHETYPE-EVALUATING TALENT (Part 2)

So, if you are an organizational leader, what are you looking for in the questions on the previous page? Here is a suggestion of a possible answer to each question, that might look like that team member demonstrates qualities that show they can play an archetypal role. Compare the responses of those you interview for these archetypal roles with what is suggested below. Here is what their answers should tell you about them:

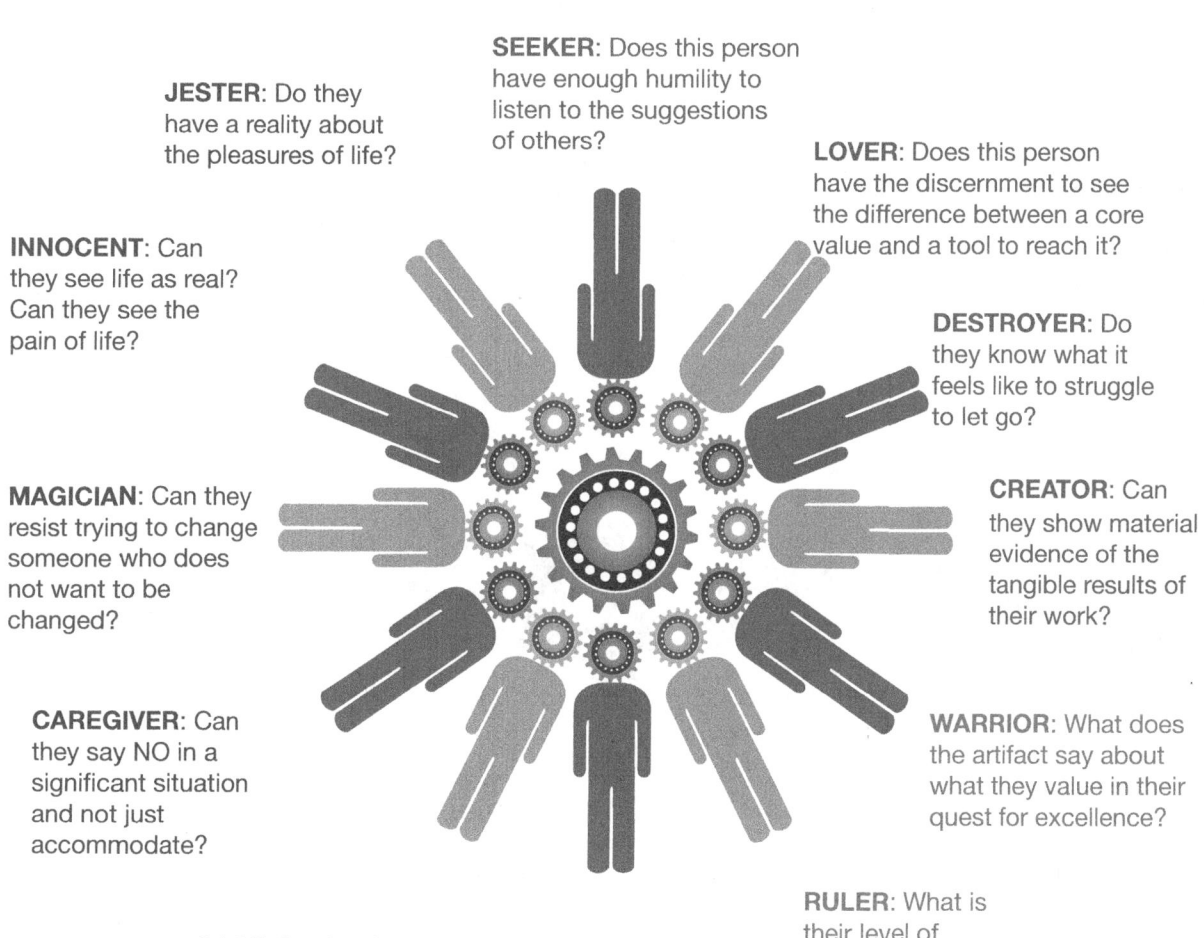

JESTER: Do they have a reality about the pleasures of life?

SEEKER: Does this person have enough humility to listen to the suggestions of others?

LOVER: Does this person have the discernment to see the difference between a core value and a tool to reach it?

INNOCENT: Can they see life as real? Can they see the pain of life?

DESTROYER: Do they know what it feels like to struggle to let go?

MAGICIAN: Can they resist trying to change someone who does not want to be changed?

CREATOR: Can they show material evidence of the tangible results of their work?

CAREGIVER: Can they say NO in a significant situation and not just accommodate?

WARRIOR: What does the artifact say about what they value in their quest for excellence?

SAGE: Do they have practical knowledge that allows them to impact change?

ORPHAN: Can they convince others to change on top of spotting danger?

RULER: What is their level of accountability?

CONCLUSION(S) - ARCHETYPE-EVALUATING PROCESS

As the drama of change unfolds, the leadership of the team will need to make constant adjustments and changes (see steps 8-11) above. But what should the leadership be looking for in regard to each archetype and the archetypal teams (Developmental, Structural, and Attitudinal)? Below is a script to follow for what you should be evaluating as the drama of change unfolds:

SEEKER: Does the *idea* have evidence of multiple voices speaking into it?

CREATOR: Do they show an obsession about the creation that they can't let others own?

WARRIOR: Do they show a concern for the struggle others have in the process?

SAGE: Are they providing practical insights, truths and knowledge that is improving the change.

CAREGIVER: Are they showing restraint by allowing others to do their own work and supplying help in areas others *can't* do?

JESTER: Do they show a desire to be serious about the work? Are they engaging with the other archetypes to discover what they need to enjoy their work?

LOVER: Are they showing an ability to blend old values with the new values the change suggests?

DESTROYER: Are they showing some sensitivity to the concerns of those who are still not ready to let go?

RULER: Are they crafting the rules to actually bring stability or to quench their inner need for the satisfaction for order or structure?

ORPHAN: Are they using good skills to warn and persuade others about the dangers they see, so that people are responding rather than just rejecting their warning?

MAGICIAN: Are they showing restraint in regard to manipulating others and the system to create some change they want?

INNOCENT: Do they show any evidence that they see the reality of the change initiative? Are they engaged with other archetypes to understand what they expect from the change?

CONCLUSION(S) - ARCHETYPE-CURTAIN CALL

You can always tell how a change initiative unfolds by the stories that are told by each archetype. Each archetype has a mission and a desire. If the change initiative starts by using the archetypes with intent, the story can be positive. They will see the change as energizing and valuable. They will play their roles in the strength side of their archetype. If, however, we ignore the archetypes and simply move through the change drama hoping for the best, each of them *might* play their role ... but in the shadow side of their archetype. This guidebook is written in hopes that the leadership of an organization will use the archetypes with *intent* and in the *strength* side of their roles. If they do, here are the stories you should hear from each archetype, because they had a successful role during the change drama. Following these scripts can assure that each archetype will act out their roles during the change initiative with energy and in their strength role. Here is what you would hear if they are in their strength role, answering this question, "It was a great change because I was able to ..."

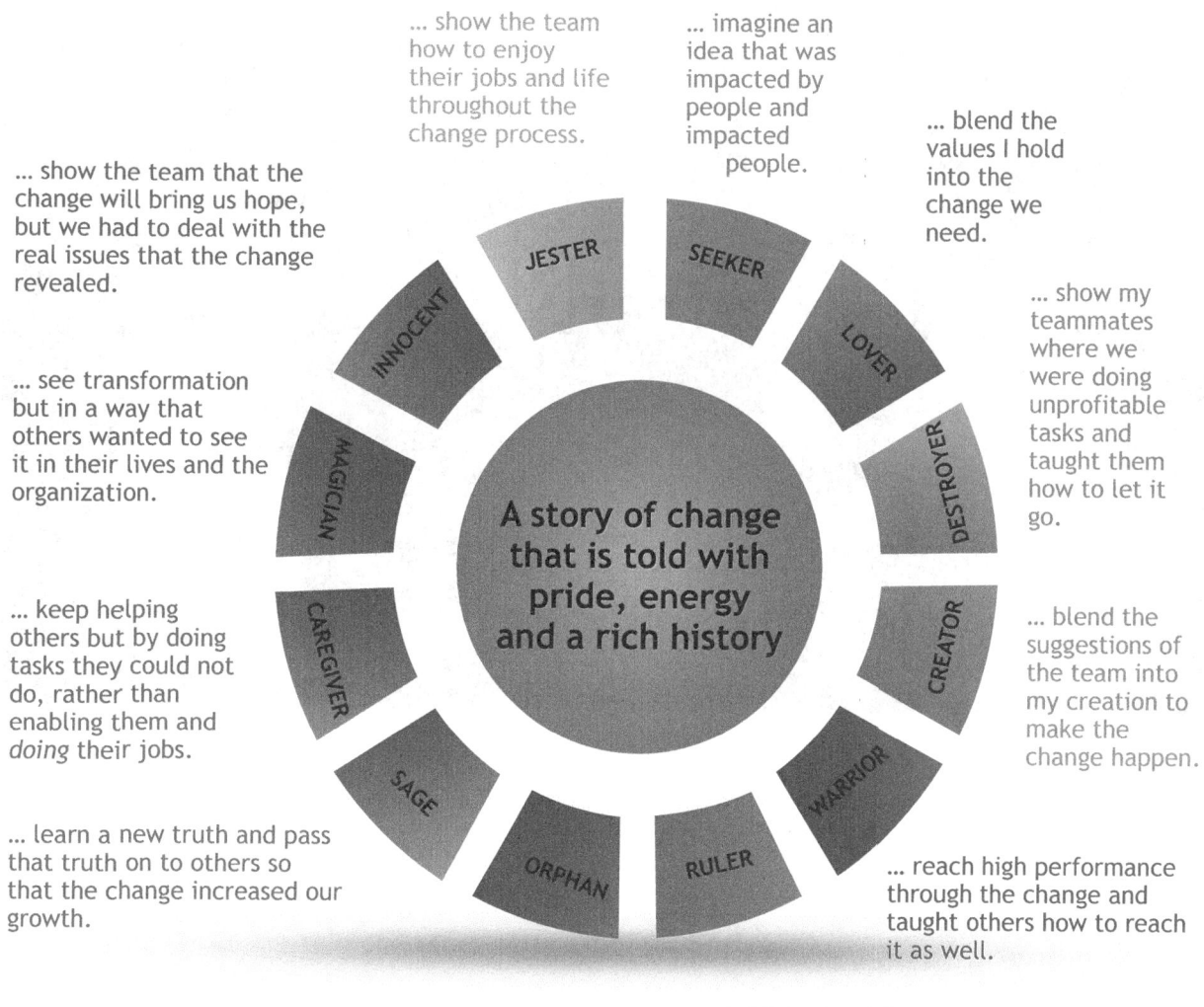

JESTER: ... show the team how to enjoy their jobs and life throughout the change process.

SEEKER: ... imagine an idea that was impacted by people and impacted people.

LOVER: ... blend the values I hold into the change we need.

DESTROYER: ... show my teammates where we were doing unprofitable tasks and taught them how to let it go.

CREATOR: ... blend the suggestions of the team into my creation to make the change happen.

WARRIOR: ... reach high performance through the change and taught others how to reach it as well.

RULER: ... established stability as the change unfolded while making sure there was flexibility in my approach to allow my teammates to flourish and grow.

ORPHAN: ... point out the dangers in the change, but in a way that allowed others to hear me and me to hear them.

SAGE: ... learn a new truth and pass that truth on to others so that the change increased our growth.

CAREGIVER: ... keep helping others but by doing tasks they could not do, rather than enabling them and *doing* their jobs.

MAGICIAN: ... see transformation but in a way that others wanted to see it in their lives and the organization.

INNOCENT: ... show the team that the change will bring us hope, but we had to deal with the real issues that the change revealed.

A story of change that is told with pride, energy and a rich history

The Drama of Change is real. Those who go through change have felt it and experienced the fluid, murky and muddy waters it creates. If we are willing to do the work and assign the roles of the archetypes to willing, eager and abled teammates, with intent, we can see success and change the drama so that it doesn't harm the team. By using the archetypes with intent, we can build the team, complete the change and impact those involved in the Drama of Change.

Addendum

Addendum 1 - The Innocent Archetype descriptor change: The Pearson-Marr Archetype Inventory is going to change the descriptor of the *Innocent* to the *Idealist*. The assumption is that there is much evidence to make such a change. However, since this author has no experience with this descriptor, for the sake of this work, the choice was made to continue with the term *Innocent*.

Addendum 2 - The Orphan Archetype descriptor change: The Pearson-Marr Archetype Inventory is going to change the descriptor of the *Orphan* to the *Realist*. The assumption is that there is much evidence to make such a change. However, since this author has no experience with this descriptor, for the sake of this work, the choice was made to continue with the term *Orphan*. The term *Orphan*, however, can provide such a rich image as to what the archetype is all about. I have decided to continue to use the term *Orphan* for this reason. The *Orphan* term gives so much energy to the *Orphan* voice.

Addendum 3 - The Destroyer Archetype descriptor change: The Pearson-Marr Archetype Inventory is going to change the descriptor of the *Destroyer* to the *Revolutionary*. The assumption is that there is much evidence to make such a change. However, since this author has no experience with this descriptor, for the sake of this work, the choice was made to continue with the term *Destroyer*.

The term Destroyer, however, does signify the work of the archetype. When the archetype is in full motion, they are moving away from something. To those who are being asked to *let go* of something by *Destroyer*, there is a feeling of destruction. To them, the term *Destroyer* fits appropriately. It should be noted that when you *let go* of something, you really still don't have a *Revolution*. A *Revolution* needs to let go of something and bring something else in to replace it. So, a *Revolution* is the *result* of the *Destroyer* and *Creator* working in balance. You can't have a *Revolution* by just letting go of something. To have a *Revolution*, you must move away from one thing and bring in another. This is why I would prefer to keep the *Destroyer* descriptor for this work.

Addendum 4 - Goal Association Work: Goal Association Work is one of the most powerful tools of leadership and a key tool for archetype work. Goal Association Work states the following. Imagine that you are a *follower*, and I am the *leader*. Here is what Goal Association Work would sound like:

As my follower, you will never take one of *my* ideas if I keep presenting to you *my* ideas in a way that you believe that you incorporating my ideas will help *me* reach *my* goal.

But if I present to you, my follower, my ideas in a way that allows you to see that my ideas will help you reach *your* goals, you will go through a wall with *my* ideas.

When we present our ideas and tasks to others, we have this powerful tool. We have to connect our ideas to the goals others have for themselves. If we can't connect our ideas to the goals of others, we have one or more of these problems:

1. We simply have a bad idea. We can't connect the idea to their goals because our idea lacks merit or something necessary to make the connection. Solution: *Improve the idea*.

2. They have bad goals. We can't connect our idea to their goals because our idea is good, but their goals are poor. They come to the table with goals that make it a struggle to connect with meaningful ideas. Solution: *Improve their goals*.

3. You have a great idea, and they have great goals, but you are failing in communicating your idea to their goals. The issue is communication. Solution: *Improve the communication*.